JOHN BARRINGTON is an established storyteller and author. For many years he was a hill shepherd, living in Rob Roy MacGregor's old house in the heart of the Scottish Highlands. He herded 750 Scottish Blackface sheep on the 2,000ft Perthshire mountains above Loch Katrine. Successful at sheepdog trials, shepherd and dogs have given demonstrations of their ancient craft at two Garden Festivals and many shows, galas and Highland Games.

In 1998, the Scottish Qualification Authority asked John Barrington to design a course in sheepdog handling and management, which took two years to complete. The first classes were run at Oatridge Agricultural College, near Edinburgh, in 2000, the author at the helm. Students were enrolled from Ireland, England and all parts of Scotland.

With a good eye for sheep, John Barrington has judged classes of sheep at the Highland Show in Edinburgh and has made several judging trips to Europe.

Like most shepherds, Barrington is a natural storyteller, a gift he exercises at schools, clubs and societies, and as an after dinner speaker. Stories are recounted on the move during daytime guided tours and twilight ghost walks, and as a commentator at a dozen or so Highland Games each year. Stories told to enliven his whisky tasting sessions are always presented in the right spirit! *Red Sky at Night,* his first book and a UK bestseller, won him a Scottish Arts Council book award. His latest book, *Of Dogs and Men,* will be published soon.

The chapters in this book are numbered according to a shepherd's count (1 to 10), a pre-Celtic rhyming method of counting sheep, thought to be the oldest language still in use in the British Isles.

By the same author:

Loch Lomond and the Trossachs (2006)
Out of the Mists (2008)
Of Dogs and Men (2013)

Red Sky at Night

JOHN BARRINGTON

Luath Press Limited

EDINBURGH

www.luath.co.uk

To Gran

First published 1984 by Michael Joseph Ltd
Paperback edition first published 1986 by Pan Books Ltd
First Luath edition 1999
Reprinted 2003, 2006
New Edition 2013

ISBN: 978-1-908373-37-3

The paper used in this book is acid-free, neutral-sized and recyclable.
It is made from low chlorine pulps produced in a low energy,
low emissions manner from sustainable forests.

Printed and bound by
Bell & Bain Ltd., Glasgow

Typeset in 10.5 point Sabon by
3btype.com

Illustrations by Paul Armstrong

Contents

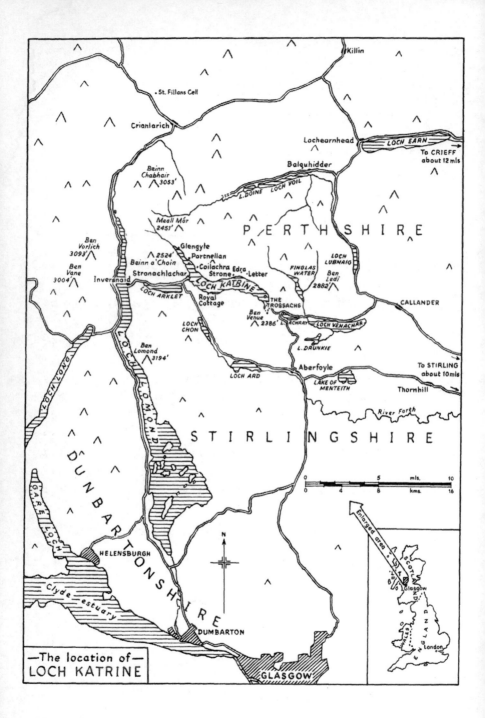

—The location of—
LOCH KATRINE

vi

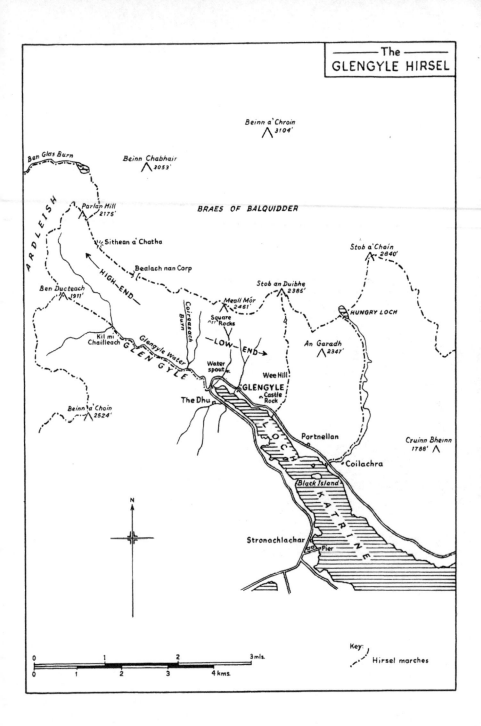

The GLENGYLE HIRSEL

Beinn a' Chroin
3104'

Beinn Chabhair
3053'

BRAES OF BALQUIDDER

Ben Glas Burn

ARDLEISH

Parlan Hill
2175'

Sithean a' Chatha

Bealach nan Corp

HIGH END

Ben Ducteach
1911'

Kil mi Chailleach

Stob a' Chain
2640'

Stob an Duibhe
2385'

Meall Mór
2461'

Coireasach Burn

Square Rocks

HUNGRY LOCH

LOW END

An Garadh
2341'

Glengyle Water

GLEN GYLE

Water spout

Wee Hill

GLENGYLE
Castle Rock

The Dhu

Beinn 'a' Chain
2524'

LOCH

Portnellan

KATRINE

Coilachra

Cruinn Bheinn
1788'

Black Island

Stronachlachar

Pier

N

0   1   2   3 mls.
0   1   2   3   4 kms.

Key:

Hirsel marches

vii

Preface to the 2013 Edition

THERE IS NO doubt that Loch Katrine, and the highlands encircling this sparkling jewel in the Scottish landscape, is a marvel of nature. I consider myself to have been remarkably privileged to herd generations of sheep over the Glengyle hirsel, ably assisted by my collie dogs, and surrounded by the best nature had to offer. Those days are gone, a 21st century Highland Clearance sweeping away livestock and people alike. What was a large, vibrant community is no more, the local school has closed and, once the daily visitors have departed, the hills brood in silence.

Scottish Water was the first to abrogate their responsibilities, only too willing to relinquish control of the land bestowed by a 1919 Act of Parliament. It became apparent that this organisation had lost sight of one important fact. The grazing of 12,000 sheep and 200 cows was integral to land management in the catchment area of Glasgow's principal reservoir, suppressing natural tree regeneration. Deciduous leaf litter in a reservoir is the last thing you want. Along came the Forestry Commission, intent only on establishing trees, with no thought or care of wider environmental issues. All the while, the National Park Authority simply nodded through these catastrophic changes, at the very heart of their domain, steadfastly ignoring at least two of their legal obligations.

Originally written as a contemporary account of day to day life in the Highlands, *Red Sky at Night* has become more of an historic document. Such have been the recent changes that have swept across Scotland. However, one contentious issue is still very much a hot topic – culling badgers to control tuberculosis in cattle. My views remain unchanged. Publication of this book opened many doors and certainly broadened my horizons. It also brought me into contact with many wonderful people who, over the decades, greatly enriched my life. Although too numerous to mention individually, I have a soft spot for a London couple who read my book, then bought a farm in Scotland.

Now a good few years retired and residing just south of the Highland Line, from time to time I become one of a host of visitors to Loch Katrine. The mountains still rise majestically from the very edge of the loch, to be enjoyed on foot, by bicycle, or from one of the cruising vessels. You may be fortunate enough to see some highland cattle, brought in by the Forestry Commission in an attempt to control the rampant vegetation. Fine beasts, but they are not sheep.

My thanks, as always, to the countless people who have helped me along life's way, especially the editorial team at Luath Press. But most of all, my debt is to each and every one of my dogs, without whose help none of this would have been possible.

John Barrington
Croftamie
2013

Preface to the 1999 Edition

WHEN RED SKY AT NIGHT was published by Michel Joseph, London, my editor told me that the book would eventually find its way to a Scottish publishing house, probably in Edinburgh. How prophetic those words turned out to be and I have to thank Gavin MacDougall and Luath Press for their faith in me.

Since publication time has marched on, and there have been significant changes in the glen. My own family left to find pastures new and, after a number of years, I married a lovely lady, Marjory Owens. I was offered and accepted early retirement, whatever that means. I seem to be busier than ever. There are always sheep to tend, Highland cattle to look after and I have just designed the first ever course in 'sheep dog handling', for the Scottish Qualification Authority.

Many of my old friends have retired or moved on and not all of them have been replaced. The local primary school is reduced to a handful of children and a large number of houses lie empty and lifeless. An area of outstanding natural beauty, once described as Scotland's first National Park, now has an air of neglect.

Farming has fallen into a black hole. With sharply declining returns and ever escalating costs, drastic action has followed. The hill cows have all been sold and, for the first time since the coming of the MacGregors, there are no cattle in Glengyle. The number of shepherds has been more than halved. However, this is still the largest sheep farm in Britain (27,000 acres and 12,000 sheep) and the only way to herd high ground flocks is to lace up a good pair of boots, take up a cromach and, with dogs at heel, go to the hill.

John Barrington
Glengyle
October 1999

To Begin at the Beginning

THE STAR-SPECKLED BLACKFACED night of the first day of December begins to break as the light of the new day gently touches the eastern sky. Ice thickens and the white frost tightens its early morning grip. In the shelter of the drystone-dyked fank, the Glengyle tups, still cudding on last evening's hay, begin to stir themselves, heads lifted high, nostrils held to the sharp edge of the wind. Beyond and above on the still dark hill, 38 score of ewes will already be foraging, hungry for the first bite of the short winter day, their ground about to be taken over by strong-horned mates. Dawn inches up over the night sky; a new year for the flock of the forked glen is about to begin.

Frost-crisped grass scrunches softly under my feet as I make my way to the fank. Alerted now, 16 tups tug long wool staples free from the frozen ground and scrabble to their feet. Four sheep-dog muzzles push enquiringly between the lower spars of the gate; Old Bo, Mona, Gail and Boot size up the job in hand. At this intrusion the tups bunch tightly in the middle of the pen, their smoky breaths merging into a small, grey cloud. I pause at the gate, leaning over the top to study my charges, making sure that all is well before taking them out to the hill. Each tup in turn shakes himself vigorously, sending a shower of fine ice prisms flying and glinting into the first slanting shafts of sunlight.

The success, or otherwise, of the Glengyle flock in the coming year depends upon the performance of my tups during the next six weeks. Having satisfied myself that these fellows seem to be sound in wind and limb, I lift the snek and allow the wide wooden gate to swing open. Particles of white hoarfrost shower from the metal hinges. Three dogs dart inside to bring the tups out. Two or three heads turn defiantly to face up to the threat, but are quickly turned back again under the strong-eyed gaze of the collies. Guided out through the gate, across the bridge, a left flank by Mona and Gail

turns the sheep to the right, and up through the park we go, towards the hill gate.

The sun lifts itself above the hills which fringe the south shore of Loch Katrine. The water sparkles. A small herd of whooper swans swims, dabbling for food in the sheltered, shallow lagoon in front of Glengyle House. A cold, north-westerly wind blows directly down the glen, bringing hints of ewes in season to the tups and a tingling to my fingers. Mona and Gail head off the tups and bring them to a halt. Bo and Boot guard against any retreat as I open the gate to the hill. Eager to fulfil their roles, 16 curly-horned heads turn onto the low-end of Glengyle. Last summer's lush bracken, burned brown by back-end frosts and battered flat by autumnal gales, crackles underfoot.

The hirsel of Glengyle covers almost four square miles, more than 2,000 acres and lies between the loch shore at 384 feet and Meall Mór summit, 2,451 feet above sea level. From the north-west, the Glengyle burn flows down the ice-chiselled valley into the dark, deep water of Loch Katrine. My ground stands to the north of the water which gives it the considerable benefit of facing south into the life-warming sun. Across the burn, on the aptly named Dhu (Black-side), much of the ground does not see the sun for six long winter months.

Mountain grasses, together with bilberry and a little heather, provide most of the grazing on this rock-strewn ground. Each one of my ewes requires over two acres of pasture to secure sufficient food. Sheep do not just wander over the hills feeding at random, but have a firmly established grazing pattern. No matter how often a flock is gathered in, once they are returned to a hill, they all make for their own particular ground in the vicinity of their birth place. All the ewes are directly descended from long family lines. Each small family unit grazes over an area of 100–150 acres and, normally, is never found off this ground. Several units will co-exist on a section of the hill, their territories overlapping, forming a cut or heft of sheep.

It is to each of these hefts that I now introduce a tup, his coat dyed bright yellow to help me to see him from a distance, as I walk my daily rounds. The traditional number of tups for Glengyle is 16;

six on the low-end and ten on the high-end. The number of tups put out is critical. Too few, of course, means that ewes in season may well be missed, while too many tups on the hill can also give rise to poor lambing results the following spring. The danger lies in the fact that some tups may not be able to take sole charge of a heft, but be forced to spend valuable time fighting off challengers, leaving the females' needs unsatisfied. In-bye shepherds – those whose flocks are always close to the buildings – usually put out an odd number of rams, as they call them, into a field of ewes. Then, in the event of battles breaking out between pairs of tups over the attraction of the moment, there is always one extra to do the necessary.

My stock is predominantly of the Scottish Blackface breed, a very hardy type of sheep and numerically the strongest in Britain today. The origins of the Blackface breed are shrouded in antiquity. They are first mentioned by Hector Boethius in 1460 who wrote that until the introduction of Cheviots, only the rough-woolled, black-faced sheep were to be found in the Vale of Esk in Dumfriesshire. In 1503, records assert that King James IV introduced 20,000 Blackfaces into the Ettrick Forest in Selkirkshire; unfortunately, no mention is made of where this enormous flock came from. Up until the 19th century, it was the custom for flockmasters to call their sheep by the name of the locality rather than by the breed. Thus, the Blackface was known simultaneously as the Linton, Forest, Tweeddale and Lammermuir, amongst others. Each area naturally believed that its flocks were the principal strain of the breed.

Blackface sheep did not appear in this part of Scotland before 1770. Previously the Highland grazings were stocked mainly by a small, old Celtic type of sheep, with a white face and soft Moorit (tan) wool, which can still occasionally be found on some of the offshore islands. There is a legend of an inebriate Perthshire publican who bought a few Blackface sheep which promptly escaped to the hill. Through sheer neglect, they were allowed to remain untended on the hill throughout the following winter. As it was the custom to house the Moorit sheep each night, the fact that these Blackfaces survived surprised many people and awakened interest in the breed. This story may only be a fable, but it is a fact that by 1767 Dumfriesshire flockmasters were renting many sheep-walks in Dunbartonshire and Perthshire. In 1770, there were around one thousand Moorit-type sheep in this parish of Callander, and by 1790, the total had exploded past the 18,000 mark. Unfortunately, this increase in sheep numbers in the north and west of Scotland was accompanied by the enforced emigration of the human population – the iniquitous Highland Clearances had begun.

My four collies hold the tups tightly together just outside the hill gate. I use Mona and Gail to shed off two from the group, and start driving them in the direction of the Wee Hill. Bo, these days more usually called 'Gran' because of her 15 years, and Boot will watch over the others and stop any of them straying while I am away. Boot is a novice, still learning his job. He circles keenly round the tups, not allowing them the slightest chance to escape. Wise old Gran lies back a bit and watches, one eye on the tups, the other on me as I make my way towards the rising sun.

A little way ahead, a handful of sheep are grazing peacefully. Two or three look up at our approach. I call off the dogs and the two tups quickly come up, sniffing hopefully from one to another. Nothing doing here. Mona and Gail move them on.

A big ewe, tail-twitchingly in season, comes running down the hill towards us. Both tups oblige her in turn. No fighting; proper gentlemen. This gives me the ideal opportunity to split them up. I want to leave the younger tup at the bottom of the hill so that I can easily keep an eye on him. While he is busy with his paramour, I use the dogs quietly to work the other fellow, together with a few ewes, further up the hill. This tup ought to be able to cover the top ground of the Wee Hill.

Gran stirs herself, yawns, stretches and wags her tail at my return. Boot is still patiently 'wearing' the sheep in his charge as they pick at the grass shoots still to be found, sweet and succulent, under the twisted skeletons of fallen bracken. Mona separates out another pair of tups and Gail cuts in to help her take them straight up the hillside, en route for Meall Mór (Big Rounded Hill). The first of these I leave immediately above Spit Dubh (Black Spout), this morning a magnificent mare's-tail of silver, ice-sheathed water, highlighted against the backdrop of sheer black rock. The second tup has to keep climbing to come within sight of An t-Innean, the majestic Square Rocks which crown the summit of Glengyle.

A herd of red deer, suddenly alert to my presence, are startled into flight. Following their leader, they file away into the Braes of Balquhidder, white tail patches flashing in the bright sunshine as they go.

I descend by way of Allt na Bruiach (Steep Burn) which will bring me down a few hundred yards further up the glen. It is noticeable that the Scots were not very imaginative when it came to naming things. Indeed, the majority of Celtic names give either the simplest description of the place, or describe some prominent feature: big (mór), little (beag), black or dark (dubh or dhu), speckled or spotted (breac), crooked (cam), point (stron) as in Stronachlachar, Stonemason's point. Big hills (meall mór) and dark lochs (loch dhu) abound throughout Gaeldom. The Gael was also fond of giving the names of animals to many places associated with them. The Gaelic for a cow is 'bo', as in Baelach-nam-bo – Pass of the Cattle – through which the old drove-road passed between Loch Katrine and Ben Venue; Loch Chon is Loch of the Dog; Brig O'Turk is Boar's Bridge. The list is apparently endless.

On the shoulder of Spit Dubh, 500 feet up, I have a clear view of the small group away down to my left. The tups browse whatever food they can find, still only yards from the hill gate. A couple of whistles pierce the crisp, clear air, riding down the wind. Gran rises to her feet and starts the tups moving towards me, along the well-worn sheep path at the back of the stone dyke. Several times Boot tries to pass the sheep and progress is interrupted. Each time I direct him back behind, the tups come on again. After yet another unscheduled stop, I decide to call him to heel and, once he has left the sheep and is safely on his way to me, I head for the bottom of the hill, leaving Gran to do the rest.

The red post-bus wends its way along the road to Glengyle with the morning post.

Boot is soon at my side, looking very pleased with himself. I make a fuss of him – reward is all important, especially during the early stages of training.

Near the foot of the hill is a small knoll (Cnap beag). By the time I reach it, Gran and the sheep are already in sight. The Steep Burn flows along beneath an overcoat of ice, and the tups carefully pick their way across. We move along between the top fence of my West Park and the last stand of birch trees in Glengyle. Long ago, the whole glen floor would have been well wooded with birch, oak, pine and alder. Man cleared the ground in the name of progress. Today, only the dark fingers of alder groves, pointing out the course of even the smallest flow of water, and a few isolated stands of birch and oak, remain in the glen. Lower down the strath, the wider part of the glen, modern plantations of fir trees have been established, with little regard for the eye or the delicate balance of nature.

The next stop is at the Coireasach Burn (said, Cor-ech), which probably means 'Water flowing from the Corrie'. This divides the low end of Glengyle from the high-end. Before going on, I must put out the last pair of low-end tups and on the lower slopes, I leave an old lad that I have some reservations about. During last summer, he had an attack of pneumonia and, although he responded to treatment with penicillin, he is probably not 100 per cent fit. This heft is very open and it should be a simple matter for me to watch him closely. The sixth, and last, low-end tup is stationed on the terracing, 1,500 feet up, in front of Meall Mór. His ground runs back into the large corrie at the head of the burn.

Crossing onto the high-end, and into the afternoon, my task becomes somewhat easier. My ground is a lot narrower at this end of the glen, gradually reducing from a width of one and a half miles to only three-quarters of a mile, over its four-mile run. Now I can put the tups off in twos and leave them to separate themselves. This is exactly what I do at the next dispersal point, a wide green gully which angles up for 750 feet through the rocks, to a broad shoulder levelling at 1,500 feet. At the back of this plateau, the ground rises steeply once more to the 'drium', or long back of the hill, 2,100 feet above sea level. My march or boundary with Balquhidder on the east and Ardleish – on the eastern tip of Loch

Lomond – to the north, runs along the watershed between us. Only land which drains my way is officially mine – it is a pity that the sheep do not always seem to realise that. My other two marches, with the Dhu on the west and Portnellan to the south, simply follow 'march burns' down to the loch.

The sun has followed on my left shoulder all day long. Shining directly onto the full face of Glengyle, the sheen and sparkle of the ice-hung crags has to be seen to be believed. Now and then, a sun-loosened icicle crashes to loud, echoing, prismatic destruction.

There is a rough-hewn road, negotiable only by Land Rover or tractor, running halfway along the high-end. It was constructed in 1963 to allow the Electricity Board to erect power lines when 13 massive metal pylons were planted in the glen. They look like some science-fiction monsters marching southwards along the way of the ancient drove-road, climbing from the glen from Glenfalloch and disappearing in the direction of Stronachlachar. At first I found the pylons and cables a bit of an eyesore, but I soon became used to seeing them around. They do have their uses too. Apart from being landmarks, I have been known to tether an uncooperative ewe to one at lambing time while trying to persuade her to accept a lamb. Foxes also find them handy. One of the local dog foxes used to regularly patrol beneath the wires in search of birds which had accidentally flown into them. This must happen fairly frequently to make such expeditions worth his while. Once, I beat him to it and brought home a nice plump grouse.

The dogs turn the tups onto Eves Road, named after the con-tractor who built it, and we head on towards the most prominent feature of the glen, Ben Ducteach (said, Dochty). The name liter-ally means Holy Hill, so called because of the nunnery which was founded at her foot in the 14th century. Robert the Bruce, in grat-itude for his victory over Edward II at Bannockburn in 1314, where the English army was completely routed, dedicated a priory and ecclesiastic college at the site of St Fillan's cell. (The cult of St Fillan was sufficiently important for the Scots to carry his arm relic to the field of Bannockburn, and to attribute their victory to the saint's intercession.) In conjunction with that establishment, a nunnery was founded eight miles due south, at the confluence of the waters

A local dog fox

of Glengyle. The Wise Women, once quite famous, are long, long gone and only a few ruins remain as an epitaph to the community of Kil-mi-Cailleach (Cell of the Nuns).

Two more tups are left at the Sandy Burn. There are plenty of ewes near at hand to draw them up the hill, and they certainly need no prompting to go. In fact, the dogs have their work cut out to prevent the whole lot breaking away and taking off. Mona and her kennel mates manage to maintain full control, and we continue steadily on our way.

The tups prefer to travel alongside the road as sheets of ice have covered most of the stone-strewn surface, like cold, hard, polished porridge. Walking on it is virtually impossible. We gain height all the time, until we reach the 700-foot contour, and the final parting of the ways.

This is Bealach nan Corp (Pass of the Dead), sweeping down from the heights of Balquhidder. This is the way by which the notables, from as far away as Strathyre, were carried to Kil-mi-Cailleach and their last resting place. Cairns still mark the places where the cortège would pause and take refreshment. At each stop, everyone would add a stone to the resting cairn. Highland funerals sometimes entailed journeys of considerable distance, often over very rough terrain. I have been told of one funeral where the body was carried 73 miles, arriving at its destination on the third day of travel. The mortal remains would have been wrapped in a blanket of blue dyed woollen cloth. Charles II introduced a statute which decreed that every person be buried in just such a shroud. It must have done wonders for the wool trade of the time.

On the lower reaches of the Pass of the Dead, six very much alive tups stand and wait, quietly held by my four collies. What I plan now is a three-way split. A single word, and Gran moves in to shed two off on the right; a whistle, and Mona cuts two away to the left; Boot and Gail drive the very last pair straight ahead, up the glen. Gran plods up the Bealach, pushing her tups before her. Mona drives her two downhill, across the Glengyle water and up onto the face of Ben Ducteach.

The glen divides at this point. The Dhu ground forks away west, past the nunnery, and runs another mile to the top of the 2,000-ft Stob nan Eighrach. My ground continues to the shaded north-east side of Ben Ducteach.

The road, such as it is, comes to an end at this point. Only caterpillar tractors venture any further, leaving tracks through the soft peat as evidence of the routine maintenance visits by the Electricity Board engineers. A small, sturdy wooden hut built beneath pylon number seven serves as a base during operations in the glen. Needless to say, I often find it very useful, too.

Mona and Gran respond to my 'That'll do!' command, the whistles echoing along the narrowing glen. Ahead, the power lines appear to squeeze their way between the opposing hillsides. Beyond lies the day's final destination.

Here, Sithean a' Chatha (said, she-an a catha), a fairy hill, stands to my right, and behind it the long shoulder of the Parlan Hill, her 2,175 ft summit astride the far end of my march. The sun-shielding tail of Ben Ducteach forms the opposite rim of this broad basin, enclosing the best grazing of the Glengyle hirsel or ground. The last two tups are left to their own devices as I turn, dogs at heel, and head for home.

Above me, a pair of eagles soar, seemingly higher than the sun. Their glinting, golden nape feathers and the white underwing patches of the barely mature male are conspicuous in the late afternoon sun. This piece of my ground forms only a part of the territory belonging to these mighty birds; at least four other adjoining hirsels also share this privilege. I know of three eyries on Glengyle, and two more on neighbouring hills. The actual nesting site is changed every year, so that only occasionally will it be located in my glen. Unfortunately, the breeding record of eagles in Glengyle is abysmal. Nobody can remember a single eaglet being successfully reared and there are many tales of deliberate slaughter, as well as natural catastrophe contributing to this sad state of affairs. I hope for better things next season.

The sun slowly slides down the back of the Dhu, sending the evening shadow climbing up the face of my hill, like a giant sundial. As the gloaming gathers, I cannot help but reflect on the many people who have lived in this glen through the eons of time. Early tribes of hunter-gatherers probably moved frequently through the natural passage of the glen. Eventually, some of them settled inside their hill-top forts, or on the safe man-made islands, called crannogs, built out on the lochs. Primitive farming settlement followed and the natural forest was gradually cleared. With settlement came industry, and iron was smelted in the glen up until the 18th century, further depleting the local woodland.

In 1499, the warrior clan MacGregor came to these secluded parts, and their colourful, chequered career was to span more than 400 years. Finally, in 1855, by Act of Parliament, the Glasgow Corporation became the owners of the Loch Katrine water, and by 1954, had become the Lairds of the entire catchment area. The names may change but the game's the same. Nowadays, the control is in the hands of the Strathclyde Regional Council (Lower Clyde Water Board). These nameless people employ me as shepherd to the Glengyle flock; a marvellous job in a wonderful place.

I 'flitted' into the glen with my family on a white winter's dark night early in 1975. Wife, Maggi, and children, Jamie then aged six and Victoria, three, had never seen the place before. In fact, it was the next day before they could see anything because it was so late when we arrived at our new home. I wouldn't be surprised if they thought that they had come to the end of the earth!

About now, Maggi will be taking in the house cow and her two calves, and the children will be tumbling out of the school bus and making a mad, head-long dash for the warmth of the house. The frost begins to curl my beard as Venus becomes a beacon in the deepening western sky. I leave my glen to the care of the night and quicken my pace towards the guiding lights of Glengyle. I can almost smell the soup that I know will be simmering away on the Rayburn.

Early evening in the living-room is one of warmth and noise; rich, hot soup, boisterous children, dogs stretched out on the floor, cats looking for a lap to nap on. The radio news is lost behind school stories – who pinched whose hat, who punched whose nose, who nearly got the strap. Soon tea is on the table, always our main meal of the day, always plenty of it and excellent too. 'The Archers' compete with spelling homework before, at last, Jamie and Victoria squabble their way off to bed.

The evening changes gear. Soft music is punctuated by gently snoring dogs and the soft pedal of Maggi's spinning wheel. Little by little, wool is worked rhythmically into hanks of yarn. I sit in my comfy old armchair reading, listening and, finally, snoozing like the cats napping on my knee.

Eleven of the clock. Time to go out into the dark and feed the dogs. I like to spend a few moments with the stock in the byre last thing at night, topping up their hay and collecting my thoughts together.

And so to bed.

Each day now falls into a similar pattern. The tups seem to have spread out well. The weather is fine and open, and each morning I set out to turn in the sheep off the very high ground at the back of my hirsel. It is mostly the youngest sheep on the hill, gimmers, two-year-olds, who get away up there. They are extremely fit, never having lambed; the problem is that usually the tups are not prepared to climb all the way up to the tops when there are plenty of other females closer at hand. Older ewes often go looking for a tup when they need one; not gimmers though, so I have to hunt them down nearer to the tups. Even then, gimmers are 'shy breeders', and it often requires an experienced and persistent tup to complete a service successfully. Young tups, or a less than fully fit tup, frequently give up. Shepherds have an old saying, 'Old tup with young ewes; old ewes with a young tup'. It makes a lot of sense, that.

Small flocks of snow buntings flit amongst the rocks and hummocks, their silvery, rippling song well in keeping with their plumage and undulating flight. Winter colours consist of a reddish crown, dark brown back, creamy underneath and, in the male, conspicuous white wing patches. From the ground or a boulder perch, the call is a loud, short warble or sometimes a single 'tu' note. Snow buntings are very welcome winter visitors to Glengyle.

While on my daily rounds, I drive any straggling sheep back to their own ground. The ewes on each hirsel are marked with a brightly coloured identification 'keel' on a particular part of the fleece. Glengyle ewes are keeled with a scarlet spot on the near (left) hip. The other keels which I am most likely to see are: blue, near hip, on Portnellan ewes; green shoulder – Braes of Balquhidder; blue kidney Ardleish; red shoulder – Dhu. Tups, too, carry a keel mark. In their case, it is a contrast colour to the ewes' keel, for ease of locating them. My tups have a blue hip keel, but on the far (right) side, to avoid confusion with Portnellan ewes. If I discover someone else's tup on my ground, I make every effort to return him from whence he came.

Tupping time is a good opportunity to work with my less experienced dogs. Mona, my top dog, always accompanies me just in case I encounter a tricky situation, such as trying to move an intransigent tup. The ewes are very fit this year. A mild autumn with plenty of grass has ensured that they have come into the winter in fine fettle. They will stand a fair amount of 'dogging' from the younger dogs.

I have nine dogs in my kennel at the moment. Bo – or Gran – the old matriarch, is now semi-retired and, at 15, has a life of tremendous achievement behind her. Her grand-daughter, Gail, who like Bo is a black-and-tan collie, continues the line. Gail has a son and daughter in the kennel, Boot and Juno. Juno, in turn, is the mother of Owen and Gwen, a couple of six-month-old pups. Maggi

Du (Black Maggi) is a daughter of Bo's full sister, and, as her name suggests, is nearly all black. She is in pup to Boot, and is due to whelp at Christmas. Mona and her son, Max, complete the team. These are the only bought-in dogs, the others are all home-bred.

Recently Mona has replaced old Bo as my top dog. It has been a revelation in dog behaviour to watch as the old bitch has rapidly slipped down the 'pecking-order'. Even young Gwen will bully her now. I try to make sure that she does not get into corners of conflict, especially with the younger dogs. Of course, Bo lives in the house, not the kennel, along with Mona. It is a privilege of only the best dogs.

A smuttering of snow has capped the high ground during the night. Hill shepherds are quite pleased to see the 'Big White Dog' from the sky at this time of year, as it brings the high-flyers down off the tops. The ideal is about a foot of snow to well cover the ground, followed by some hard frost to stop the sheep scraping and digging down to find food. This time, there isn't much at all, but there could be plenty yet, especially after the turn of the year.

The tup which had seemingly recovered from his summer attack of pneumonia is not working. Each time I pass through his ground, I find him standing all on his own. I gather up some ewes to join him, but a while later they will have moved off, leaving him alone once more. He will have to be changed as soon as possible and taken home for further antibiotic treatment. If, as seems likely, he survives until next month, he will be sold in Stirling as a cast tup along with any other old boys who have come to the end of their useful working lives. I telephone the head shepherd for a replacement and Iain Campbell brings me a strong two-shear Blackface tup in the back of his Land Rover. It is a simple job to change him for the ailing fellow.

Hard night frosts set in and continue until the moon begins to wane. In the cold night air, at dog-feeding time, the moonlight is like a sculpture. The red deer are well coated against the winter elements by their thick, grey double coat. The long, hard guard-hairs of the outer layer successfully resist both the driving, horizontal rain and snow of the west Highlands. Red deer calves quickly learn to dig through the first light snowfalls of winter. Hinds and calves appear to be hardier than the males of the species, keeping to the highest ground, often choosing to stay well above the snow-line. Maybe the stags are still recovering from the stresses and excesses of the rut.

No sooner has the full moon passed than the weather breaks. Two days of solid, torrential rain. Rainfall averages around 12 inches for December. The burns tumble and froth downhill in a

Red deer hind

spate of white water. These are just the conditions to demonstrate the hardiness of the hill sheep. Dry cold is no problem to them at all. They do not mind rain too much either. But wet and cold together, particularly prolonged wet and cold, driven in on the teeth of a gale, takes its toll. My flock has had its hardiness considerably improved by the introduction of Swaledale blood.

The Swale is similar in appearance to the Blackface, and undoubtedly, many years ago, came off the same stock. These country cousins from the Pennines of England have been selected for two attributes, extreme weather resistance and abundant milk yield.

Many traditional Scottish flockmasters will not entertain the idea of using the Swaledale at any price. In my experience, however, the stock resulting from using Swale tups on Blackface ewes show classical hybrid vigour; they forage well in bad weather, milk well on precious little food (invaluable in seasons of late spring) and mother up their lambs beautifully.

Even though in the plant kingdom, it is the middle of winter with most species at their mid-winter rest, there are several exceptions to this apparent situation. The intriguing world of mosses, liverworts and lichens is worth a peep.

Anywhere in the vicinity of water, whether it is a puddle, pool or running burn, mosses and liverworts are likely to abound. Some of these simple, non-flowering plants have separate male and female forms. In other species, they occur together on the same plant. The male produces a motile reproductive cell which swims through the film of surface water, hence their affinity to damp places, homing in on chemicals secreted by the female organs. The fertilised female receptacle develops into a spore-producing capsule.

Mosses have their leaves in spirals or in two rows; liverworts are either flat lobe or have three rows of leaves. Lichens are even more fascinating. In reality, a lichen is not one plant, but two entirely different kinds of plant; a fungus growing in association with an alga. They need each other in order to survive.

Maggi collects some species of lichen for dying wool.

Ewes begin to come into breeding condition as the days shorten. Unless tupped successfully, they return to oestrus every seventeen days. On the 17th day of tupping, fresh 'chaser' tups are delivered to Glengyle. I use eight chasers, four on each end of my hill. These reinforcements will, hopefully, mop up any missed ewes and act as an insurance against any of the original tups being infertile. I do not dye the wool of these chasers, just keel them well. This way, they do not become confused with any of the first batch.

It is customary for a shepherd to keep a few sheep of his own, and these are known as the shepherd's 'pack'. Mostly they are orphaned lambs, hand-reared by the shepherd or his wife. It is the wool from my pack which Maggi spins during the long winter evenings.

I run a Suffolk tup with my own sheep. This has several advantages. The cross-bred lambs which I sell make more money in the ring than pure Blackface lambs. The quality of wool on the sheep I keep for breeding is better than the rather coarse, hill-type fleece. Finally, the carcasses that end up in the freezer are larger and meatier.

To make sure that the pack will receive adequate attention at lambing time when I am always very busy, I use a harness on my Suffolk tup. This holds a coloured raddle, a sort of large crayon, on his chest and each time he serves a ewe, a distinct mark is left on her rump. Every day during tupping, either Maggi or I will look through the pack and note the name of any ewe that has been tupped. Now, after sixteen days with a green crayon, it is time to change the colour of the raddle to red. The new colour will show over the paler green, in the event of a ewe returning to the tup. In this way, I know on which date each of my ewes is due to lamb – 147 days after tupping. As I only have a small number, every one of them can be sure of individual attention. If I am away on my hill, then Maggi is quite capable of coping.

High up on Meall Mór, 2,000 feet above the house, I often, quite literally, stumble upon ptarmigan. This strange member of the grouse family is seldom seen below this contour level. In winter, both sexes are entirely white, apart from red wattles above the

Ptarmigan in complete winter plumage

eyes and black or dark brown tail feathers. The males can be iden-
tified by a thin, black eye-stripe. Even when there is no snow at all
on the ground, the camouflage is very effective. Ptarmigan are surprisingly tame, especially considering that they are game birds,
and will sit tight until danger is almost on top of them. Then... an
explosive launch, followed by a burst of rapid, whirring flight.
Such behaviour is probably adequate in deterring potential predators; even a momentary 'start' would give the bird a good chance
of escaping. It never fails to startle me.

Christmas is suddenly upon us. On the Friday before Christmas, I
take the local youth club members carol singing. We go around all
the houses of Stronachlachar, a small Water Board community. It
rains. The carol sheets, which Maggi so carefully typed out this
afternoon, gradually disintegrate until the choice is reduced to any
carol you like – as long as you like 'Away in a Manger'.

The club meets at Stronachlachar Lodge which was built as the
New Hotel at the end of the last century, during the second phase
of development by Glasgow Corporation. The old hotel was bought
by the Corporation for £5,500, and renamed Invergyle House. It
was used by the Corporation until, in 1919, the level of the loch was
again raised, when it was demolished. The new building, along
with other properties, was taken over by the Corporation in 1920,
the year following the compulsory purchase order on the whole
catchment area. It was vacant at the time, and has never since been
used as a hotel. Today, the Lodge is home to three families. In
addition, there are two, large public rooms, where assorted societies hold their meetings, parties and dances.

Tonight is disco night for the younger members of the community. Hot punch – non-alcoholic, I hasten to add – and an oven
full of mincepies await the carollers' return.

On Christmas Eve, the children break up for the holidays.

Early risers are our children, especially on Christmas Day. The
floor is soon covered with pretty patterned paper. Later, the task
of trying to match gift labels to miscellaneous presents quickly
becomes a lost cause.

Christmas day or not, the stock still have to be tended. An

hour sees the morning routine completed and then it's back to the kitchen. To me, Christmas Day, more than any other, is a family day. Jamie and Victoria exhaust their piles of parcels from under the Christmas tree. After a while, although it seems like hours at the time, the tempo slackens a little. Jamie is just beginning to wonder what to do next – play with something or annoy Victoria – when his mother, always a master of timing, wheels in his red, shining, brand-new racing bicycle. The look on his face is a complete picture. Makes my day, it does.

Christmas dinner – the living-room table fairly groans under the quantity of traditional fare. The black bitch, Maggi Du, chooses this moment to start whelping. Each course is followed by a rush out to the barn to see what progress is being made. After numerous sorties to the steading, the bitch has four fine puppies; three bitches and a dog. We have consumed a considerable amount of food, and yet the table appears undiminished.

Everyone joins in doing the evening chores. Sheep are fed and checked; cow and calves are safely housed for the night; dogs given an early supper, and the evening's supply of logs brought in. Maggi Du barbs her pups with her rough tongue as they nestle and suckle along her belly.

Appetites have been restored, and the evening passes, as I suppose the evening passes all over the country, the world.

The days following Christmas turn raw. A damp chill pervades the air. The head shepherd decides to start giving the hill cows some supplementary feeding. Until now, they have been foraging for themselves on the lower slopes of the hill, occasionally browsing through the woods. Every morning from now, right through to the end of May, my hill cows will be fed hay, straw and high protein cobs.

I expect the first of my spring calves to arrive early in February, long before spring itself. Most of the Glengyle cows are big, Highland type. None of them is very young, so I do not expect any calving problems with them.

The first of my tups begin to come in off the hill. Some of them make their own way home and arrive at the hill gate virtually demanding to be let in; others need to be herded back to the steading, sniffing the air all the way for just one last ewe. I try to leave the chasers out for a little longer since they should still be quite fit. Once a tup has returned safely to the fold at Glengyle, he is fed a small quantity of hay each morning. Soon the number of tups in the East Park begins to grow. The Portnellan tups come back to Glengyle too; it is easier to manage them as a large, single group.

I really enjoy going away to the hill at this time of year, especially if the weather is on its best behaviour. I do not mind the cold, clad in warm tweed and continually moving, and I seldom notice any harshness in the wind. Wandering peaceably around my hirsel, I am never surprised by anything I might see. The red deer are quite used to seeing me with my dogs, and just melt away as I approach. Even if I happen to chance upon them suddenly, they never seem to get into a panic, quietly cantering off towards the nearest cover. Once out of sight, however, they usually pause to take stock of the situation. Some resume feeding almost at once. I have ample opportunity, if I stalk with great care, to watch and study their behaviour. It is not unusual for there to be three score or more red deer on Glengyle. I can see them any time I want to, and plenty of them. But if I have somebody with me, usually with the expressed intent to watch deer, they simply vanish off the face of the earth.

The resident, deep russet dog fox sometimes comes up quite close to me so long as I see him first and the wind is in my favour. Although Mr Tod has relatively poor eyesight, tending to be short-sighted, the eye of the fox is a highly-adapted organ. The retina at the back of the eye is well endowed with sight cells; rods which pick up the slightest movement, and cones which provide full colour vision. It is during the hours of darkness that the wily predator comes into his own since the night vision of a fox is surpassed only by that of an owl. A specialised reflective layer immediately behind the retina returns the image, transmitting light back to the light sensitive rods and cones for a second time. This has the beneficial effect of doubling the light available to the eye. It is this layer, called the *Tapetum lucedum*, which is responsible for the green eyeshine that becomes apparent when a fox (or cat) is caught up in a beam of light.

I keep perfectly still. The dogs lie quiet. Foxy prowls closer and closer. He still has no inkling of my presence. His eyes are set no more than fourteen inches above the ground so his natural horizon is fairly close. Lacking long-sight, his vision is further impaired by the absence of a *macula lutea*: in eyes equipped with a *macula*, an area of maximum visual appreciation is present and without it a fox is unable to focus on a stationary object for more than a brief moment. My collies regard this rather aromatic creature without concern until Gwen suddenly pricks up her ears. Exit fox, stage left.

Hogmanay, derived from the old Norse expression for a new season, is the highlight of the Scottish calendar. It may not have the same historical associations as some of the other festivals but faded memories of ancient traditions still persist. Children in some places continue to form into gangs on the last night of the year and go from door to door reciting a poem, demanding a Hogmanay bannock. One old custom, which has died out, was for a man to dress in a dried cowskin and, carrying a torch made from a tightly-rolled sheepskin smeared with tallow, walk three times around a house in a sunwise direction. Each person of the household would then come outside and singe a piece of the hide with the torch. The acrid smoke had to he inhaled by all, including the cattle in the byre. This, I understand, was the ritualistic sacrifice of a god, by fire, to ensure the safe return of the sun to the cold, northern sky.

The more modern style of celebration at New Year centres on the drinking of large quantities of whisky. People divide into two camps: those who stay at home with a few bottles, waiting for visitors, and those who carry the whisky forth into the night to 'first foot' their friends and neighbours. A dark-haired man should be the first person to cross your threshold once midnight has been struck. He may bring a small lump of coal or peat which he throws onto the fire to bring luck, thus maintaining a tenuous link with the fire rituals of the past. Drams and toasts will be exchanged long into the new year.

Already my new year is more than a month old. Thirty-four busy days have passed since I put the tups to the hill. Most of my

Whooper swans on the loch

ewes will be in lamb by this time, but there are always some who, for one reason or another, are still empty. During my first years at Glengyle, I used to leave the tups out a little longer before bringing them home. Even if the weather remained fine and open and most of the ewes had been given a third chance to take the tup, I felt that, come lambing time, the number of eild ewes was far too high. Last year, I changed my policy, and brought everything, ewes and tups, into the parks at Glengyle for the best part of a fortnight. This reduced the eild count by five per cent, but there remains much room for improvement in this department.

Each morning, once I finish in the byre and have fed the cows, providing the hill is clear of mist, Maggi and I set off to gather sheep. I work with Mona and Boot, while Maggi handles Gran and Gail. Given a few good days, between us we bring in most of the flock.

Glistening Glengyle

THE BLIZZARD STRUCK FROM the north without warning, as sudden and brutish as a Viking raid. The wind tore at everything, searching out any weak point in a quest for absolute destruction. The stout walls of Glengyle house stood firm, but outside, who could tell what havoc the furies of the night were wreaking?

I am usually careful about securing doors and gates about the place, anything left unfastened will soon be reduced to kindling wood. Nevertheless, I cannot rest easy until I have been out to check. Pulling on several layers of protective clothing, and with torch in hand, I set out into the storm. Like Captain Oates, I may be a little while.

The forces of Hades almost overwhelm my flashlight. Snow flows soft and deep across the land, but the flying flakes which reach my bare skin feel like fine grapeshot. This is the kind of cold that makes teeth ache and toes shriek for mercy. A quick circuit of doors and gates confirms that all are fast and secure.

I reach the sanctuary of the black byre; no electric light in here. Tansy belches loudly, her neck chain chinks as she chews on her cud. The sweet smell of her breath and warmth from her body reach out towards me as I draw near. I top up the hay rack for the night. Felix, the farm cat, materialises, rubbing herself against the back of my legs. I hand-draw a saucerful of milk, a nightly ritual, this. A little uddercream is smoothed into the cow's teats; between my daily handmilking, the calves' vigorous suckling and the winter winds, they have a hard time of it. Tansy stands perfectly still while I gently massage her vessel, my forehead resting against her warm flank.

It is a wrench even to think of going back outside. The wind is quite unabated, all Hell is on the loose out there. However, once the calves have been suppered, the dogs must be fed too. Doors lead from the byre, through the old stable, clipping-shed and into

Glengyle Blackface ewes in hard weather

the barn, and here I fill a pail with dog meal from a large kist. And then out into the worst of the night and a rapid round of the kennels. With all fed and everything secure, I turn my back to the tempest and beat a new trail to the house. Unlike poor Oates, I make it back safely. I close the door behind me and leave my footprints outside, catching snowflakes.

The Rayburn exudes welcoming warmth. Maggi presses a mug of steaming, piping hot broth into my numb hands. On the radio they are broadcasting storm warnings. We already know. At this time of year the larder is always kept well stocked, just in case of emergencies. Even having a Land Rover is no guarantee against becoming snowed in for a spell. We could stand a fairly lengthy siege, relying on porridge, potatoes, turnips and, of course, lamb. Of these four commodities, the only one which we have to buy in is porridge oats. That comes in halfhundredweight bags, enough to out-last the severest spell. The dogs' feed is mixed up every month, and unless I am caught at the very end of a batch there is no problem. If I do run short, they have porridge like the rest of us.

Blackness suddenly plumps down on all of us. Maggi conjures candles out of dark drawers and a box of matches brings them to life. The children love power-cuts. Victoria bought me a roll of candlewick for Christmas. (Is there a message there, somewhere?) So, indeed, a few of these candles are home-made. They are easy enough to turn out. There is always plenty of sheep fat from our butchered lambs (mostly used to feed the birds in winter) which I melt down and pour into half-pint beakers. I add a little bees' wax or a few bog-myrtle buds to give the burning candles a lovely aroma. Wicks are suspended from above, usually from a pencil across the top of the mug. The finished product is a three-inch thick candle which will burn for many hours. Maybe Jamie and Victoria are not the only children here tonight.

Snug in the flickering light, we all sit round and tell spooky stories. One of the marvels of modern technology, the transistor radio, plays to itself in the background. Maggi makes mouth-watering toast over the glowing charcoals in the Rayburn. Outside these thick, stone walls all of nature battles against the night, fighting to survive.

In the earliest, colourless light of the still day, earth and sky seem as one: no top, no bottom, no sides to the world. The silence is breathtaking. After the war of last night, the day is peace; for the eternity of a moment nothing, but nothing, moves. Even the waterfall is stilled. Glengyle is in deep freeze. Smoke from the chimney wends its way upwards, blending into the sky. There is life inside this ermine cocoon.

As soon as I open the door the dogs bound out to wake the world. Mona leaps and bites into the funny, fluffy stuff which melts in the mouth. Bo skips and rolls through it, sending up great flurries of this magical snow that makes her young again. The first great tit of the morning flies past my head to feed from the fat-filled coconut shell hanging at the living-room window. The coconut clacks gently against the glass.

Hearing the sounds of breakfast, Hazel, my proud red rooster, flaps off his perch and out through the door, disappearing into a drift in a plethora of snow and feathers. The worried hens simper for their missing husband. Hazel flounders back to the safety of the hen-house. I have to plough, knee-deep, through the snow and scatter their corn inside the wooden house. A couple of red-breasts and a host of sparrows pirate a share.

The cowshed is still in deep darkness, the skylights blinded by the blanket which keeps it extra cosy. I hand-milk Tansy while she munches her way through a bucket of cow-cake. Cow and calves breakfast on hay while I return to the house for my daily porridge. The ample winter menu does not vary much in house or byre.

In less than a month, the first calf will be born. I increase the feed this morning to compensate for the extra hard conditions and also to allow for the rapidly growing, embryonic calves. A calf makes up 50 per cent of its birth weight during the final two months of pregnancy. Usually, these hardy hill cows will forage all day long, making considerable contribution to their daily ration. But, with this depth of snow, even in the shelter of the Glenygyle wood, there is little chance of finding much in the way of food. Today, and for several more days I should think, they will be almost totally dependent on what I bring out to them. I will not let them go hungry.

My pack push and jostle around my feet as I fill up their hay-net. The hand-reared members of this flock are no respecters of personage. Before I reach the trough, they are lined up waiting for the tasty concentrates. If I do not put the feed out fast enough, they soon let me know; Penny and Susie will get their heads into the bag and practically clamber inside it.

There was no sunrise this morning. Only the hands of the clock tell them it is late. Then, faintly at first and gradually growing stronger, the sun melts its way through the icy heaven. The sky turns from grey to pale blue as the first hint of colour tints the canopy. The deepening hue behind the brightening sun transforms the whole landscape. The flat, plain, matt white snow comes alive, and a glistening Glengyle lies in front of me.

The radio tells of blocked roads with motorists marooned in their vehicles and communities completely cut off. The blizzard had swept down the country from Caithness to Dunbartonshire, burying the land under a swathe of deep, drifted snow. Farmers and flockmasters are reporting heavy losses, with large numbers of sheep unaccounted for. Sheep are prone to being buried alive in these conditions because they habitually graze with their tails to the wind and are driven ever forward until the way is barred. Trapped on the windward side of the barrier, where the snow builds up into drifts, they are always in danger of becoming snowed under. Deer and cattle, on the other hand, feed into the wind and eventually find shelter on the lee side of an obstruction.

Our electricity is still off although, no doubt, the engineers will be working flat out to repair the damage. No matter what conditions are prevailing, these men brave the elements as they endeavour to get everyone switched on again. The longest break we have had at Glengyle is three days. That was a result of my Hereford bull knocking out a transformer by rubbing himself rather vigorously against the pole. Thinking that it was a general power-cut, I did not bother to report it. On the third day, the cause finally dawned on me, and the engineers rectified the fault in twenty minutes.

All the other dwellings along the north shore have diesel-driven generators which supply them with their own power. These engines churn into life at the first touch of a switch, and pound away until the last demand is turned off. The noise is quite considerable, even with the units being situated as far from the house as possible. People who have them say that they are invaluable, and that they do not notice the noise after a while. Our electricity is supplied by the Hydro-electricity Board which covers the north of Scotland. In days gone by, they generated cheap electricity from water power, at a fraction of the cost of conventional stations. Nowadays, the hydro generators only produce a small proportion of the total requirement. The result is that our bills have become as high as anywhere else in Britain. I have often considered the possibility of making our own electricity; after all, there is a burnful of energy flowing right past the door.

The loss of power is no great handicap. Log fires heat the house, and the Rayburn does most of the cooking anyway. Maggi has the freezer well insulated with tinfoil, but if necessary we could cache the contents in a snow-hole. Any saving on the quarterly account will be very welcome.

The herd of whooper swans has grown overnight, increased by refugees from the storm. Ice has sheeted over the upper reaches of the loch, reducing their feeding area, but they dip and feed in the shallows still available to them.

In the Glengyle wood, I find my first casualties of the gale, a tight tangle of prostrate pine trees; I shall cut them up for firewood. To the eye of the casual visitor, there may appear to be abundant timber growing around the lochside. Even so, apart from an occasional thinning out, I don't believe in felling standing trees. There is always plenty of wind-blown wood lying about, sufficient for my needs, anyway. I have heard tales of the legendary 'Big blaws' going back for many years, 1968, 1953 and 1917 being the most notable ones. The last day of January 1953 is known as the day that the forests fell, all 50 million cubic feet of them.

Natural regeneration is virtually impossible because of the sheep and anything that the sheep miss will be cleaned up by the cattle or deer. Red deer will chew off twigs up to a quarter-inch in diameter. Unless saplings are protected, they have no chance of growing any more than mouth high.

Practically the entire, original forest of birch, hazel and alder, as well as Caledonian pines, was annihilated by earlier inhabitants of the glen. Trees were felled and burned to clear the ground for farming. Houses were no more than simple wooden huts with wattle and daub walls. Wood, of course, was the chief fuel throughout the millennia, although peat and turf were used to some extent. But it was not only the home fires which ate up the surrounding woodland: an ironmaster, working a single open-hearth bloomery, accounted for 125 acres in each 12-month – gobbling up a square mile every five years. A royal charter of 1291 mentions the extreme scarcity of firewood. Many laws were passed, aiming at the preservation of old timber and the planting of new. Some of the penalties were rather strange, to say the least: if a fire, horse or dog were brought into a wood, eight cows were to be forfeited, while if goats were found to be at large, one was to be hanged from a tree, by the horns. I am afraid that it was to no avail: in 1617, Sir Antony Weldon believed that Judas could not have found a tree in Scotland whereon to hang himself.

These present-day trees have been established during the last 300 years, through the endeavour of successive, far-sighted land-owners. At the end of the 17th century, the Duke of Montrose began to actively encourage the planting of oak trees on his land. Oak bark, which was used in leather tanning, was peeled off the trees during the summer, giving welcome employment to the local population. The best bark was taken from trees which were between 20 and 24 years old. Once trees had reached this stage, they were felled and replaced. The oaks still standing are survivors of that bygone industry.

Two hundred years later, the Glasgow Corporation planted a great number of hardwood trees to enhance the landscape. Magnificent chestnuts and beeches still stand as a testament to the services of those gentlemen who supplied Glasgow with the purest of waters. Rhododendrons introduced from Asia, though not useful, add extra colour to the roadsides during the weeks of early summer. More recently, the Corporation established large tracts of alien conifers. Cutting up these fallen fir trees to feed the Rayburn is a pleasure. After too many years of labouring with assorted hand-saws, I made one of my best investments: I bought a power-saw. It will not take me many hours to tidy up here.

The strident song of a jenny wren penetrates through the roar of the power-saw. Such a vigorous scolding of my rude intrusion of his territory.

Beneath the chill blue January sky, life goes on. For some, like the short-tailed vole, life becomes a little easier as the snow-cover protects them from their enemies. For the predators, life is hard. If their prey is not exactly buried, they might just as well be. On the high tops, hares and ptarmigan lead invisible lives, concealed from view by their white winter coats.

Standing in the deep snow, leaning easily on my crook, I spy a thin, diagonal line being etched onto the opposite hillside. A cut of my ewes are on the move, looking for food. In single file, they follow their leader who instinctively knows every twist and turn of the obscured track, down the steep slope. Through my telescope, I can make out the frozen snow encrusted on their long winter wool.

I am looking for embedded stock. Mona has a good nose for finding sheep but Gail is exceptional. If there are any sheep under the snow, providing I go to the right area, these two will find them. I do not expect many, if any, of my ewes to have been buried. This is one advantage rugged, boulder-strewn Glengyle has over the lower, more rounded hills. In the face of a storm, my flock breaks up into numerous small groups, a few sheep sheltering here, a few there, and so on, this way avoiding the danger of a large number becoming trapped in any one place. On smoother hills, the opportunities of finding shelter are far less. Large numbers of sheep are likely to crowd into the fewer available places, sometimes with tragic results.

In the severe winter of 1962–63, when I was working in Wales, I saw the consequences of just such behaviour. On a neighbouring farm, a couple of score of ewes had taken refuge in the only cover they could find, piling into a steep gully. The blizzard buried them. When they were located and dug out, a dozen or so at the bottom had been smothered by those above them. Suffocation is the greatest danger under these circumstances. An individually-wrapped sheep, or two or three together, will come to no harm for a considerable time, even under a great depth of snow. Sheep have been known to survive under a drift for more than 50 days, although these are exceptions and two or three weeks would normally be the limit. The metabolic rate of a buried sheep is naturally reduced by the low temperature surrounding it. The entombed sheep is sustained by a complex digestive system. There are two sources of nutriment: from the coarse highfibre food which has been eaten, and from the direct absorption of tiny, micro-organisms which live in the stomach.

The stomachs of ruminants, such as sheep, cattle and deer, are made up of four chambers. In the largest, the rumen which holds the coarsely-ground food, the micro-organisms begin to break down the cellulose into a form digestible by the sheep. After a while, a small quantity of cud at a time is regurgitated and chewed 60 to 70 times into a finer state. Mixed well with saliva, the cud is swallowed a second time; the finer particles bypass the rumen and travel via the reticulurn and omasum into the abomasum where conventional digestion takes place.

Meanwhile, back in the rumen, the micro-organisms are themselves feeding on the cellulose and multiplying profusely. These rumen flora can be absorbed directly into the blood-stream anywhere along the digestive tract, providing the sheep with an additional and valuable source of nutrition. In order to maintain this function when the supply of fibre begins to run out, the buried sheep will resort to eating her own wool. However, under experimental conditions, ewes have been examined after a fortnight beneath several feet of snow, and were found to have their rumen still two-thirds full of roughage. This surely shows that a buried sheep relies almost entirely on this bacterial source of food.

The Water Board has ploughed open the road. Unscheduled holidays are over and Jamie and Victoria go back to school. The electricity supply has been restored, and life slowly returns to its normal rhythm.

Crisp, moonless nights are held by stars like silver steel fingertips. The snow on the hill glitters a little longer each day, unfolding to me the stories most people never know.

Here an ermine-clad stoat has stalked and killed a rabbit more

The stoat in his white camouflage coat

expertly than a master butcher and, having drunk its fill of warm blood, moved on. Rabbit stew on tomorrow's menu. I follow the trail: four close footprints, showing five splayed toes, every 15 inches indicating the normal bounding gait of this killer. The stoat is our only hunter who changes into a white camouflage coat. Suddenly, the trail digs into a snow burrow which opens out right amongst a cluster of mouse tracks.

A fox trail shows almost daily use. It is about ten inches wide and it runs in an uncannily straight line for considerable distances. On the first day after this snowfall, a single track of paired prints told me of his – for I am quite sure that this is the path of a dog fox – passing this way. Each successive day has usually added to the trail, confirming my belief that they have been left by a dog and that this is his personal boundary line.

During December, the dog will have renewed his interest in the resident vixen. If last season's male had moved on, or been removed by one means or another, a new dog would have made her acquaintance. They would not have been observed much in each other's presence. At the approach of mating time – and here it begins in the latter part of January and runs through into February – the dog begins to take his territorial tasks much more seriously. He patrols the outskirts of his ground at dawn and dusk, barking out his characteristic quick, three-syllable yelping call. It is called out so fast as to be heard as a single shout, and is repeated after a pause, continually around the whole of his march.

This is a warning to his neighbours that he is very much at home. Dog foxes bark out against each other but, here at least, confrontations seldom occur between land-holders. Territories do not meet directly, there seems to be a no-man's-land between them. Any conflict is usually with a roaming male, looking for a territory of his own. Any such battle between males is normally won by the resident fox. He has all the advantages. A fox without territory has more difficulty finding sufficient food; often he will be young, in his first season, and will not be very adept at hunting anyway. The Laird will usually see off these inferior intruders without much bother.

His boundary will be reinforced by special 'no entry' signs. Mr Tod will leave frequent, highly-scented droppings, politely called scats, on his rounds. Strong smelling urine will also help to define the limits of his home range. The fox is well equipped with glands which label his scats and urine, and he also has glands on the soles of his feet. Scraping earth is not an attempt to cover his toilet but it is to help impregnate the soil with scent. It also increases the surface area, thus releasing a stronger, more potent smell.

All through this activity, the vixen has been quietly living within the confines of the territory. Quietly, that is, until she is ready to mate.

Tonight, the hairs on the back of my neck fairly stand on end. It does not matter how many times I hear a vixen outscream a banshee, it never fails and never will fail, I can assure you, to freeze my blood. Tomorrow I shall expect to find more proof of the intended nuptuals. While the rest of Scotland is busy piping in haggis, and toasting the immortal memory of their great poet, Rabbie Burns, my pair of red foxes will be celebrating something far older, far more beautiful. The rutting ritual has begun.

Burns Nicht is yet another excuse for drinking whisky – along with the consumption of haggis and neeps, and large helpings of poetry. The Bard himself became immortal in 1796, and not before or ever since has Scotland produced the like. Perhaps it is just as well that the Welsh do not revere their poets in the same style.

The morning light shows me two sets of fox prints in the snow, side by side.

Boot and Juno gather up the tups in the East Park and sweep them tidily into the fank. Glengyle and Portnellan tups mill about as the head shepherd looks at them with me. The oldest tups, and any others unsuitable for further breeding, are drawn out and put into a side pen. They will be sold off as cast tups, along with those drafted from the other hirsels on the lochside. Four of my tups and three from Portnellan are taken away in the trailer behind the head herd's Land Rover.

I return to the fank to check the feet of the remaining Glengyle tups. I catch each in turn, sitting them up on their tail-ends while I trim back the hooves. This is one job where a strong, sharp knife is essential. One or two have a touch of foot rot, a highly contagious infection picked up from the ground. It is the result of a complex arrangement between a bacterium and a fungus, working in unison to the detriment of the flock. Fortunately, foot rot is not the same problem for the hill shephed as it is for the in-bye sheepman. The old adage about a sheep's worst enemy being another sheep is perfectly true. When sheep are crowded into fields and parks, the problems of disease are magnified. The horny shell of an infected foot will show a degree of separation from the hoof, and may contain pus. I pare back shell thoroughly in an attempt to remove all traces of the infection. A little proprietary ointment is applied to speed recovery and counter any lingering organisms. It is a laborious task but one which is well worth the shepherd's while. A shepherd may be judged by the feet of his flock.

The end of January is reckoned to be the middle of winter. Many farmers will be casting an anxious eye over their stores of fodder, and working out just how long they will last out. With the hard weather, many people have begun feeding sooner than usual and in greater quantities. Already, there is a tidy hole in the Glengyle barn. Every day, each cow eats her way through 15 lbs of hay, 6 lbs of straw and 4 lbs of cobs. The tups account for a further 2 lbs of hay and ½ lb of cereal per head. At least the Glengyle flock does not need any supplementary feeding. The south-facing crags and boulders which break through the snow-mantle absorb warmth directly from the sun, melting back the snow cover to reveal green strips for the flock to forage on. This is another advantage my rough-hewn hill has over more gentle sheep-walks. Only a few miles down the lochside, the snow lies deep and crisp and even, too deep for the ewes to easily scrape through to find food. These sheep have to be hand-fed hay every day, and supplied with high-protein feed-blocks to lick at. This is essential to the well-being of the flock but rapidly depletes the winter food reserves.

The time has come for the mid-winter clean-out of the calves' pen. For the past month, the daily dung from the byre has been barrowed directly onto the enormous rhubarb patch, alongside the steading. The rich manure from the calves' pen goes out the same way and to the same place. Once the job has been completed and the dung spread out in a thick layer, the hill cows are brought into the paddock to trample it well in. It seems that you cannot be too severe with rhubarb: the harder you treat it, the better it grows.

January is usually the wettest month of the year but this month, instead of inches of rain, we have had feet of snow. In fact, this has been the coldest January since 1963, with night temperatures as low as 24°C. The bright, sunny days have been very welcome to both man and beast.

The first day of February is the festival of St Bride. Or is it? This is a clear case of a Christian institution being built onto the ancient celebration of a pagan deity. Brid was the Celtic Goddess of Fire. The Gaels of old had a predilection for fire and fire-worship which has been handed down to the present day, in various forms. February 2 is Candlemas Day (fire, again), a day when the weather should be closely watched. If the day is fair and bright, winter will have another fight. If the day is cloudy and wet, winter ills you can forget. Candlemas Day is fair and bright.

Scotland is a land of innumerable lochs and lochans, but only one lake – The Lake of Menteith – and the news from the lake is of a curling match, arranged for next Wednesday. No ordinary match, for this is to be a Grand Match. Word has been sent out far and wide and the call will bring curlers from ' 'a the airts' to this, the thirty-first Bonspiel. Teams from north of the River Forth will compete against teams from the south. If only the weather holds.

For the past two days, and much of the nights, officials from the Royal Caledonian Curling Club have been hard at work on the arrangements. By first light on Wednesday, more than 300 rinks will have been marked out. The first Grand Match was held as far back as 1847, but the vagaries of our climate have limited the total to just 32 more. The last one was, as you might expect, during the arctic conditions of 1963. Last year was one of the many near misses. Ice had refrigerated across the surface of the lake to the required minimum thickness, and for 48 hours rinks had been etched out, one after another, but a thaw set in the night before the match. I have no fears for tomorrow's Bonspiel, the moon is still waxing and a thaw is a long way off.

The morning of the Grand Match is perfect. I have finished feeding the stock as the sun strikes the top of Glengyle. The children climb rather reluctantly into the school bus; Bonspiel or not, they have to go to school today. The low, early-morning sun slants in through the windscreen, and the borrowed set of curling stones bump about in the back of the Land Rover. I go equipped, just in case there is a chance of taking part in the festivities.

The narrow roads are chock-a-block with traffic. Everyone, it seems, is of the same mind. Farms are deserted, shops closed, offices empty, as curling takes precedence over all else for the day. The make-shift car park in the field adjoining the lake is already dark with serried ranks of parked motors of all description. It takes quite a while to join them.

This is my lucky day. I answer a call over the public address system for a spare player. I explain to the skip that I have never actually curled before, but Allan Lauder is prepared to give me a chance anyway, and I am all set to take part in the Bonspiel. There are thousands upon thousands of curlers, and it looks like most of them are here today, but I wonder how many have made their debut at a Grand Match.

Captain Anderson, president of the Royal Caledonian Curling Club, reads out a telegram from the Queen, which conveys her

warmest good wishes to everyone at the Bonspiel. Promptly at
1.00 p.m. Lord Elgin fires the traditional cannon to signal the start
of the match.

I was forewarned by the widow of the late Colonel Archie
Douglas that his stones which I had borrowed were rather on the
fast side. That was understating the issue: I would classify them as
being rather on the fast side of very fast. I cannot pretend to be in
control of these burnished bits of heavy granite. The line and
direction are no trouble, but finding the range is quite another
thing. No matter how careful I am with my swing, my stone gathers
speed along the ice. Outpacing the valiant sweepers, it passes out
through the head at the far end of the rink, before disappearing
into the distance. Maggi makes the suggestion that I should label
my stones in case I lose track of them altogether. The game is
played on the same principle as team bowls, only using ice instead
of a green. A crucial difference between the two codes, however, is
the liberal application of whisky in the northern version. Before
the last echo of the cannon's blast has died away, hip-flasks appear
as if by magic and are passed around.

The booming, moving ice makes the nervous jump. The old
hands at this outdoor game and those experienced in the ways of
ice only worry if the groaning and cracking stops. The ice is holding
up somewhere around four hundred tons of curlers and their
equipment for a start; in addition, there are more than six thousand
spectators and, on the far side of the ice, a couple of dozen skaters.

The authorities have relented and all the primary schools have
come here for the afternoon, countless small children laughing and
larking about, each delighting in the unexpected free-time and in
the strange ways of the ice. Most of them skid and slide their way
to visit the islands held fast in the centre of the ice-sheet.
Impromptu history lessons are given at the priory of Inchmahome,
the largest of the three islands. It was an abbot of Inchmahome
who banished the 'little people' to the confines of Loch Katrine.
The priory, founded in 1238, long played an active part in
Scotland's life. Mary Queen of Scots, at the age of five, was sent
here for safe keeping after the battle of Pinkie in 1547. A garden
known as Queen Mary's Bower can still be seen. On Inch Tulla,

the ruined castle, once the seat of the Earls of Menteith, is eagerly explored.

After five ends, we adjourn for a little light refreshment. Sandwiches are produced and disappear again almost as rapidly. Bottles are taken out of bags and hampers; everyone has brought their favourite malt or blend, and the picnic becomes a whisky-tasting session. The sun is warm and the ice very bright.

Flasks are refilled and the game restarts. The ice is very keen now, and the film of melt water on the surface speeds up every shot. My stones are stronger than ever, much to my frustration and my skip's amusement. At long last, I manage to get a stone to stop right on the head. It is a pity that it is the far away head of the rink behind ours. I do not score with any of my stones, but I am quite good at knocking out any of the opposition stones which are lying up. Eventually, after a dogged struggle, we lose. But it has been a great experience and lots of fun. The Grand Match must surely qualify as the Match of the Day. Television cameras have been in attendance – maybe we will all be on World of Sport, or some such programme. There were 2,560 curlers on the ice, a match of 1,280 a side. The final result will not be known for a while yet.

As people stream homeward, the Lake Hotel is packed to bursting point, doing its best trade for many a day. In the noisy, bustling bars, shots will be recalled in instant action replays and whole games relived. Techniques will improve and stones raise, draw, guard and wick to perfection as the night wears on.

The earliest reference to curling is, perhaps, to be found in Pieter Bruegel's 16th-century paintings, 'Hunters in the Snow' and 'The Bird Trap'; the first Scottish account of the game is dated 1620. Stones of long ago were small, hand-sized and irregular in shape, often doubling up as loom weights. Gradually, stones became larger, culminating in the massive jubilee stone, at 117 lbs. Round stones were introduced during the 18th century, allowing a much more skilful game to develop. The only quarry producing curling stones today is at Trefor in north Wales, but they are still dressed in Scotland.

Many villages in this area have outside curling ponds, shallow basins which can be flooded when Jack Frost is about. There is even a local trophy which is played for at a mini bonspiel whenever the conditions are suitable. Nevertheless, the game has moved indoors and is more usually played on immaculate ice. Quite a few expert curlers had as many problems as I did trying to come to terms with the uncertain outdoor rinks.

The weather eases, and a good thaw sets about clearing away the winter whiteness. Snowdrops, the fair maids of February, shake their heads above the receding snow. It amazes me that these Mediterranean plants, introduced by the invading Romans, thrive so well in these harsh climes. I love to see them because they remind me that spring will come. The snowdrop is not alone, however, in proclaiming better times ahead. The robin becomes even bolder and begins to chirp out his familiar song from an open perch. Blackbirds, song thrushes and dunnocks form a hedgerow chorus behind the longtime, redbreasted soloist. In the evening gloaming, a solitary pipistrelle bat takes to the wing in search of insects. A good feed or two now will help to carry it through to the real spring. After dark, when the bat has given up his hunt for the few snowdrop-pollenating insects, the tawny owl sits scritching in the old beech tree, watching out for larger prey.

A small, yellow-flecked, white face nuzzles into the cow's udder. The first calf of the year has arrived. His mother, number 191, has produced a bonny, big bull calf, and both are well. Four legs shake and wobble precariously as he takes in the life-sustaining milk.

The first milk is called colostrum, or beestings, and is essential to the calf. Not only does it provide nourishment, but also antibodies against any harmful organisms that may be around. During the last three weeks of her pregnancy, the cow has been producing these antibodies and storing them in her colostrum. For some reason, no immunity is passed to the unborn calf and after birth, the calf can only absorb antibodies from the gut during the first 24 hours, so an early feed from his dam gives him the best chance of fighting off infection.

191 licks the calf's dark red coat until all traces of calving mucus have been removed and the short hairs stand upright along his back. The placenta has already been eaten by the cow. This is

done immediately after producing the calf and serves two purposes: the first reason is probably obsolete now as it was to remove all traces of the birth and reduce the risk from predators; the second intention is to give the cow a boost of important vitamins and minerals after her ordeal.

For the past six Fridays, my weekly telephone call to the Rugby Club has met with the same response – all games off. But tomorrow there are two games for Stirling County at Ardrossan, down on the Ayrshire coast. The bus leaves at 11.45 a.m. and I have been picked at wing-forward for the 2As. Travelling away from home with the 1st xv is always an experience, even if you are not turning out for them. The atmosphere in the team bus is one of cigarette smoke and winter green, and anticipation.

By the time the bus is heading into the night, back towards Stirling, things are a little different. Beer and songs weave in and out of rugger talk. Two smiling, scantily-clad cardboard ladies, kidnapped from a wayside inn, stand at the back of the bus – the spoils of victory. Somewhere along the road, the inevitable, tradi-tional cry goes up. Roy, the driver, pulls up and half the occupants pile out and line up along the side of the bus, in regulation fashion. Bodies clamber back aboard, and somebody casually observes that we are parked in front of the local police station.

As we leave the effect of the mild coastal strip behind us, the Atlantic rain turns to snow. Winter has returned so soon. I am thank-ful to have a Land Rover waiting for me back at the clubhouse.

First thing on Monday morning, there is an urgent message for me to go to Harthill where my hoggs are being wintered. It seems that the sheep have broken out and have eaten rhododendrons, with dire results. I put Mona and Bo into the back of the work's van and head for Lanarkshire as fast as the law will permit. I have a bottle of multivitamin solution and a couple of hypodermic syringes in my pocket. I may just need them since rhododendrons can be deadly poison to livestock. It all depends on the quantity they consume dur-ing their first meal of the plant. If it is just a nibble here and there, then there is usually no problem. On the other hand, if the first feed is a large one, then it quickly proves to be fatal.

Andrew Graham has taken the Glengyle hoggs for many years and always looks after them well. Marauding dogs, let loose from the nearby housing estate, often cause some mischief during the winter let, but rhododendrons are something new.

Andrew is waiting for me and looks rather worried. He thinks that he has managed to drive most of the sheep out of the neighbouring wood where the troublesome plants abound, and back into his own land. I gather up the hoggs. Then Mona and Bo bring the sheep between Andrew and me as we take a count of them. Eight missing.

The two bitches hunt through the dense undergrowth in the dastardly wood where rhododendrons have been allowed to grow un-checked for many years. I wish now I had brought Gail with me. Her excellent nose would soon find the missing sheep, alive or dead. Eventually, between us, we locate them all: six are dead but two are still living, just. This is where the bottle of multi-vitamin is needed. I sit each of the surviving hoggs up on her tail and lie the head back across my knee. By pressing the side of the animal's neck with my thumb, I detect a vein into which I inject 2 ml of the solution. One recovers quite quickly and returns to her companions. The other one doesn't look too good. Andrew and I carry her to the fence and lift her over to the proper side. I inject another 2 ml into her vein and make her as comfortable as possible before leaving.

The treatment is simple enough, if given in time. The active harmful agent in rhododendron leaves interferes with the animal's vitamin balance, inducing a deficiency. A small amount of vitamin injected intravenously restores the equilibrium.

I set off to drive the 70 miles back to Glengyle, while Andrew has six sheep to bury and a boundary fence to straighten.

Sometimes, even the hardy, weather-resistant red deer are forced off the hill tops in search of food and shelter. An interesting aspect of red deer is the fact that they used to be woodland dwellers and have changed their way of life to one of moorland existence. Clearly a successful case of adapt and survive. However, in times of great stress, they will return to the woodland.

In the Boathouse Wood, there are plenty of signs that red deer have been in residence. They browse at a higher level than sheep, not that there is much left to ruminate on at the lower level, with birch and rowan being preferred to any other tree. Occasionally, they gnaw the bark from the trunk of the tree and, of course, if they remove the bark in a complete ring around the bole, the tree will die. Sheep and goats are also guilty of this practice in hard weather or when the diet is short of minerals. Both the red and the roe deer find the lichen, *Parmelia physodes*, a delicacy. This grey-green lichen is widespread, growing profusely on older tree trunks, fence posts and heather stems.

During February, if a vixen has been successfully mated, there will be important hormonal changes taking place. The Glengyle vixen is obviously in cub, and I do mean obvious. She may even dig out a completely new den, but she will not decide which one will be the nursery until the very last moment. This behaviour only lasts a few weeks; she will not want to betray her intentions by digging out fresh soil immediately prior to cubbing.

By the end of February, six of the hill cows have calved; three bull calves and three heifers. These old cows of mine are a good sort. I have a few younger ones but they are a different type altogether. The old are bred out of Highland cows by using a Shorthorn bull. The chief asset of a Highlander is its ability to thrive in these bleak, wet hills of the west Highlands. Daughters of a Shorthorn sire, my cows have better milk yields than their dams, but have lost none of their hardiness. I cross the cows again, this time with a Hereford bull. The cows produced from this union are still tough enough to outwinter at Glengyle and grow quickly during the time they remain on the farm. Calves by the Hereford bull are popular in central Scotland, and there is always a good demand for them at the Stirling markets.

March comes in like a lion. This is supposed to be the lengthening month that wakes the adder and blooms the whin, but for the moment, winter's grip holds fast onto Glengyle. Even so, it is impossible to ignore the tell-tale signs of the coming season.

The ravens are already nesting on the Square Rocks, high above the house. Four pale-blue, speckled eggs lie in a nest of twigs and heather stems. The construction is cemented to the rock face with mud and peat, and has a soft lining of grass and wool. These birds, Britain's largest member of the crow family, are mainly carrion feeders and this year there is plenty of food lying out on the hills. Many deer, both young and old, have perished during the winter. On the slopes of Ben Ducteach, below the Netted Rock, I find two dead ewes; their carcasses will add some variety to the ravens' menu. It looks as though they were buried alive in the January blizzard, and faded away peacefully. The Government has promised to pay compensation for casualties such as these. If I have only lost two sheep to the storm, I will not have done too badly and neither will Her Majesty's Treasury.

Below the Square Rocks, the gorse adds a touch of colour to the lower slopes. In the woodland, only the brave alder has been standing sentinel to the spring season, catkins hanging to catch the wind. On the ground, the goblet-shaped grey stalks of the cladonia lichens are brimming over with scarlet spore-producing structures.

Maggi Du's puppies have grown well. I weaned them completely last week and now they are ready to go to new homes. I shall not be keeping any of this particular litter, although I like to keep track of every dog I sell, in case I need to buy one back again.

Out on the loch, in front of Glengyle House, pike nets have been surreptitiously submerged to trap the voracious predators as they swim into the shallows to spawn. Nothing in or on the water is safe from ambush; ducklings by the dozen and trout by the score fall prey to them every year. A 5 lb pike is believed to have an annual intake of about 50 lb of other fish, mostly trout. Pike is the largest freshwater fish in the British Isles, and this part of Britain appears to produce the biggest pike. One weighing 47 lbs 11 oz was reportedly taken from Loch Lomond and a 70 lb pike has been claimed from Endrick Water. Last year at Glengyle 131 pike, weighing half a ton, were taken from Loch Katrine.

Every cat in the lochside is well-fed at this time. However, very few local people bother to eat these fish as they require a great deal of work. Pike are ugly, slimy fish, not at all nice to touch. This can be rectified by soaking the pike overnight in a bowl of salt water containing a few soda crystals. The numerous needle-sharp bones are a bit more of a problem: sometimes Maggi spends ages de-boning a cooked fish to make smashing fish-cakes. Recently, quite by accident, we discovered that if we leave the fish slowly baking in the Rayburn for two whole days, all the bones decalcify completely and are safe to eat. Maggi usually stuffs the pike with potatoes mashed with herbs and adds a little dry cider or white wine to the casserole.

The sun climbs a little higher and stays up a bit longer every day, warming and waking the cold earth. Daffodil buds open into full flower.

Snowdrops – the fair maids of February

The First Gather

ALTHOUGH THE FIRST OF the summer migrants, the diminutive olive chiffchaff, has arrived at Glengyle, the winter visitors to the loch are still very much in evidence. A large flotilla of brown-headed pochard ducks keep to the deep water mid-way between Glengyle and the Dhu, diving to feed on underwater plants. Another diving duck, the goldeneye, prefers to pursue small water animals and insects closer to the shore than the pochard. In the quiet woodland, the soft, furry pussy willows emerge and the yellow lambs-tail catkins hang from hazel branches, teasing me that spring is almost here. Elsewhere in the country, lambing is well under way, but here at Loch Katrine we are only now thinking about gathering the sheep for the spring dipping.

Towards the end of each winter, the ewes are gathered in, hirsel by hirsel, starting with Letter at the end of the loch. The name means Land on a Slope. The flock is treated to make sure that it is free from pests and parasites, and protected against as many sheep diseases as is humanly possible. Through these endeavours, the shepherd gives his sheep the chance to be in good body condition and in the best of health by the time lambing comes around.

After his dogs, the most important item a shepherd possesses is his boots. They are relatively expensive, costing the best part of a week's pay, so it is imperative to look after them well. If treated properly, a good pair of leather boots will last a long time; my present pair of Hawkins boots are more than eight years old. Before the gatherings get under way, I give my boots a thorough going-over. I remove the leather laces before coating all the external stitching with wax polish. This gives extra protection to the yarn and helps to prevent the dubbin softening and so weakening the leather around the stitches. Then I give the outer surface and the tongue a spare application of dubbin, just enough to soak into the leather.

The first gather

Leather contains natural oils which effectively keep it waterproof. Dubbin replaces these oils which frequent wetting, particularly in the acid water found in Scottish peat bogs, takes out. When the dubbin has had time to soak in, I polish the boots well, the wax putting a thin skin onto the outer surface. Inevitably, this is soon scuffed off as I walk through bracken or clamber over rocky ground, but it does afford a little extra protection for a while. The golden rule in leather care is to avoid heat of any kind. More boots are damaged this way than by any other factor, even a normal centrally-heated room can cause damage. When my boots are wet, I leave them in a cool, airy place to dry off. If necessary, dubbin can be laid onto damp leather – in fact, it is better to do this as the pores will be opened up – rather than wait until the boots are completely dry. Ever since I was taught as a youngster by my father and grandfather, I have found that dubbing should be done occasionally and sparingly, and polishing with ordinary shoe polish should be the order of the day.

After an early bowl of porridge, the north-shore shepherds, together with their dogs, assemble in the Edra close. This is where today's host, young John McDougall, the Letter shepherd, lives with his parents. His father, John sen. and always addressed as Jock, is the Edra shepherd. The rest of the team under the direction of Iain Campbell from Strone is: Charlie MacLauchlan, Coilachra; Alec McLellan, Portnellan; and myself from distant Glengyle. My four dogs, Mona, Bo, Gail and Juno, mill around with the others as we wait to get started. The day will be divided into two parts: this morning will be spent hunting sheep out of the Letter Woods onto the open hillside and, after lunch, we will gather in the flock off the hill itself into one of the stone-walled parks.

On every gather, each man is responsible for a particular section of the ground to be covered. It is traditional for a shepherd to do the top of his own hirsel with the others strung out below him. I make a start from a point almost three miles along the loch shore where the old sawmill is situated on the edge of The Prison. This is a well-wooded peninsula named from the time of the MacGregors, who found it a useful place for hiding large numbers of reived cattle which could be easily guarded by a couple of men. Apart from their lowland raiding, the MacGregors founded a protection racket based on the local black Highland cattle. In those days, cattle were not only used as a guide to a man's personal wealth, they were also a main source of currency. The passing of coin as a means of payment was commonly known as 'silvermail'; the use of cattle, 'blackmail'. The MacGregors levied blackmail against their neighbours in return for guaranteeing the safety and protection of their cattle. If the offer was refused and payment withheld, the livestock in question inevitably went missing from their usual pastures. However, as soon as the premium was safely in the MacGregors' hands, these beasts would quickly appear again. On rare occasions, cattle would be stolen from fully paid up clients and the Gregarach would take up arms in the pursuit of the reivers, always returning the correct number of stock to the rightful owner. In 1691, these irregular affairs were put on a legal footing with the formation of the famous Glengyle Watch under the captaincy of none other than Rob Roy himself.

The Coilachra shepherd is below me and the Portnellan man above me as I leave the road and climb up into the mature conifer plantation. Flashes of yellow from the restless flitting of a small bird catch my eye. The chiffchaff has spent the winter in sunny Africa and, as always, is the first of the woodland migrants to return for the breeding season. This bird is very similar to the yellow warbler, and not unlike the slightly larger wood warbler, both of which will arrive later; then I have to rely mainly on the voice to make my identifications. The call-note 'hweet' is close to the 'hoo-eet' of the willow warbler but its song is completely different, comprising a monotonous 'zip-zap-zip-zap' which gives the bird its name. Now and again, the song is interspersed with a quiet churring. The male chiffchaff likes to sing from a perch at least 15 feet above the ground, but the hen will build her domed nest of moss and grass, lined with feathers, in dense undergrowth.

There are no ewes to be seen. It is clearly a case of not being able to see the sheep for trees. Gail barks and barks. Below me I can hear Charlie's big grey Beardie, Paddy, giving voice while beyond me Alec has his Jean doing likewise. A pair of roe deer bound down the slope in front of me and swing back the way I have come, crashing away through the trees to safety. The sheep, I hope, are drawing away forward. My dogs work out on both hands to make sure none is left hiding.

After our midday meal, we turn out again to gather the Letter Hill. This time John and Jock go away to the west, the shepherd touching the 2,000-ft contour at the back of his hirsel. Iain and Alec swing around on the east flank, while Charlie and I take the centre ground, quietly driving the in-lamb ewes out the way until John and Iain come together behind the sheep. The flock is then turned for home along the route I had followed out. Eventually, the sheep funnel in through the hill gate into the park where they will wait overnight.

The loch darkens and it looks as though rain is not far away. March is surprisingly only the eighth wettest month of the year, averaging a little over 6.6 inches. It was the plentiful water that brought the Glasgow Corporation to Loch Katrine in the first place. By the early 19th century, the city of Glasgow (the name comes from an obsolete Gaelic term for precious water) was bedevilled with polluted drinking water from an archaic system of wells and open burns. Robert Stewart, who lost his fiancée through typhoid fever, swore that he would devote himself to the task of securing and implementing a supply of the purest drinking water for the city. Stewart became Lord Provost of the Council in 1851 and he was successful in guiding his project through some very stormy times to a very satisfactory conclusion before his term of office ended in 1854. On 2 July 1855, the necessary Act of Parliament received Royal Assent and work on the Loch Katrine scheme started almost at once.

Under the Act, the level of the loch was to be raised by four feet and a 26-mile-long aqueduct constructed to carry the water to holding reservoirs at Milngavie (said, Mul-guy) on the outskirts of the city. Thirteen miles of the aqueduct are tunnelled through some of the hardest rock imaginable; at one stage, the contractors, working 24 hours a day, were progressing at the rate of just one yard a month. There are almost four more miles of iron piping and the remainder is open waterway. On 14 October 1859, amid scenes of great ceremony, Queen Victoria inaugurated what was then by far the greatest water works in the world. The engineer in charge throughout was John F. Bateman, who was at one time assisted by no less personages than Robert Stephenson and Isambard Kingdom Brunel, engineers of considerable repute.

In 1885 and again in 1919, further Acts of Parliament allowed the level of the water to be raised by five feet at a time, to stand at its present level of 14 feet above the original water-mark. A second aqueduct was constructed during the second phase of development which was completed in 1895. Today, and every day, 100 million gallons of the softest, purest water will flow down the pipeline to the thirsty city of Glasgow which, in one respect, now lives up to its name.

The overnight rain has cleared away and the morning sun has only a few clouds for company. The Letter ewes are herded the half-mile along the road to be handled in the Edra fank – dosed against worms and liverfluke, innoculated against eight diseases and, finally, dipped to kill external parasites. Sheep suffer from a multitude of complaints mainly due to the fact that they are stocked at a far heavier density than would naturally occur. From earliest times, shepherds have searched for remedies to cut down their losses. Flockmasters of bygone ages had various treatments for sheep maladies and were surrounded by a mysticism which kept them aloof from other farm workers. Some remedies were in general use, others were known only to the flockmasters and the secret carefully guarded. In those days, each shepherd was his own veterinary surgeon, and therefore a man whose flock suffered fewer losses than those of his neighbours was held in high esteem.

The favourite stand-by in a shepherd's medicine box was simply bluestone, copper sulphate. This compound was used effectively in drench-form against stomach worms, and also to prevent swayback in newborn lambs. A footbath of bluestone solution was equally useful for treating footrot and, as a powder, it was a powerful antiseptic for dressing wounds and lambs' navels. More complex by far was the concoction used to combat the deadly bacterial disease known as braxy. In the early winter and again in the spring of the year, it is not uncommon for certain districts to lose a number of sheep in otherwise good condition. These outbreaks are often associated with night frosts and in some cases losses may be very serious. Under pressure from this annual visitation, a preparation was evolved by trial and error, and that intangible something called intuition, which significantly reduced the incidence of braxy. Dung from a pregnant sow fed on a mash of milk and selected vegetables was mixed with cow's milk and the sheep at risk drenched at the appropriate season. This proved to be an efficient, if primitive, vaccine.

Nowadays, a shepherd has things a great deal simpler. In recent years, the results of painstaking research have done much to combat disease, even to the extent that the single 2-ml vaccination we give each ewe will protect her against eight different ailments: dysentery, struck, pulpy kidney, blackleg, black disease, redwater, tetanus and, of course, braxy. Antibodies produced in the colostrum of ewes on this system will protect their lambs against lamb dysentery, pulpy kidney and tetanus, provided the lamb suckles normally within the first 12 hours of life. This protection lasts for three months and will cover the period of greatest risk.

Besides receiving the Covexin 8 injection under the skin, behind the shoulder, each sheep is given a combined oral dose against roundworm, tapeworm and liverfluke. Roundworms probably cause the greatest single loss to the sheep industry: a poorly thriving sheep is often a sign of worm infestation, in most cases associated with scouring. A number of dirty tails and hind-ends usually indicate the presence of insidious worms which do their greatest damage by depressing the sheep's appetite and stunting growth without necessarily producing a dramatic appearance of ill health, although such disastrous outbreaks do occur causing a number of fatalities.

There are ten or 12 different species of roundworm and their life cycles are basically the same, each one specific to the stomach or intestines. Eggs laid by adult female worms pass out with the droppings. Under favourable conditions, the eggs hatch within 24 hours, the larvae feeding on the available moisture and bacteria. In a short time, two or three days, the larvae shed their coats and reach the second larval stage; then in a further three to seven days, the third infective stage is reached. The larvae climb to the top of the nearest herbage and wait to be eaten. They can survive there, it is thought, for three months. Mountain sheep on extensive upland pastures tend to be less affected than heavily stocked in-bye flocks. However, regular treatment proves to be beneficial and more than repays the initial cost.

Tapeworm too can be a problem, particularly from June to September. Infestation is more easily recognised because segments of tapeworm can be seen easily in the droppings. Like all worms of this type, sheep tapeworms have a complex life history. Hermaphrodite adults shed mature segments of their own body, and the cover quickly disintegrates exposing the eggs. Tiny pasture mites eat the eggs which develop inside these secondary hosts. Sheep consume these mites along with the grass, the larvae break free inside the primary host's intestines and develop into adult worms. The old-fashioned treatment was with a drench of copper and nicotine sulphate and was very successful. Today, the active ingredient is contained in a single worm fluke dose.

Liverfluke is another hermaphrodite and the flat adult worm is found in the bile ducts of infected livers or gall bladders. It is shaped rather like a leaf or fluke, from which it gets its name. It has the most complex life-cycle of all the internal parasites. The eggs, like those of the other worms, pass out in the faeces. In nine days or so (under less than favourable conditions, it can be as long as five months), the eggs hatch into first-stage larvae. They swim in the film of surface water until they are picked up by a small snail with a 'left-hand-thread', most commonly *Limnam truncatula*. Snails with a right-hand spiral never act as secondary hosts. The fluke larvae take six or seven weeks to develop into the second stage, whereafter they leave the snails and climb to the top of near-by plants. They can survive in this state for a year or more. Once they have been ingested, the larvae penetrate the intestine wall and in four or five days they reach the liver of their host. There they burrow through the tissue, growing larger and larger until they are almost able to cover a one-pence piece. After five weeks or so, they reach and enter the bile ducts having wreaked considerable, irreparable damage on the way. It takes a further six weeks for the new flukes to attain full maturity, after which they can live for 11 years, producing as many as a million eggs each year.

The effects of the invasion of a sheep's liver by flukes will depend mainly on the actual numbers present. An otherwise healthy animal can tolerate a low level of infestation; there comes a time, however, when the degree of damage caused to the organ clearly manifests itself by chronic ill-health or death. Until comparatively recent times, it was easier to attack the problem by attempting to eradicate the secondary hosts, the small water-loving snails. Good old copper sulphate was broadcast by hand over the wettest ground. As it is quite impossible for the parasite to be passed from sheep to sheep except through the agencies of the secondary host, reducing the snail population was an effective method of fluke control on a small scale. However, on the vast tracts of wet upland sheep-walks, the problem was considerable until the advent of modern drugs. Some flockmasters used to treat their liverfluked sheep with a weekly dose of 4 oz of salt or a monthly treatment with Male fern (*Diyopteris filix-mas*).

The Male fern is the second most common fern, after bracken, found at Glengyle. It favours a damp woodland position and similar shady places. There are many old beliefs about the power of this particular plant; apart from its medicinal role, its spores were supposed to confer invisibility to the carrier. On St John's Eve (26 December) its roots were dug up and carved into the shape of a hand and baked to make a charm to ward off witches and other evil forces.

Before the sheep are returned once more to the hill, they are bathed through the dipping tank. This expedient will protect them from the attentions of external parasites, particularly from lice and ticks. Infestation of lice would cause loss of both wool and body condition, while ticks, apart from their nuisance value, can transmit several nasty diseases to the sheep.

It is, perhaps, in the field of sheep-dipping that modern husbandry techniques have made the greatest strides. For every 50 gallons of water in the tank, I open and stir the contents of an 8 oz packet of fine powder into a bucket containing a little water. With each packet of dip, there is a sachet of copper sulphate, proudly proclaimed to be a bacteriostat: the addition of the copper sulphate helps to prevent postdipping lameness which sometimes occurs especially if the solution has become highly contaminated. The mixture is stirred into the tank, the whole operation taking only a few moments.

A magpie's comfortable perch

In days of yore, it was necessary to brew up a concoction in a large cauldron which was fired alongside the dipping tank. One local recipe for the production of 85 gallons of dip required the heating of 2 lbs of arsenic with the same weight of soda, and bringing it to the boil. Then 5 lbs of soft soap was added and the whole lot stirred into the bath water. Another of the countless preparations was to heat 1 gallon of spirit of tar, half a gallon of carbolic acid, plus 1 quart of soda and add to 80 gallons of water. It was claimed that the advantage of this mixture was that the smell would deter livestock from either drinking water or eating grass contaminated by the highly-poisonous dip. In addition to all that palaver, some flockmasters further complicated the business by insisting on the addition of an oil, such as whale oil, to the dip. They believed that this was beneficial since it enabled the fleece to throw off rainwater more readily. In this case, all that happened was that the oil floated to the surface of the tank and was carried away by the first few sheep, leaving practically none for the rest of the flock.

Even in quite recent times, proprietary dips still required melting down in the old boiler prior to being added to the water. Thankfully, I missed out on this particular treat. Present-day dips, besides being so much easier to work with, have many advantages over the old types. They are longer lasting and, provided the solution is given a chance to dry on the animals after dipping, they are not washed out of the wool by the first downpour. Neither is the wool stained or damaged in any way. Modern dips cover a broad spectrum of pests, both killing off and preventing re-entry of the parasites. Most important of all, perhaps, is that they are no longer such a health hazard to man and beast. Sheep tolerate the dip so well that very young lambs may be safely treated. Also, there are no lingering residues in the meat and sheep may be slaughtered for human consumption three weeks after going through the tank.

The middle of March sees the new fishing season come in, although the hire-boats will not be going out until the beginning of next month. The water still bears its winter chill, and for a while anyway the only way I can tempt out one of Loch Katrine's lovely brown trout is with a juicy worm. Shepherds and boys alike set about bringing a little variety to the daily menu; there is nothing quite like grilled, freshly caught brown trout. Anglers up and down the land will he busy preparing their tackle, tying flies and making up casts, ready to commence their campaign, and contemplating the ones which will not get away.

As a simple shepherd, my fishing bonnet contains just two flies, tied for me by my good friend, Walter Kennedy. The Collie Dug, dressed with the long, blue-black hairs plucked from Bo's flank, is an excellent salmon fly. As there are no longer any of these majestic fish swimming in Katrine's deep water, I only use my trout fly on this loch, the Tup's Indispensable. Even though this fly is one of the best-known dry flies in the angler's armoury, it never ceases to amaze me that absolute horrors are sometimes passed off as a Tup's. The secret is in using real hair, wool and grease taken from the scrotum of a tup. Old flies should only be re-oiled with genuine grease, as there is no doubt that it is the taint from this which makes it such a fatal lure to the quarry.

The pike nets have been taken out of the lagoon in front of Glengyle. The season's tally is 168 pike, weighing in at more than half a ton. This must represent an appreciable conservation factor for Loch Katrine's trout and wildfowl.

The weather has turned much colder and the day is rather on the raw side as we head away to gather the Edra hirsel. On the way out, the other men disturb a large herd of red deer. I count 105 hinds and yearlings as they troop off the top of Edra, down the hillside in front of me and swing away into the comparative tranquillity of Balquhidder. This is a difficult time of the year for the Highland red deer and, logically, is the period of highest natural mortality. Food is scarce and many of the inexperienced calves succumb at this time, together with some of the old-timers who have reached the end of their days. Weather does not make a lot of difference to the death rate although, like sheep, deer seem to prefer the hard, dry cold to the strength-sapping perpetual wet.

Another major contribution to the death toll is made by the heavy burden of parasites involuntarily borne by deer, the control of which is left to nature's own devices. It is believed that, again like sheep, an otherwise healthy deer can tolerate a certain level of parasites, but in a weakened animal with its threshold of resistance reduced, it may prove to be the final straw. Besides the usual run of parasites held in common with the sheep, red deer play host to a few more, very nasty beasties. First, there is the mass of small, white, thread-like worms which take up residence in the lungs and windpipe. Although seldom assuming the serious proportions of stomach worm infestation, this can cause much coughing, symptomatic of the invasion, and restricts the breathing.

Next on the list is the warble-fly, specific to deer although there is a close cousin which attacks cattle. The large white grubs of the warble fly emerge through the skin along the back of the host in March and April, and drop to the ground. Adult flies will emerge from their pupae in the summer and, after mating, the females will deposit their eggs on the long hairs growing on the back of the host's legs. The larvae burrow into the skin and migrate to the throat where they pass the winter months before resuming their journey to the site of exit. This parasite appears to have the least harmful effect on its host, except that the hides are effectively ruined for commercial purposes.

The last in the group certainly is the most vile creature of all – the nasal bot-fly. This fly is on the wing during the summer and, by alighting on the nose of its intended victim, injects a drop of fluid containing minute larvae into the nostrils. The larvae quickly attach themselves to the inside of the nasal passage and gradually make their way to the pharynx, a chamber at the back of the nose. There they feed on the mucus and grow steadily larger. By mid-March, they are almost ready to emerge and can measure as much as 1½ inches by ¼ inch. At this stage, when there can be 50 or more of these larvae *in situ*, they must be responsible for a great many deaths. If, however, the host is fit enough to withstand this terrible pestilence, the larvae eventually loosen their hold and are either sneezed or coughed out to continue their horrendous life-cycle elsewhere.

As the shepherds reach the outer limits of the hirsel, and turn for home with the sheep before them, plumes of grey smoke begin to rise up. This is the age-old practice of muirburn. Even though the sky is heavy and threatening snow, the older stands of heather and the white, weathered foliage of last summer's Flying Bent-grass is dry enough to burn. On the other side of the loch, too, on the slopes of Ben Venue, the shepherds are busy setting fires. I watch a chain of small fires linking up to form easily regulated lines, burning their way across the hillside.

While we work the Edra ewes through the fank, the smoke mingles with the low cloud cover, shrouding the twin peaks of the Ben from view. Controversy as to whether burning is beneficial or not has raged for as long as muirburn itself. I am a firm believer that controlled burning of heather is a sound practice, whereas burning anything else is probably not. Very young, regenerating heather shoots provide valuable feed for grouse, hares, sheep and deer. As the plant matures, first the grouse and then the hare begin to find it too tough; after seven or eight years, even sheep begin to find it too coarse. If it is burned again at this stage, the whole process returns to square one. This is sound husbandry providing that the shepherd makes sure that his sheep do not kill out the young shoots by overgrazing.

On the other hand, burning acres of Flying Bentgrass (known to hill men as white grass) has little to recommend it. If it produces more grazing, it does so at a time when grazing is already adequate, and it obviously reduces the amount available in late winter when food is always in short supply. It also has a tendency to increase the dominance of this plant at the expense of better grasses. Burning the vestiges of last summer's bracken ash is one of the best natural fertilizers and does nothing more than promote the growth of more bracken. As an agronomic measure, the burning of bracken and white grass may be dismissed as a relatively harmless form of pyromania.

In the early hours of Sunday morning, following the third Saturday in March, the clocks are put forward one hour and Summer Time has arrived. So does the snow. Out on the dark hillside, grouse will be facing the storm and treading like mad to melt the snow under their feet. On the Ben Ducteach eyrie, my golden eagle will be sitting tight on her new-laid single egg, while high on the Square Rocks the raven will be protecting her precious clutch, now quite close to hatching. Somewhere, enveloped in the night, the red deer will be lying up, invisible in their snow overcoats, and my sheep will be sheltering as best they can, or standing, spending a miserable night with their tails to the wind.

The last of Maggi Du's pups leaves Glengyle to go to a new home. I have sold Juno, too, to a rugby colleague who farms on the good arable land beyond Stirling. She will find working in closed fields completely different to the vastness of the open hill. But it is not all one-way traffic: I keep my kennel up-to-strength by recalling Dust from a friend who had her on loan. Dust is another of Gail's offspring and, like her mother, is a useful hunter.

I have often heard the old country saying, 'There is no good shepherd without good dogs'. There is more truth in this statement than meets the eye, especially when made with reference to the hill shepherd. A collie (the name might be derived from 'colley', the old Scots term for a mountain sheep or from the Welsh word coelio, meaning faithful) can carry out duties which would tax the temper and agility of a handful of men, and do it better too. A good dog at once establishes an authority over his charges, an authority which man can never hope to match. When, on the odd occasion, I have had no dog at heel and it has been unexpectedly necessary for me to move sheep, I come to appreciate exactly how little respect they have for a two-legged dog. No matter how much I whistle, shout, clap and wave my hands, stamp my feet or run about myself, I have a minimal effect. The sheep largely ignore me until I am forced to give up and go home for a dog. Immediately the dog appears, the sheep group together nicely and take off in the required direction.

Britain is undoubtedly the cradle of the sheepdog world. As far back as Saxon times, the sheep-herd tending his flock, in conjunction with his dogs, was a familiar sight. Over a long period of time, several distinct breeds of working dog developed on our farms, each evolved by careful selection to be best suited to the countryside and stock that they were expected to handle. On the high upland sheepwalks, where there are great distances to cover in search of fast and elusive sheep, speedy and hardy dogs were needed. Where heavier sheep had to be worked under enclosed conditions, bigger and more powerful dogs were preferred. In the days before roads and railways, drovers, who moved livestock the length and breadth of the land, were the main agents responsible for introducing new blood to remote areas. Nowadays, it is possible for a shepherd to jump in a car and take his breeding bitch to a dog almost anywhere; for a price, the best bloodlines in the country are available to him. One drawback resulting from modern transport, however, has been the practical extinction of some of the old strains. Dogs like the Welsh Hill-man have been crossed so much with the Border Collie that it usually resembles his northern counterpart rather than his native ancestors.

The extremely clever Border Collie is the best-known sheepdog on the farm today. Many of the early breeders, and the shepherds who used these dogs, were from the border marches of England and Scotland. Since those days, this breed has found its way all over the British Isles and to a great many other parts of the world.

Officially it is spring; it said so on the radio, and as if to celebrate this fact, both the willow warbler and common gull arrive at Glengyle. For the next three months, the diminutive willow warblers will weave their distinctive, fluent chains of melody into a veritable tapestry to be hung about the trees. The common gull, despite the name, is one of the least numerous of our gulls, but it is the only member of its family which bothers to pay us a visit. They fly in from their coastal wintering to nest in isolated pairs on the islands of Loch Katrine. They will mew and scream and heckle and, at the end of lambing, lay eggs for my breakfast.

The wind returns to its south-west quarter and the weather suddenly improves. We gather and handle the head shepherd's Strone hirsel, and move on unhindered to do the same with Charlie's sheep at Coilachra. The last fall of snow still lies on the top of the hills; Stob a' Choin wears a white mantle down to her shoulders. Below the snowline on the Stob, fresh earth heaps testify to the subterranean activity of the moles. Males and females appear to lead a solitary existence, only associating in late March in order for the sow to produce her annual litter of three or four young about six weeks later. The females throw up their molehills in a random pattern as they search for the nearest worm; the

The female mole throws up her mole hills in a random pattern

boars, on the other hand, leave their molehills in a straight line as they search for the nearest female.

With a feeling of spring in the air, I turn my attention briefly to the garden. I lift out the last of the leeks, swedes and parsnips, before putting in my pet sheep to clean up the ground while I go to Stirling to play rugby. This weekly excursion also gives me the opportunity to buy my new seed potatoes and assorted packets of vegetable seeds. Back home again, I lay the seed potatoes in a wooden tray and leave them on our south-facing bedroom window-sill to start sprouting. Meanwhile, the sheep are doing a great job in the garden; no gardener should be without one. A dozen queens of the Small Garden Bumblebee are busy on the flowering currant.

The start of the Portnellan gather brings us onto the home stretch, so to speak. Traditionally, the sheep from this hirsel are brought to the Glengyle fank to be handled. Providing this spell of settled weather holds, we shall all be finished by the end of the week. Driving the blue-keeled ewes along the top of Portnellan, towards the place where we all come together, I cannot help but notice the profusion of purple saxifrage growing in one particular place. The surprising thing about seeing this plant here, apart from it being in flower so early in the year, is that it only grows on lime-rich soil and, as an area, this is anything but lime rich.

The underlying rock is composed of old, very old, crystalline material, laid down under the sea as silt sediments, more than six hundred million years ago. Now, exposed high above sea level, it is apparent from their present state that those deposits were sub-jected to tremendous pressure and stresses during the rising and folding of the land which took place at the time the Scottish Highlands were formed. This activity caused a considerable rise in the temperature of the original sedimentary rocks and produced a marked recrystallisation of some of the minerals. In this case, the metamorphosed rock is mica-schist and it is the main component of the Dalradian series, named after the ancient Argyllshire king-dom of Dalriada. By nature, this silica-rich bedrock is rather acid.

Later volcanic action forced molten lava through the bedrock, giving rise to zones of harder, igneous rocks. The characteristic bands observed in surface-cooled felsites are formed by the minerals sinking through the magma as it cools and accumulating in layers. Felsites are formed from acid lava rocks which weather down to an acid soil. Even the occasional intrusion of the neutral granite, diorite, does nothing to alter the general acid condition of the area. It is, however, the third kind of lava rock, dating from the very end of the volcanic period, which is interesting. A large number of whinstone dykes, composed of dolerite, were intruded into the bedrock, usually in a south-west-north-east plane. Dolerite is an alkaline rock and where one of these dykes reaches the surface, the distribution of plants growing there changes dramatically. It is on one of these dykes that the lime-loving purple saxifrage is thriving.

Alec takes the Portnellan ewes to one of his parks for the night, making the following Glengyle gather a little bit easier for the men bringing in the Wee Hill heft. I give the pens in the fank a good brush out before fetching my pets up from the garden and giving them the same treatment as the rest of the sheep. I also pay particular attention to their feet, trimming back any overgrown toenails. Maggi, as usual, helps me with our own stock, taking great pleasure from pushing them under as they swim through the dipper. The pets are left standing overnight on the green behind

The ring ouzel chatters angrily

the byre, allowing them to expel their worms before I turn them onto clean pasture tomorrow.

The home hirsel gather starts with the weather set fair, which is unusual for Glengyle; it always seems to rain when we reach here. The low-end first: Jock and Charlie go away to the Wee Hill, while Iain, John, Alec and I head away to start the steep climb at the Coireasach Burn. In a few well-sheltered spots, hidden from the teeth of the wind but open to the sun, the first tightly-furled bracken fronds can be seen peeping out of the ground cover. Another newly-arrived migrant, the ring ouzel, chatters angrily at our invasion of his summer territory. Once up on the top of Glengyle, I take a quick look into the Braes of Balquhidder to make sure none of my ewes has wandered away over. Gail and Dust speak up in fine voice, and start things moving.

A dog fox, still in his best winter coat, leaves his cover and takes off downhill. The dogs sniff at the place where he has been lying; a strong musky odour hangs in the air. It has been said that a fox stinks, yet I have to be within a few yards before I can smell anything of Mr Tod. On the other hand, he would be well able to get a whiff of me at 500 paces. The fox is gifted with an extraordinarily keen sense of smell. Individually, it is probably the most important of the five senses and, allied to a well-developed ability to interpret not only wind direction but wind strength, is the animal's ticket to survival. The nose of a healthy fox is cold and moist; it must be thus for the reception and correct reading of the information carried to it, even on the most breathless of days. I have often watched vixens lick their noses as soon as they emerge from their earth to take the air. A dry nose could mean disaster, not only less chance of locating food but less warning of any approaching danger. A fox does not track its prey in the same way that it would itself be hunted by foxhounds. Instead, he homes in on his food as if by radar. In this manner, well-concealed sources can come to light. Mummified fruit has been discovered under tangles of weeds in an orchard as well as deeply-buried bodies of all kinds. Hence the high walls around the Glengyle graveyard.

As I sweep my sheep past the Square Rocks, it looks as though the ravens are bringing feed to the nest. This is a bird of ancient mythology, legends lingering on since the days of the Viking raiders. The Norsemen were reputed to have carried a plain woven banner into their battles and during the conflict the image of a raven, the symbol of Oden, the god of war, would appear on the fabric. If the bird was seen in an aggressive posture victory was assured; if, on the other hand, the raven appeared to be dejected, then the day was lost. The omens are good: the Glengyle ravens are definitely not dejected today, prucking aggressively from on high.

The low-end sheep safely in the Middle Park and the gate secured, the shepherds make their way to the house for lunch. After the soup, Maggi serves shepherd's pie as the main course, followed by apple crumble and custard. Tea and biscuits round off the meal before we all troop out again to tackle the high-end of my hirsel.

Alec and I take the Land Rover out on Eves Road to Ben Ducteach and start driving the ewes out the way towards the Parlan Hill. As this is my ground, I take the highest ground again, up amongst the flurries of snow buntings, with my neighbour below me. The silvery, rippling flight-song of these snow birds will be lost to the hill any day now as they begin to return to their breeding grounds in Iceland and Norway. At the head of the glen, we swing the sheep around to the north side of the Glengyle water and herd them in the direction of Bealach nan Corp, Alec carefully policing the Ben Ducteach sheep to prevent them making any sort of break back to their own ground. By the time we arrive at the Pass of the Dead, the other four shepherds are waiting with the rest of the ewes, having driven them out from the Coireasach Burn to meet us.

This time we take the sheep home in two cuts. Iain and I bring the second lot, while Alec drives behind us with the Land Rover. The ewes are left in the West Park and everyone adjourns once more to the house, this time for tea. Maggi has been every bit as busy as ourselves, and we sit down to a feed of fish and chips, gallons of tea and enormous slices of home-made cakes.

Overnight, the sheep stand safely in the parks. Early morning sees Maggi giving me a hand to bring the ewes closer to hand; the low-end sheep are put straight into the pens and the high-end stock put into the paddock below the fank. While I handle Mona and Boot, Maggi works well with Bo and Gail. With the arrival of the other shepherds from down the lochside, the Glengyle handling gets underway. At 11 o'clock, Maggi provides a mid-morning cup of tea with toast, biscuits and pancakes. Lunch at 1 p.m. features roast lamb and mint sauce, served along with peas and baked potatoes. By mid-afternoon, we have finished dipping and administering the jabs, and I return the sheep to the hill.

After sweeping out the pens and generally tidying up the fank, I open the stop cock and let the dip out of the dipping tank. Even though this dip is one of the safest available on the market, if it got into the burns it would be deadly, not only to fish but to most of the other aquatic life forms. Soon after my arrival at Glengyle, I saw at first-hand exactly the dire consequences of sheep dip being inadvertently allowed to drain into the waterways. The morning after there were hundreds upon hundreds of frogs, feet up along the loch shore. Immediately afterwards I dug a series of ditches across the lower paddock to hold the released dip allowing it to drain slowly into the ground. This keeps the solution well away from the drains and ditches where the frogs are already laying the first of their spawn.

Where you find a congregation of mating frogs, the noise can

The male frog clasps the female in a hold called amplexus

be quite considerable as males vie with each other in order to obtain a mate. From observation, it would appear that the loudest wins fair maid, clasping her around the body in a hold known as amplexus, while she sheds between two and three thousand eggs into a pool. The male fertilises the eggs as they sink to the bottom of the water, prior to swelling up into the mass familiar to every child. In some years almost every rain-puddle contains frog spawn and I regularly find some in hilltop pools above 2,000 feet.

Palmate newts too are in the throes of breeding here, although they are much more surreptitious about it. The male develops a brightly-coloured tail which he displays to attract a mate. The female lays about 300 eggs singly on leaves of water plants, enclosing each one in a protective coat of jelly.

One of my younger cows, a cross Hereford-type, is having a spot of bother calving. The front feet have been showing for some hours but she doesn't seem to be making much progress. Fortunately she is quiet enough to let me approach to make a cursory examination: it is all as it should be, just a big calf trying to pass through the proverbial eye of a needle. I attach the ends of a single calving rope to each of the calf's front legs, the loop hanging low enough for me to put my foot on. I lubricate my hands and arms with lambing jelly, and begin to ease the head out of the passage; as the cow pushes during her contractions, I press down on the rope with my left foot while working the head clear. Working with the cow, I soon have the head and shoulders clear and the rest of the calf almost falls out; a good bull calf. The cow mothers up her offspring and he is soon on his feet, suckling at the udder. Now another problem arises since the cow has not expelled the placenta – retained afterbirth can mean possible infection and inability to breed. This is the second cross-Hereford that has failed to cleanse properly this year. I shall have to watch them closely.

This is only one of the problems I am faced with as the Hereford-type cows gradually replace the good old Highlanders where calving troubles are practically unknown. Another point, relevant on a farm like Glengyle, is that Herefords are nowhere near so hardy or able to eke out a living on next to no grazing. They are fussier too, not keen on anything but the best quality hay and virtually ignoring the straw offered to them. I agree that Herefords are less likely to be eild and, all things being equal, will drop a calf most years. But taken over their working life as a whole, a Highlander will produce more calves simply because she will live and thrive many more years under these conditions. I hope that one day the management will go back to restocking with Highlanders.

Every year at this time, the gamekeeper enlists the shepherds to act as beaters on fox-drives through some of the mature stands of conifers on the north shore. Lines of standing guns are stationed ready to blast any fox which bolts from cover. Rumours of huge populations of foxes building up, especially in areas where they have had some sanctuary, inevitably turn out to be unfounded. One such area not far from my own hirsel, where there has been no fox hunting for many years, was believed to be full to overflowing with foxes. Last year, a great foxdrive was organised to clean out the ground. A large force of men and guns came from far and wide and, although a possible den was discovered, not a single fox was seen that day. Quite simply, foxes naturally space themselves out according to the food available. The best controller of fox numbers is the fox.

A whirlwind tears its way along Loch Katrine, dragging up a column of spiralling spray. Suddenly the infernal wind changes direction, leaves the loch and rages through my garden at the back of the house. It rips small branches off the trees and sends them up the roaring vortex. Then it is past and twirls its way towards distant Ben Ducteach. A strange tranquillity settles on Glengyle.

I hike out to visit the Ben Ducteach eyrie in the hope that the whirlwind did not do any damage. All is well and the female sits tight as I spy down on her from a discreet distance. I carry on walking around the top of the high-end. Snow still lies deep in some of the north-facing hollows and crevasses. On my way, I pick up a couple of good red deer antlers, one of them with seven points. The horn is very good for making such diverse things as handles for walking sticks and buttons.

Mature stags are casting their old armoury before beginning the growth of the new, improved versions during the mid-summer months. Younger stags will cast their antlers on, some holding onto theirs until well into May. Why deer cast their antlers only to regrow them annually is not known. What is understood is the consequent drain on the body resources in providing calcium for the new growth. However, animals have a marvellous capacity for balancing mineral deficiencies; in this case, a stag can increase the amount of available calcium by chewing up not only cast-off antlers but also any old bones found lying about on the hillside.

March came in like a lion and is certainly going out like a lamb. Near the loch, a great grey shrike is sitting in an undressed rowan tree, curved black beak glinting in the sunshine. At the mouth of a small burn, a dipper braves the cold water, disappearing into the current and walking to and fro along the bed of the burn. Rather him than me. Out on the open water there is some excitement amongst the mallards. A group of the ducks were going through their pairing ritual when unfortunately for one of the females the system broke down and she is now being subjected to what can only be described as a gang-bang. Such brutal rapes are only known in this species of duck, and often the victim is half-drowned into the bargain. Far out on the loch, I get my first glimpse of the newly-arrived male goosander as he swims and occasionally dives to feed. The wintering pochards and goldeneyes have become weary of waiting around and have left Loch Katrine to go in search of spring.

Waiting for Spring

SPRING HAS NOT YET MANAGED to find her way to Glengyle. Take a trip to Stirling, though, and you can see countless young lambs gambolling on the rich grass of the lowland farms. Most of the brown, ploughed ground contains the swelling seed of future harvests. While the in-bye ewes graze over the plentiful green pasture, my hill flock has to search for a mere picking. The Glengyle grass still slumbers on in deep winter sleep. This is where the prowess of these blackfaced sheep begins to tell. True, the very weakest are likely to become crow bait, but the hardiest of them will live where even the crow will die.

The first winter for the hoggs is one of the most crucial periods of their lives. Life on the hill is hard at the best of times but during the long winter conditions becomes extremely difficult; for young inexperienced animals, doubly so. Going away to a less harsh environment is obviously the answer to this problem. But where can such a utopia be found for thousand upon thousand of Highland hoggs? However, at the onset of each winter, dairy farmers throughout Scotland house their stock, leaving the grass fields empty for several months. By their very nature, dairy farms are situated in the more favourable parts of the country, on the fertile arable lowlands and on the milder coastal plains, and many of these dairy farmers take hoggs for the winter.

The Glengyle hoggs have been wintered with Andrew Graham at Harthill since well before my time as shepherd here. Andrew's farm is right in the heart of the Scottish lowlands, almost half-way between Glasgow and Edinburgh. It is ideally positioned to supply fresh milk to the area of greatest demand, Scotland's industrial belt. One of the less welcome aspects of this ready market for milk is the number of post-war housing developments which have sprung up with the resulting problems of litter, vandalism and uncontrolled dogs. I am not saying that the people who live on the

Falcons' cartwheel of love

estate adjoining my wintering are responsible for an out-lying barn being burnt down so many times that Andrew has given up rebuilding it, or that the dogs which chase my sheep come from there, but they do come from somewhere.

There are several benefits in taking sheep onto a lowland farm for the winter. The ground receives a liberal application of valuable manure which improves soil fertility; the grass can benefit too by having all the previous season's leaf growth removed, preventing frosts and disease damaging the plant. All this promotes healthy and vigorous new growth the following spring. The financial remuneration to the farmer is not to be overlooked, either. The hoggs themselves benefit by being adequately fed during their period of maximum growth, between the ages of four and ten months and those which safely return home are usually in good fettle and ready to join the breeding flock.

The first of April is the date traditionally set for the return of the Glengyle hoggs from their winter quarters. Not until they are sold off as cast ewes, to end their days on easier, in-bye ground, will they find food so readily available. For the past few weeks, my hoggs have found fresh succulent grass shoots sprouting up at every turn. However, Andrew would far rather see his black and white Friesian cattle grazing over the land, getting the value of the nutritious spring grass, instead of my ravenous, woolly hoggs.

The Water Board have three lorries stationed at Stonachlachar and with their stock-carrying bodies, called floats, attached, they will cover a great many miles during the next few days, carrying hoggs homeward. My driver this morning is Andy Donaldson, and we are ready to set out soon after day-break.

As the big, blue British Leyland lorry pulls out of the yard and begins the long haul to Harthill, Mona, Gail and Boot curl up on the floor at my feet, while Andy's large golden labrador settles next to me on the seat, surveying the passing scenery. The journey will take fully two hours and sitting high up in the cab I enjoy the different view from usual. From my vantage point, high walls and screening hedges around private gardens present no barrier and some of the gardens belonging to the big houses on the outskirts of Aberfoyle are well worth seeing. Many of these impressive houses on the shores of Loch Ard were built in the last century by prosperous industrialists who had their business interests in Glasgow. Already a few trees of the spectacular flowering cherries are in blossom above manicured lawns coloured with crocuses and hosts of golden daffodils. Spring certainly has arrived at Aberfoyle.

At Harthill, while I gather up my sheep, Andy busies himself putting up the collapsible sides on the top of the float. This provides us with a third deck, the inside of the float already being divided into two decks. Some of my hoggs are running on the far side of the A8, Glasgow-Edinburgh road which cuts the farm in two. Since the parallel M8 motorway was opened a few years ago, the flow of traffic along the old main road has been greatly reduced. However, driving sheep across it can still be a hair-raising experience. Motorists speed along, the wide straight stretch of uncrowded road being an obvious invitation to push down the right foot. The last thing that these drivers seem to expect is a flock of sheep trespassing on their domain. How dare they? appears to be the general attitude these days, to sheep and shepherd alike. Like the White Rabbit from *Alice's Adventures in Wonderland*, they are all dreadfully afraid of being late.

Andrew Graham and Andy Donaldson help me by flagging down approaching vehicles. Even with their assistance, I am worried that one of my charges, or worse, one of my dogs, will be run down by an impatient driver. So far, I have been lucky but a while back the Water Board very nearly lost a shepherd. Charlie, the Coilachra shepherd, was away with some of the other herds, to move hoggs when a car hurtled out of a dip in the road and birled him round and round.

Once I am safely across the road with the sheep, the delayed motorists roar off to keep their appointments with destiny and I quietly gather together the rest of my hoggs. The dogs work the hoggs steadily into the farmyard where Andrew and I count them. This count is important because payment for the wintering is made on the number of sheep returned. We are agreed on the total, but it is one more than expected. I walk through them, slowly, and there she is, a straggler sheep. A faint green keel and a different ear mark confirm that she does not belong to me. I catch hold of her and Andrew shuts her in a shed until he can find from which of the neighbours the animal has strayed.

Mrs Graham provides Andy and me with a welcome bite of lunch, while Andrew telephones to the surrounding farms. In next to no time he tracks down the place the straggler has come from and arranges for the farmer to come over to collect her later.

Andy reverses his float into the mouth of the close and drops down the tail-door. Each deck is sectioned by gates into three separate compartments. We try to load the sheep evenly, the same number into each section. By dividing the sheep into small lots, we reduce the risk of injury through crushing and trampling. The hoggs are counted onto the float to confirm the first count. With the hoggs safely on board, Andy starts up his lorry and we set course for the dark, distant Highlands to the north-west. I think that Andrew is quite glad to see the back of the Glengyle hoggs for another year.

The afternoon sun dips on our left-hand side and warms up the cab. Dogs and shepherd settle down to nap happily as the float drones homeward.

Between Stirling and Aberfoyle, we pass by the wide, flat expanse of the strangely-named Flanders Moss. Up until 200 years ago, this place was an almost impassable swamp, with the castle at Stirling controlling the one convenient route to the north. This was the reason why Stirling was fought over with such determination and ferocity: he who controlled Stirling had authority over much of the realm. However, with the failure of the Jacobite cause, the destiny of Scotland was to be drastically altered. The country was full of broken men. The remaining landholders, mostly Hanoverian sympathisers, quickly realised that sheep were taking over the hills and glens where previously countless families had lived and worked. There was little hope for many, except by emigration as thousands were already doing.

One man, Lord Justice Kames, dreamed up a revolutionary scheme to improve his land and to help some of the displaced Highlanders. He conceived the idea that the peat covering much of his estate could be removed and the underlying land reclaimed for farming. The dispossessed MacGregors, MacFarlanes and MacLarens from Glengyle and Balquhidder were amongst the first to become tenants of the 'Moss Laird'. About ten acres of moss was let to each tenant on a 38-year lease. For the first eight years, no rent was required, with only a nominal payment for the following 11 years. After this time, rent was due for each acre under cultivation, plus 2/6d in old money for every acre still in peat. The Laird supplied his tenants with enough oatmeal to sustain life, timber to build a dwelling and wooden spades with which to dig and chop the peat which could be up to 20 feet deep.

The first settlers came in 1767 and by 1774 13 tenants had cleared 104 acres. The cut peat was floated, peat does float, down an ingenious system of water-filled ditches to the River Forth. Other landlords followed suit and many Belgians were believed to have come as colonists, hence the name Flanders Moss.

Apart from uncovering fertile farm land, the history of the moss was revealed. Oyster shells and whale bones pointed to the fact that at one time the area had been under the sea. Oak trees, some with enormous girths and as black as coal, were found lying on their sides above their own roots. The wood was still sound, although it must have been buried for 1,500 years; many clearly bore the marks of small Roman axes. Along with the oak, the peat covered felled birch, hazel, alder, willow and pine; all testimony to the theory that the woodland had been cleared by the Romans in order to remove the cover which it afforded to the native Celts who opposed the Roman occupation. The Romans built a road from east to west across the moss, constructing a causeway over the boggiest ground. Part of the road which we have just driven along, to the west of Thornhill, runs directly above a section of it.

Of late, the Forestry Commission has been draining more than one thousand acres and planting lodgepole and Scots pine. Using modern machinery the Commission has shown that the Moss can once again grow trees; they look to be healthy and doing well enough.

At Aberfoyle, we leave the lowlands behind us and enter the Highlands by way of Strath Ard and the back of Ben Lomond. Three hours of heavy pull have passed by since we left Harthill before Glengyle hoves into view. Andy backs the float to the gate of the paddock below the fank and the hoggs are unloaded. They will stay in here overnight and be close by for handling tomorrow.

A male woodcock flies overhead on his evening roding flight, the first I have seen this year. He defines his territory by flying at dawn and dusk, uttering a continuous t'wick, t'wick, punctuated by a low-pitched frog-like croak.

The morrow dawns cold and blustery. Sudden, stinging squalls of hailstones clatter off the dry-stone walls as the smoke from the freshly-lit brazier curls away on the wind. Mona and Max drive the hoggs into the fank, ready for making a start.

The other shepherds arrive. Sheep are brought forward into the handling pen; the brazier is stoked up and branding irons pushed into the heart of the fire. A score of hoggs are confined in the small handling pen and work commences along production line principles. Jock and I both catch the sheep; John punches a hole in the centre of their left ears so that we can insert a coloured self-locking identification tag. Each hogg in turn is passed to Iain who holds her steady while Charlie injects 2ml of Covexin 8 under the skin just behind the shoulder. Alec then doses her with a worm drench and pops her through a side gate into a holding pen. Soon the line is in full swing and one penful follows another until the gate shuts behind the last hogg.

Then it is back to the beginning for the hoggs and we start to run them through the handling pen once more. This time Iain, Alec and John catch and hold the sheep while Jock passes glowing red-hot branding irons to me and Charlie. Each of my hoggs is carefully branded on the right horn with the letter 'G' for Glengyle, together with the last number from the year of her birth. A good hot iron will brand a half score or more, before becoming too cool. The way in which the sheep are held is most important: they must be absolutely secure and still, or else... At the first touch of a fresh iron, a flame will flare from the horn. The animal, however, feels no pain at all, the outer shell of the horn containing no nerves. The worst that can happen is a singeing of the hairs around the base of the horn, and this doesn't hurt either.

In the days before plastic ear tags, branding used to be the only way of permanently marking a sheep with her age and hirsel. Nowadays, it is still a useful back-up system. Often all that remains of a dead sheep on my hillside is a rickle of bones and a little wool, strewn around. The ear tag is rarely to be seen and I have even recovered them from fox droppings before now. However, I can usually find the horn with the brand and from this I can identify and make a note of the victim.

To conclude the proceedings, the hoggs are plunged into the dipping tank, ducked under a couple of times before being allowed to swim out and stand in the dripping pen. This ensures that any parasites living on or in the skin will be killed off, and any smouldering fires extinguished.

I turn 206 hoggs out onto the hill; hale and hearty, free from nasty pests inside and out, and sporting their bright ear tags and brand new brands. Unfortunately, I don't think that they are very enamoured with the hillside. After all the grass they had in front of them at Harthill, the cupboard at Glengyle is decidedly bare. Suddenly caught in a sharp hailstorm, this place must seem like the end of the earth.

As I make my way back to the house for lunch, I notice the first pale primrose of spring, growing on the sheltered bank of the nearby burn.

By the time I reach the house, the other herds are already seated around the dining-table, tucking into one of Maggi's magnificent meals. Rich steaming soup is followed with roast leg of lamb accompanied by mint sauce. A set of big bowls containing cabbage, carrots, roast potatoes and one holding a mountain of creamy mashed potatoes, together with a giant jug of thick gravy, sit in the middle of the table. In no time at all, the contents have been demolished and Maggi follows on well with generous helpings of rhubarb crumble and custard. Rhubarb was introduced to Britain in the 18th century by a Scotsman. Doctor Mounsey was physician to the Russian court of Catherine the Great and it was he who brought this strange 'vegetable' to these shores.

After lunch, we all pile into the head shepherd's Land Rover and head down the lochside to work with the hoggs that have come home to Edra. The choppy Katrine water looks dark and menacing, with wind-driven white horses racing each other down the loch towards the Trossachs.

At Edra we can handle the hoggs in comparative comfort, under the cover of a big shed. As we work through the sheep, periodic bursts of hail-stones rattle against the roof. This time I take a turn to catch and hold hoggs while they are being branded. I like to stand astride the sheep's neck, and back her into a corner of the pen. Then, grasping the left horn firmly in my right hand, I pull her head round and present her right-hand horn to the man with the branding iron. My left hand holds the hogg's nose securely against my left leg: this, I find, keeps them absolutely still. If a sheep was able to jerk or jump, then someone could be badly burned, probably me.

In the days that follow, we handle the hoggs from the remaining hirsels, and they are all turned out onto the hill to fend for themselves as best they can. At some of the handlings, there are a few homewintered hoggs which are all markedly smaller than their contemporaries. There are endless discussions and comparisons as to whose hoggs have done the best this winter. This year, I believe that the Coilachra hoggs, wintered across the road from mine, have done very well indeed. They are well grown, with no obvious exceptions amongst them.

The evocative sound of geese on the wing has me craning my neck. The strident 'wink-wink' sound of pink-foot geese reaches my car long before I can pick out the long, straggling skein against the southern sky. For the next month, these harbingers of spring will pass overhead on the way to their northern nesting grounds in far away Iceland and Greenland. The grey geese which pass over the snow-capped hills of Glengyle are usually either the deep-throated greylag or the lighter-voiced pink-foot species. By flying in the characteristic 'V' formation, geese conserve much of the energy normally wasted by birds in flight. Each goose receives a fair amount of lift from the slipstream of the bird in front. Only the leader has to battle on unaided, but the leadership changes periodically during a flight, spreading the task.

The constellation of the mighty hunter, Orion, is lost from the sky at night. He has come to the end of his winter stalk across the northern hemisphere and disappears behind the Dhu of Glengyle to hunt out the summer elsewhere. Already gone with him, or soon to follow, are his animal companions: the Great Dog, Little Dog, Hare, Bull, Lion and Unicorn. Saturn shines with a steady, yellow radiance, conspicuous in the early evening but clearly visible for most of the night. Venus is a bright morning star, lying now in the south-eastern sky, just before dawn.

The mallard duck are nesting. The green-headed drakes still swim on the loch, forming themselves into a loose bachelor flock, dabbling for food throughout the day. The dowdy females are nowhere to be seen. They will be sitting on clutches of six to 18 buff-olive eggs, secluded in a clump of rushes or under a bramble brake, some way inland from the shore. The nest is built solely by the female, a hollow lined firstly with leaves and grass and covered with a layer of down and feathers. Incubation, also, is carried out by the female alone, and takes 28 days from the time the clutch is complete. Until all the eggs are laid and at any time she leaves the nest, the duck will carefully cover her eggs with down.

My solitary remaining pair of goldeneye are still on the loch in front of Glengyle. The drake has begun courting the duck, performing a complicated ritual which includes his swimming round and round the object of his affection, tilting his head right back, uttering gutteral grunting noises and occasionally kicking up showers of spray. Nonbreeding pairs have been known to summer in Scotland sometimes, but I hope that maybe these two will go a stage further and breed here.

One thing which is more of a certainty is the breeding potential of the new arrival on the Loch. Last month saw the return of one of our two saw-billed ducks, the goosander. Now its close cousin, the redbreasted merganser has turned up again. In winter the red-breasted merganser migrates to the coast, preferring the salt water to fresh water. The duck is feathered in simple brown and grey with a white bar on the wings. The drake is a different kettle of fish altogether: he has a bottle-green head with a proud double crest; chestnut breast, black mantle and wing tips; white collar, belly and wing patches. Red eyes (yellow in immature birds), red legs and a long red, slightly hooked, serrated beak complete his colourful covering. Identification of this bird is never a problem. Small rowing boats, hired from the Water Board, bob about here and there on the water as anglers take time out to challenge Katrine's keen brown trout. Each of the fishermen has to pit his wits against the trout; some always row away to the same place, others try to read the signs and vary their location according to the prevailing conditions.

Jamie has the right idea; he keeps things very simple – a rod, a line and a worm. He casts from the shore in front of the house, and waits for the fish to come to him. And they do, in large numbers. Every morning, as soon as he has tumbled out of bed, he goes straight down to check his rod. The same each afternoon, the moment he gets off the school bus, he is away to see what he has caught. The evenings often seem to be peak fishing time; I have seen Jamie bring in five or six trout an hour when the fish are really biting. Smaller fish, anything under ½ lb if they are unharmed, are returned to the water. Now and again, Toria is bitten by the fishing bug, and for several days enthusiastically sets out her line. It is Toria, of course, who catches the biggest trout, much to her brother's annoyance. The local youth club fishing trophy is for the heaviest fish caught on a hook during the season. The advantage of this rivalry is to be seen in the way the deepfreeze is filling up, as surplus fish are frozen for consumption at a later date.

The last of my expected calves has arrived. In the final count-up, I have one more heifer than bull calves. The one cow which I have long suspected of being barren still seems to be that way. Although the bull was running with the cows until the end of August and, in theory, she could calve up to the first week in June, I am afraid that she is far too prosperous-looking to have a calf inside her.

One eild cow a year is about average for Glengyle. The reasons can be various and sometimes complex. The Highland cow, from which my old girls are bred, are naturally eild about one year in three. Even by using Shorthorn crosses in this herd, the problem to a lesser extent still remains. Other causes of infertility can be generally classified under three main headings: injury and/or infection from the previous calving; poor body condition; lack of available minerals or vitamins. The barrenness of this beast could stem from her Highland ancestry, although she may have been a little backward in condition, or simply short of minerals during the last breeding season.

Several weeks after the frogs have resumed active service, the more stolid toads eventually condescend to leave their hibernating quarters. From beneath logs and boulders, out of dry-stone dykes and disused rabbit holes, knots of these pimply-skinned, earth-coloured amphibians emerge and set off for their spawning ground. During this season, migrating toads will travel night and day, and some have been known to be on the road for ten days or more. The Glengyle toads do not have to go far to reach suitable water. Even so, they sometimes appear to journey further than necessary by passing one or two apparently ideal situations. Unlike the frog who will spawn in almost any puddle, toads return faithfully to the exact spot where they first saw the light of day. All around the lochside, the light croaking of both sexes can be heard.

Toads often pair on the way to the water. The smaller male climbs onto the back of the egg-swollen female and clasps her firmly under the armpits. They can stay like this for several days until the female lays her long string of eggs; the double row of about seven thousand tiny, round, black eggs is contained in a strand of clear jelly eight to twelve feet long. Toads require deeper water than frogs and must have plants because, as she lays her eggs, the female swims about and winds the spawn around shoots and stems of these water plants. After a week, the eggs will have become oval and a few days later the embryos will begin to take on a recognisable tadpole shape. Although toads spawn later than frogs, the tadpoles hatch out at roughly the same time. Toad tadpoles can emerge from the jelly in as little as a fortnight, but three weeks is nearer the normal length of time. It all depends on the temperature of the water.

Once mating is over, the toads disperse, each to its own territory. A toad's homing instinct is well developed. The summer home is a little hollow dug into the soil by the judicious use of the hindquarters, usually under a root, log or flat stone. For several years a very large, warty female toad, with beautiful coppery-red eyes, has lived out the warmer months in my vegetable garden. Every evening she sets out hunting and may travel some distance during the night, but before morning she is back snug in her form under a large flat stone left for exactly that purpose. Her diet includes flies, beetles, caterpillars, slugs, snails, worms, wood-lice and even small mice, in fact almost anything of the correct size that moves; toads will not take motionless prey. I introduce as many toads as I can into my garden so that they will eat up all the pests. Most of them return to their own territory but I manage to persuade a few to take up residence.

April is the time for my trusty Land Rover to go to the garage at Thornhill for its annual service and MOT examination. I am quite capable of filling her up with diesel; I have been known to manage to check the oil, water and even put air in the tyres. If I really try hard, I sometimes remember to look at the batteries. Anything else I leave to the specialist mechanics; after all, I pay them enough. I do not grudge the money provided the work is done properly.

Having left the Old War Horse to get her medical, I walk the couple of miles to Bob Chapman's farm, Bo tagging along at my heel. Bob plays rugby for Stirling County and often we turn out for the same team. I plan to spend the day at the low-lying and quaintly-named Angus Step Farm, as I normally do on such days, and give Bob a hand with his lambing which, being a low-ground farm, is in full swing. The rain pours down steadily from leaden skies. The fields are saturated, pools of standing water attracting hordes of gabbling gulls.

Fortunately Bob has all the ewes which are close to lambing inside, under cover of a large court. Only the gimmers, who are a little way off lambing and lambed ewes with well-established lambs at foot, are having to face the elements. It is more than ten years since I turned my hand to an in-bye lambing and I have forgotten exactly how hectic a time it is. Every available corner seems to have a gate or hurdle tied across it, to contain some sheep or other. On the infield system, all the action is concentrated in one place; this is very different from a hill hirsel where a shepherd may walk for many hours before finding anything which requires his attention.

The morning passes pleasantly, with little undue excitement. We put a newly-lambed ewe and her twins into a small pen so that we can keep an eye on her and make sure both lambs get a good suck. We go out into the rain and get wet, walking through the lambed ewes and looking over the gimmers. Back in the court, all seems quiet with the lambers. At mid-day, Bob's wife, Jean, calls in for lunch. While we eat, Jean bottle-feeds an orphan lamb that has made itself quite at home in front of the Rayburn.

Half an hour later, the scene which confronts us is one of bedlam: seven new-born lambs are being claimed by four ewes or maybe it is five ewes with the seven lambs, or perhaps it should be five ewes with eight lambs – because by this time another lamb has put in an appearance. Bob scratches his head and mutters something I cannot quite catch. We begin to sort them out into the adjacent calfpens, now doing stalwart service as lambing pens. Two ewes each with single lambs and three others with twins. It looks about right. Suddenly one lamb decides that he is not a twin, squeezes through the bars into the next pen and becomes a triplet. Just as I am on my way to investigate this turn of events, one of the ewes reckons that she has not lambed at all, and jumps out into the court, leaving a puzzled lamb behind her. I change course and take off after her, and now an entirely different ewe does not want to be left out and jumps into a pen already occupied by a ewe and pair. The 'triplet', not getting satisfaction from his adopted mother, decides to try something new, squeezes out into the court and chases after a ewe who was doing nothing at all.

At this moment, Hector, Bob's young farm worker who has been cleaning out one of the cattle courts with the tractor and front-end loader, comes in to say that he has inadvertently severed a water pipe. The break is close to the water trough and a veritable tide is flowing freely through the court and out of the door. Of course nobody can find the stopcock, so we hammer a wooden bung into the end of the pipe and that solves that particular problem for the time being.

Meanwhile, in the far corner of the lambing area, another ewe has started and is doing her best to hang her lamb. The head is out but the front legs are back inside, preventing the body from slipping forward. The constriction around the lamb's neck is causing its head to swell and the point of strangulation is near at hand. Bob goes across to deal with her while I try to sort out some order in the pens. As I pass the end pen, I find that the ewe which had jumped out in the first place has jumped back in, alongside a ewe with two lambs that has already been joined by the ewe that has not lambed. Or has she? With a little reorganisation of the occupants of the pens, and having retrieved the wandering lamb, I end up with three sets of twins and two single lambs rearranged between the five ewes. The sixth ewe, the one without a lamb, is a thief; so close to lambing herself, she tries to steal another ewe's lamb. I shut her alone into a pen to keep her out of further mischief until she produces offspring of her own. This time I believe I have got it right.

The remaining part of my visit to Angus Step is much less frantic. I help Bob to trim any long, dangly navel cords to the new-born lambs, and dress them all with antiseptic aerosol spray to prevent infection setting into the wound. We repair the fractured water pipe in the cattle court and work through the routine afternoon jobs. A couple more ewes lamb safely. When the time comes, Bob runs Bo and me back to the garage to collect the Land Rover. What a performance!

The mild, wet weather sets in for several days; the hill tops are continually shrouded in shifting, grey mists. All at once, the stark bare larch trees take on a new, soft, green tinge. Larch is the only British pine to lose all its foliage in autumn: feathery tufts of needles begin to emerge from the bumpy knobs all along the straw-coloured twigs. Separate male and female flowers appear on the branches; the pollen-producing male flowers are like tiny yellow buttons, while the female flowers are very pretty pink or white fleshy conelets called larch roses.

Larch is a useful, durable wood which, without any special treatment, resists water and rot well. Even though it is without leaves for almost half the year, larch is fast-growing, and trees of barely forty years old can be cropped for their tough, pinky heart-wood. On the farm, the wood from this tree is widely used for buildings and fences. The Water Board grow their own timber in plantations along the north shore of the loch, and process all the wood they require through their sawmill situated at Letter.

The Scots were the first to realise and exploit the potential of the larch. James Murray, the 2nd Duke of Atholl, saw the possi-bilities of introducing the European larch from Switzerland to cover the naked hillsides of his estates in this very county of Perthshire. In 1738, the Duke planted the first larch trees in the country on his land near Dunkeld: one of these original 'mother' trees can still be seen, 105 ft high and, with a spread of immense horizontal branches, almost as wide. Saplings grown from these foundation trees were planted out on the Scottish hillsides. The new trees thrived so well that the 4th Duke of Atholl extended the project and planted out a total of 17 million trees in his lifetime. His example was followed all over Britain, and by the mid-nine-teenth century, larch had become the most important forestry plantation tree. However, widespread monoculture of any plant is inviting trouble and, sure enough, large stands of larches began to be subjected to severe aphid infestation. This problem took the steam out of many larch enterprises for a while.

The 7th Duke, as larch-orientated as his ancestors, brought in the Japanese larch in an attempt to overcome the pest trouble. He planted them alongside the long-established European variety, and in 1904 the first hybrids of the two strains were being grown. The new type of larch exhibited the classical traits of hybrid vigour and was an obvious improvement on both its parents. Not only was it faster growing but it proved to be far more resistant to pests and disease. Today, this product of Perthshire, first bred and nurtured within sight of one of the world's finest salmon rivers, is cultivated throughout the northern hemisphere.

Some of the resident British birds who find the Glengyle winter too rigorous have begun to return to their breeding grounds in the glen. The small, brown meadow pipit is one of the first to arrive, turning up in considerable numbers. I cannot walk far without flushing a pipit out of a tuft of coarse vegetation, almost from right beneath my boot. Even though this bird is very similar to others, it is readily recognised by its single sharp 'pheet' alarm note, or by its more usual triple 'pheet-pheet-pheet' call.

Along with the meadow pipit come the carriers of two sounds so characteristic of early spring time. The curlew and green plover

The curlew, our largest wader

fly in from their coastal winterings to haunt the air with their beautiful, thrilling calling over the wind. The bubbling 'clee-clee-clee-clee' of the longlegged curlew, our largest wader, soon gives way to the more familiar 'coorli-coorli' cry, from which the bird receives its name. The green plover has gone one step further, giving itself two descriptive names – peewit, from the call, and lapwing, from the striking, spring aerobatic display flying in which the wings make a loud lapping sound. Spring is surely on her way now. Easter, a morning of Holy Communion and painted eggs, is another strange mixture of Christian and pagan rites. We attend the Episcopal Church of St Mary in Aberfoyle, the Scottish equivalent to the Church of England, which was founded by the community of Welshmen who came to work the nearby slate quarry. After the service, we leave the church by the south entry, and our gaze naturally falls on the small rounded hill directly opposite, where the Rev Robert Kirk, Presbyterian minister of this parish, was carried off by the fairies on 29 May 1692.

In 1685, Robert succeeded his father, the Rev James Kirk, and settled to a successful ministry, during which time he was twice married, both times to daughters of a MacGregor. Robert Kirk was a learned man; besides translating the scriptures into Gaelic, known in those days as Erse or Irish, he was a scholar in fairy lore. His book on the subject, *The Secret Commonwealth of Elves, Fauns and Fairies*, was published in 1691. Robert was born and brought up in the Fairy Realm of Balquhidder, the youngest of seven sons, a fact commonly believed in the Highlands to account for his unusual powers.

After his book came out, the little people must have felt that the man whom they believed to be their ally had betrayed their trust by publishing their secrets. The theory that Kirk did not enter into their world voluntarily is supported by the story of his valiant attempt to return to his mortal coil. Some time after his death, he appeared in a vision to a relative, and explained that while walking on the hill of Dunshee (the fairy knowe) he had been struck down in a trance, and that while his friends believed him to be dead and buried, he was, in fact, a captive in fairyland. However, there was a way to secure the release of his spirit, and he charged his friend to see that it was carried out in the following fashion.

The christening of his posthumous child would shortly be taking place, and he would once again appear for a few moments at the ceremony. One of the guests would be his kinsman Graham of Duchray Castle and to him was to be trusted the task of breaking the spell. Immediately Kirk made his appearance, Graham was to draw his dirk and throw it over the minister's head, and the fairies, afraid of cold steel, would release his soul and return him to his friends. Unfortunately, the sight of the spectre so unnerved the Laird Of Duchray that he failed to respond to the instructions and, with a sad and reproachful look, the clergyman vanished, never to be seen again.

Walking on Dunshee hill, even in the cool, clear light of Easter Day, it seems easy enough to believe in fairies.

From my living-room window I can see old mouldiwarp mole has been busy in the garden, heaving up heaps of dark earth in the vegetable plot. Maggi has already been taking advantage of any bright spell to put the flower borders and rockeries in order. The sun comes out, the birds are in full song and I feel a sudden urge to get digging too. I had better act on it at once, or the feeling may go away as quickly as it came.

The answer to any gardener's question lies in the soil. I am a firm believer in using plenty of farmyard manure – after all, there is any amount of it about. Manure is beneficial to the ground, improving soil texture, and to the crops, providing essential plant foods. I use sheep manure as well since it contains a better proportion of potash than cattle manure.

All fertilizers are divided into three major classes: nitrogen, phosphate and potash. In nitrogen, fertilisers are principally concerned with promoting leaf and stem growth and are responsible for the development of the plant above ground level and with its healthy, green appearance. Phosphates help root development, while at a later stage in the plant's life they encourage maturity and seed production. Potash helps the other plant foods to be used in the best way and so promotes healthy vigorous growth and good resistance against disease. Potash is very important for plants which build up stores of starch and sugar in the roots, such as potatoes, swedes and carrots. Unlike expensive artificial fertilizers, manure is long-acting and does not get washed out of the soil by rainfall; it also contains the trace elements necessary to plant life.

I dig barrow-load after barrow-load well into the ground, except for one strip. This is where parsnips will follow the potatoes grown last season: parsnips don't like fresh manure but there will still be plenty of humus left in the soil from last year. Further over, I take out two parallel trenches, a spade width wide and a yard apart. I line the bottom with well-rotted manure and plant out the seed potatoes from the chitting box. A coating of fresh grass cuttings, which prevents scab forming on the skins of the new potatoes and will keep the growing plants warm in case of last frosts, is added and the rows earthed over. A satisfactory start, I think, to the annual gardening campaign.

The rhythm of life at Glengyle certainly quickens as the days lengthen. The young ravens on the Square Rocks, hatched after only nineteen days' incubation, are now a month old and well grown. Both parents fly back and forth, bringing carrion and tending to their progeny's needs. High in the Ben Ducteach eyrie, the golden eagle has just hatched out her single egg; now the eaglet is covered in a fine grey down, and in a few days' time, the youngster will have grown a thicker, fluffy, snow-white coat. For the next four weeks or so, the female eagle will close-brood her chick while the male does the hunting and brings food to the nest, mostly blue hares and grouse.

The mistle thrush, always an early bird, is already nesting high in trees and hedges. Our stormcock likes her nest to be at least five feet above the ground and sometimes as high as 30 feet. The female builds a bulky nest of grass, plant stems and roots, with dead leaves, moss and earth mixed through it for consolidation; it is lined with fine grass. Without the protection of foliage on the trees, the nests of mistle thrushes are conspicuous. The male, normally a wary bird, becomes very aggressive during the breeding season and will attack anything which comes too close to the nest. While driving to Stirling on Saturdays to play rugby, quite a number of mistle thrushes will swoop at the Land Rover as we pass through their territories.

The majority of the song birds are busy establishing their individual domains, filling the woodland with melodies all day long. Those in possession of territory will be going through their courtship displays in order to attract a mate. The complicated behaviour is not too difficult to understand; every action has a specific purpose. Firstly, it is to form a bond with the correct mate. Even very closely-related species will have a different courtship pattern, making cross-breeding virtually impossible. Secondly, each of the birds must be satisfied that its potential partner is able to perform the duties necessary to ensure a successful outcome to the season. If you watch a display closely and for long enough, you will see that every action will represent a specific task.

The cock robin feeds his mate as part of his courtship, as do most of the species where the female is solely responsible for incubating the eggs. This not only strengthens the pair-bonding, but at the same time reassures the female that the male is a capable provider; it also feeds her up prior to egg-laying and the lengthy incubation period. The peregrine falcon, above the open hillside, gives a startling display of acrobatics during a high speed fly-past. The male, called a tiercel, flies in fast and low clutching his prey tightly in his talons. His mate flies up to meet him and seizes hold beneath the victim. Sometimes there is no prey and the two birds just lock their claws together. Joined to each other in this fashion, they fly at speeds in excess of 100 m.p.h., all the time revolving around the axis of the prey. When they eventually disengage, the female carries the food back to her eyrie.

But the weather, as fickle as ever, turns cold again, just at the time when every living thing is longing for life-giving warmth. A keen, lazy wind comes out of the east, preferring to go through everything, rather than round it. In the face of the wind, the hoggs, who have never really settled since they returned home, head westwards. I found a drove of Portnellan hoggs as far away as Ben Ducteach and duly returned them to their own ground. The shepherd himself, Alec McLellan, retrieved some others from about halfway to Stronachlachar where they were making a fair speed along the road with the wind up their tails. This wind not only brings grass growth to a stop again but will burn off anything which has already appeared.

My ewes, now heavy in lamb, are having to struggle to make a living on the bleak, bare hill. This is the danger period when some of the more adventurous sheep begin to clamber onto practically inaccessible ledges, where there is a good picking of herbage to be found. Once down on a ledge, it is not so easy to get off again and sometimes I have to assist them. Dust is a brave bitch and will go in anywhere after stranded sheep. It is amazing the difference the presence of a dog makes to the efforts a ewe will make on her own behalf. However, some of the ladies, weighed down by their pregnant condition, really are stranded and I have to resort to the use of ropes to get them off safely.

With lambing almost upon us, the gamekeeper is a very busy man on the hill, trying to reduce fox numbers. By now, the vixen will have selected one of her dens and produced a litter of three to eight cubs in it. It is at this time that they are at their most vulnerable to the keeper's terriers and gun. The snub-nosed cubs are born blind and covered in short, grey hair. The vixen is a model mother, suckling and giving constant attention to her offspring, leaving the earth only to receive food from her mate. She will meet him some way from the den, depending on her own temperament. A confident vixen will allow the male to come close to the earth, while a very nervous one will travel half a mile or more to fetch her food which is mostly composed of short-tailed voles and mice.

At a fortnight old, the cubs open their eyes for the first time and about this time the vixen will begin to regurgitate partly-digested, solid food for them to eat. This is the first step towards weaning. As the cubs become more mobile and follow the vixen around the den, hardly leaving her in peace, she will take to lying on a rock or ledge out of their reach. Later, when the young adventurers have learned to climb, she may move out to another den near at hand, only returning to feed them.

The cruel east wind mercifully veers away around the bottom of the compass, to settle again in the south-west quarter. Warmth returns to the sun and the sticky buds of the horse chestnut tree are gently teased open, the long, multi-fingered leaves stretching out towards the blue sky. The rest of the trees will soon follow this example. Beneath the trees, delicate wood sorrel flowers are everywhere underfoot. Along the bank of the Glengyle Burn, in a well-secluded spot under the alders where the soil is less acid than usual, I discover some wood anemones bowing their heads in the wind. This exquisite white flower does not open until the wind has got up a wee bit, hence its country name of wind-flower. Folklore tells us that woodland fairies sleep inside the flowers at night, and that is the reason why wood anemones curl their petals at dusk.

Sand martins just beat their cousins, the house martins, back to Glengyle. Four days later, the first of the swallows takes up residence in the byre, after a long journey from the African continent. Unfortunately, one swallow does not make a summer.

The arrival of the cuckoo causes consternation amongst the meadow pipits in the glen; after all, they are the most popular host to the young of this parasitic villain. Wherever I see a cuckoo around Glengyle, it will have a mob of meadow pipits in close attendance, trying vainly to drive it away from their nesting area.

All around the house and steading, lovely, green grass is growing up in sheltered sun-traps. Out on the hill, cotton grass will be providing a very welcome fresh bite for my sheep. At last, spring has arrived at Glengyle.

A few moments old

Lambing

THE FIRST GLENGYLE LAMB of the year is born and once again a peculiar excitement courses through my veins. No matter how many lambing seasons come and go, I still get that same old feeling inside me. After all, there is something rather special, perhaps magical, about new-born lambs, even to a shepherd.

Immediately the lamb has slipped out into the big, wide world, the ewe rises and turns to vigorously lick clean the tightly-curled coat, carefully lifting mucus and membrane away from the face and mouth. In stages, the lamb staggers upright and takes a few moments more to find its land-legs. Then, through one of the wonders of nature, it makes its way towards breakfast. After a few false starts, sucking first at dangling bits of wool, then at the milk-filled udder, it finds and makes fast on a teat. The mother continues to lick and nuzzle the lamb's back-end, talking softly to it all the while. As the sweet, warm milk flows into the lamb, its tail waggles furiously.

The timing of several things seems to be ideally geared to leave me free of commitment so that I can concentrate on my lambing. The cows and calves are turned out onto the hill; I shall still feed them daily from a supply of feed stored under a tarpaulin at the far end of the West Park, but at my own convenience. Tansy has been dry for a month and is not due to calve again until the end of May, so I won't have to worry about milking her for a while. The rugby season, like all good things, comes to an end with a gala weekend of festive rugger. The last Saturday in April is the day of Stirling County REC's seven-a-side tournament, played against teams from as far away as Belfast. County win their own trophy, and this is added to the Division IV Championship Shield of the National League which the boys won in March. Disco dancing follows into the wee small hours of the morning. And all too soon it is Sunday and the turn of the mini-rugby section to hold their tournament for teams of seven- to 11-year olds. Both Jamie and Victoria regularly represent the club in their respective age groups. Toria is the first girl to play representative rugby for Stirling County, although other girls have turned up at the Saturday morning training sessions.

In what I expect to be my last spare time for quite a while, I turn my attention to my vegetable plot. I put young cabbage, cauli and sprout plants to bed in the garden; sow out carrot and swede seeds and two rows of runner beans. The potato drills are built up with a covering of dry, powdered peat which I have bagged and carried off the hill. This is my way of earthing-up the developing crop; a bonus is that the peat remains very free of weeds during the growing season. Finally, I sow a row of lettuce seeds between the tattie drills. This is a space-saving ploy, as the lettuce will be picked before the potato foliage covers them over.

Blackbirds rustle and scratch amongst the dried leaves beneath the rhododendron bushes at the back of the garden, searching for worms and other juicy morsels. But this evening there is something else rummaging about, making a lot of noise. On investigation, we find a prickly hedgie-pig also looking for food. Toria offers it a veritable banquet, putting down a dish of soppy bread and milk. Through regular dispensations of milky food, I hope to encourage it to stay around the garden; hedgehogs are a friend of any gardener, feeding on a whole host of damaging pests. I would much rather make use of natural predators as a means of control than risk upsetting the delicate ecological balances by using dangerous chemicals.

The time has come for me to get my lambing bag ready. This absolutely vital piece of the shepherd's equipment is home-made from an old grain sack, folded and stitched to form a bag with a closing flap. The flap is fastened by a pair of sheep's horn toggles, and the bag is completed with a strip of double hessian which serves as a shoulder strap. When Maggi made this bag, she put an entry through in to the lining at the front to give me an extra pocket for holding all my bits and bottles when the inside compartment is being used for carrying home an orphan lamb.

I neatly lay out the assortment of small bottles, containers and tins on the kitchen table, to make sure that I have all I need and that everything is in good order. The check list is as follows: one bottle of penicillin; one bottle of multi-vitamins; one bottle of lamb tonic; one bottle of glucose water; one tube of lambing jelly; two hypodermic syringes and tin of sterile needles; one tin of sterile suture needles and thread; one tin of sterile lambing cords; three glycerine suppositories; three antibiotic tablets (as big as horse pills); one container of antiseptic powder; two plastic containers of marking fluid (one red and one blue), and one flask of malt whisky (mainly for the shepherd). Once the bag is all packed, I hang it on the back of the door, ready for the morning.

Before turning in for an early night, I take a stroll with Maggi. Bo and Mona walk along at my heel, taking in all the scents of a world we humans can never fathom. The birds' evening chorus begins to give way to other sounds. As the last blackbird flies to his roost and the roding woodcock comes to ground, the gentle croaking of toads fills the air. Jupiter, the largest planet in our solar system, is also the brightest; a magnificent evening star in the darkening sky. The twilight deepens and the night is taken over by bats and owls. I look up at the dark silhouette of Glengyle Hill where the early lambs will be snuggled up against their mothers' warm bodies. I will soon be up there.

Soft, early-morning light filters through the mist which wraps the high hill tops. Carefully I slip out of my cosy bed, trying not to disturb Maggi. She sleeps on, oblivious of my movements. The bedside clock ticks its way past four o'clock as I dress quietly, and pad barefoot downstairs. Mona and Bo greet me warmly, tails wagging, Bo's rheumy old eyes looking intently up into mine. Direct eye to eye contact between man and dog is not always possible, but when it is, it helps to forge a really close bond of affection between the two.

Breakfast at this time of year consists of home-made muesli porridge oats sprinkled with plenty of sultanas, nuts and soft brown sugar. Without Tansy's milk, I have to resort to the bottled variety. Bonny materialises on the window-sill. I'll swear that cat can hear the sound of milk being poured at 500 yards, even my early start had not caught her napping. The moment I open the door to let out the dogs and take a look at the new day, Bonny slips in past me. A soft, cool wind is coming out of the south-west. The mist will linger on until the sun has risen to warm the day. A blackbird begins a beautiful solo prelude to the dawn chorus while, in the background, the House Burn tenors past house and steading on its way to the loch.

Bonny and I breakfast to the sounds of the BBC World Service. In another moment, her saucer is empty and she is curled up, asleep on the armchair. On with a pair of hand-knitted socks and my well dubbinned boots, and a pair of canvas gaiters to protect my legs from the early morning dampness. I make a last-minute check on the Rayburn fire before evicting the cat at her 39th wink. As I switch off the radio and lights, the whole house returns to a gloomy slumber. I lift my smock, telescope and lambing bag off the peg at the back of the door, and select a stick – the long-shanked chestnut crook which is my favourite at lambing time. Mona and Bo, understanding all these signs, know that it is time to go awa' to the hill.

Song thrush and robin are already harmonising with the blackbird melody, filling the fresh morning air with song. All the dogs come yawning and stretching out of their sleeping boxes as soon as they hear me letting myself into the kennel. I give both runs their daily clean out, swilling down the concrete with water left in the drinking pails. Then I refill the buckets straight from the burn. I like to be sure that the dogs left at home have plenty of water available. Calling out to Gail to take some of the weight off the old bitch, and slipping my lambing bag and telescope across my shoulder, I am ready to go at last. Crook in hand and three dogs at heel, I set off along the tree-lined road towards the rising sun.

Willow warbler and mistle thrush have now joined the dawn chorus. Duck swim out on Loch Katrine. Common gulls wheel and cry above the flat, grey water.

Ten minutes' walking brings me to the march burn, marking the boundary between Portnellan and Glengyle, and here the day starts in earnest. Slanting up through the oak wood, the leafless branches are alive with woodland birds: redstarts, tree pipits, chaffinches, tiny wrens and zip-zapping chiffchaffs all singing their territorial claims. The oak trees quickly peter out revealing steep, open hillside with fingers of alder indicating the downward course of numerous small rills. The more substantial march burn has eroded itself a deep gully which is lined with a wide variety of trees: oak, ash, rowan, hazel and birch as well as alder, all standing dark, stark and bare at the moment. Faded catkins still adorn the alder and hazel twigs.

As I climb, I check the burn again for victims of the long winter months. Sheep die all the year round, but there is a natural mortality peak among upland sheep at this time of year. In many respects, a mild winter can be worse for stock than a hard one because it usually means a great deal more rain. Full-coated black-faces are well able to withstand wool-curlingly cold temperatures, as long as it keeps dry. Perpetually saturated skins and sodden ground will rapidly melt away body condition, in even the strongest ewes. Pregnancy is the final nail in the coffin of a few unfortunate cases, especially if spring is late in any way. Debilitated ewes make their way inexorably downhill and are inevitably found at the bottom of glens or lying in burns. A shepherd soon learns exactly where he is most likely to find these fatalities, and this lower reach of my march burn is just one such place.

Broken bracken, the slippery skeletons of last summer's lush vegetation, makes walking a little difficult at times. Gaining height above the trees, the woodland madrigal fades and is replaced by the marvellous trilling of skylarks. It is difficult to believe that the lark's sweet song is not the result of a conscious effort at singing but is a mechanically produced sound, similar to purring in cats. Throughout the day, from April to July and again in October, a skylark will spend ten minutes or so in every daylight hour singing on the wing. Each song flight usually lasts only four or five minutes, although I have known some to go on for a quarter of an hour. The skylark is the only bird I know that sings while it is ascending. It sings while hovering on station, almost out of sight, and continues while descending. Sometimes they will also sing on the ground or from a perch.

The ewes are already grazing their way downhill. Two, I can

see, have a single newborn lamb at foot. Once again I am amazed at the smallness of the new lambs; one tends to forget how wee and delicate they can be. Now here they come again, tiny creatures on uncertain legs, struggling to keep close to their mothers. My presence makes the ewes draw away from me, moving away to my left, searching for food.

A little higher up, quite close to the burn, a ewe turns several circles and bleats plaintively. No lamb answers her call. It looks as though I have a keb on my hands – a ewe which has lost her lamb. Sometimes the lamb will be born dead, other times it will have died soon after birth. I take the dogs down into the gully, out of sight of the distraught ewe, and on command they lie down to wait for me. Quietly following a lower track until I reckon from her bleating that I am directly below her, I climb almost vertically upwards. On a small ledge about eight feet from the top, I dis-cover the lost lamb very much alive but trapped behind a tree root. Retrieving and examining the lamb, I find that, apart from hunger, all seems to be well. I carefully carry him to the top of the gully and, by imitating the high-pitched bleat of a hungry lamb, I entice his mother towards us. Keeping below the bank, out of the ewe's sight, I lie the lamb on the ground where she can see him, holding fast to his legs. The ewe, seeing the struggling lamb, has her moth-ering instincts activated and, as she approaches boldly, I release the hungry fellow who makes straight for his next meal. The ewe takes a sniff at him as he darts underneath her hindquarters. After allowing him to suckle for a minute or two, she moves off, taking her prodigal son away from this dangerous place. If only all problems were so readily resolved.

The female buzzard glides silently off her eyrie as I draw near to her tall ash tree. A single, short breast feather drifts down to land at my feet. She alights on a tree further up the hill. Although the bulky, stickbuilt eyrie is almost at the top of the tree, I can actually look down into the nest itself from the lip of the gully. In the nest, only 20 feet away, I can see three rounded matt-white eggs. The male buzzard mews from the sky above, nonchalantly disre-garding a challenge from an angry crow.

Just as I reach the shoulder of the Wee Hill, the sun starts to break through the mist. At the very top of the gully, where the march burn begins its last mad tumble down to the loch below, I see some purple saxifrage still flowering on a rock outcrop. I follow the natural run of the shoulder, using my telescope to spy out the ground below me. A little way along, I pick out four Portnellan ewes marauding on my ground, the blue keel showing up on their near hips. It should be a simple job for Bo to put them back to their own side of the march. At a word, the old bitch moves away to pass by them and take up a position at the front. A single whistle brings her to a halt; it also alerts every ewe on the hillside. The Glengyle sheep start to move away down the slope, and the Portnellan poachers try to follow but find Bo blocking their path. Momentary confusion is followed by an attempt to pass below her. Bo will have none of it, checking them easily and turning them for home. Further on, I encounter several more Portnellan sheep on the wrong side of the burn. I turn them in the right direction as I continue on my way.

The last of the early morning mist hanging about the Square Rocks evaporates in the warmth of the sun. Then I come across the first lambing mishap of the year – and I have only been on the hill for an hour. A keb ewe is standing over a pair of dead lambs. I leave her for a while, just to take a quick turn around the top of the Wee Hill, to make sure there is nothing else amiss in the vicinity. Returning to the scene of the tragedy, I put one of the dead lambs into my lambing bag, having already transferred its miscellaneous contents into the front pocket. The other lamb is deposited underneath a large stone. The dogs turn the keb towards home.

The sun is twenty minutes higher when I call off the dogs and close the fank gate behind me. Once in the confines of the small catching pen, I have no trouble in laying hold of the ewe and turning her over so that I can examine her milk potential. There appears to be plenty of milk in both quarters (even though a sheep has only two sections to her udder, as opposed to four in a cow, they are still called quarters). Now I need to find another lamb to foster onto her: this is known as twinning. On the way home from the keb, I had noticed a ewe with twin lambs near the Castle Rock. I shut the ewe into an empty pen in the byre and taking her dead lamb from my bag, I lay it down in the corner. She sniffs at the lifeless body; I leave her trying in vain to mother the prostrate form as I head back to the Castle Rock.

I find the ewe with the twin lambs at foot. One lamb is a tup lamb and the other is a bonny ewe lamb. Mona casts around to hold the ewe, fixing her with her eye, while I approach stealthily from behind. I reach out with my long crook; in an instant, the ewe lamb is popped into my lambing bag, and I am on my way back to Glengyle. The ewe will soon content herself with one lamb. The remaining lamb will grow better with individual attention from his mother. His twin sister ought to do as well on her foster mother, if all goes to plan, but if problems do arise and she fails to thrive, a backward ewe lamb is not such a financial loss as a poor wether lamb.

Back in the byre I carefully skin the dead lamb and slip his jacket onto the live one. Placing the animated bundle where the carcass had been lying, I stand back and watch. The keb sniffs; suspiciously at the now standing lamb; the scent she gets is the right one, after all it is the right skin. The lamb goes in close for a feed but the ewe moves away, then turns and sniffs the lamb again. This time she stands long enough for the lamb to find a teat and take a quick snack. The lamb is persistent and the process is repeated until it has had sufficient milk for the moment. The lamb, a strange sight in her borrowed coat, lies down on the straw bedding. A few seconds pass, then the ewe lies down alongside the lamb. Keeping my fingers crossed, I think that this twinning will be a success.

Before setting off back to the hill again, there is time for a quick visit to the house for some coffee and a bite to eat. The school bus has just left Glengyle, so the grill should still be warm. Maggi, on seeing me pass the kitchen window, puts bread on to toast and comments, 'I thought that you said you were going to get an early start.' A little later, after a steep climb to the very top of Glengyle, I look down into the Braes of Balquhidder. The view, taking in Loch Doine and Loch Voil, is breathtaking. Here is to be found solitude, but never loneliness. All around me the sad-sounding 'clu-ee' call of the golden plover can be heard. Looking through my glass, I can make out a piping bird standing on a small hummock, its black spangled, golden back feathers shining in the sun. Somewhere nearby will be a nest of heather stems, lichens and grass lining a scrape in the ground, and containing three or four eggs. Both parents share the four-week incubation period of the pointed, buff-coloured eggs with their reddish-brown blotches. The off-duty bird keeps a careful look-out and will launch itself at any intruder, or sometimes uses a realistic distraction display, feigning injury, even to the extent of lying on the ground, feebly thrashing its wings. Golden plovers are not as common on the high tops as they used to be; their breeding range has been steadily shrinking during this century.

The spangled feathers of the golden plover

There are no Glengyle ewes to be seen on the Balquhidder side of Meall Mór at this time of year, although a few Braes sheep have been drawn over to my ground by the sun on this face. When the sun has gained sufficient height to reach the north-facing side of Balquhidder, then my ewes will start straying across the march. The morning passes quietly as I follow the watershed onto the high-end of my hirsel. I watch the ewes and the first lambs enjoying the noon-day sunshine. The male eagle swoops into view, taking a good look at those who enter his dominion. The sunlight catches his white underwing patches which indicate that this is a young bird, probably four years old. He will lose these juvenile characteristics at his next moult at the end of the summer, and at the same time he will gain the true, golden nape of adult plumage.

I stop and sit for a while, delving into the depths of my lambing bag for a piece of dark cooking chocolate. It is very necessary to sustain the inner man. From my perch, high above the world, the lochs below sparkle like eyes in the earth. To the south-east, I can see clear to Edinburgh. It was from here that the outlawed MacGregors successfully resisted and defied anything the capital city sent against them.

In 1603, James VI commissioned Colquhoun, Laird of Luss on Loch Lomondside, to take up arms against the MacGregors. MacGregor, on hearing the news, brought out his men to face the enemy and in February of that year, the two forces met in Glen Fruin. The MacGregors, losing only one man of note, broke their foes with heavy slaughter and laid the Colquhoun country waste. Yet their victory was to cost them dear; it was an intolerable insult to the Crown, and the Government determined to 'extirpat and ruttit out that detestable race'. Under penalty of death, the name MacGregor was to be used no more. Anyone who captured a MacGregor or produced his head was rewarded either with a bounty or the victim's possessions. That only 36 were brought to trial and executed, in addition to six hostages in Government hands who were hanged without trial, says a lot for loyalty in the clan system.

The MacGregors became Children of the Mist, and just as elusive. Many dispersed and took other names, usually that of their adopted Laird. Others defiantly took refuge on Loch Katrine side. In 1611, King James ordered Argyll into the area to put the rebels to the sword. Argyll laid siege to the MacGregors who had retreated to Eilean Molach (Ellen's Isle), but six or seven score of desperate men broke out and carried fire and sword east and west before scattering amongst the vastness of Rannoch Moor to the north. Even though the Crown was directly responsible for the awful persecution of the clan, any woman with the name MacGregor was to be branded on the face and thereafter transported; children over the age of 12 years were to be shipped to Ireland, and younger children were sent to the Lowlands until they reached the age of deportation – the MacGregors were always to the fore when the King was in need of arms. After one such foray in the Stewart cause, Charles II restored the clan to favour. This was in 1661; but they were outlawed again in 1693, and this time 81 years were to pass before the penal sanctions were repealed and it was once more lawful to bear the name MacGregor.

Sweeping the hill with my telescope, I locate a ewe obviously in labour. She is lying on her side, head held stiffly, legs stretched out and straining. I also notice that the soft ground around about her has been well trampled, suggesting that she has been in this stage for quite some time. I quickly make my way down to where she is still struggling to produce her lamb. The ewe sees me coming as I walk softly towards her, but she is past caring about any threat which I might represent. Two tiny feet are showing from under her tail. Bo, Mona and Gail settle down to snooze while I get on with the job in hand.

I lay my lambing bag on the ground within easy reach, and kneel down alongside the ewe. I take the tube of lubricant lambing jelly from my bag and rub some of it onto my fingers. Sliding my right hand ever so gently into the ewe, I find that I have a pair of front legs in the correct presentation and position; the problem seems to be the absence of a head, which should be lying on top of the legs, facing forward towards the light. Carefully exploring further, I discover the missing head twisted backwards over the lamb's left shoulder. Using my left hand to push the lamb's legs back a little way, I am able to straighten the head and, keeping it safely cupped inside my palm to protect the ewe from internal injury, I ease the lamb out onto the grass. Working fast, I clear the slimy mucus away from the lamb's nose and mouth. This lad has been a long time coming into the world and now he is reluctant to start breathing, so I tickle the inside of his nose with a piece of grass. This makes him sneeze a time or two, and sets his lungs working, irregularly at first but after a few gasps he settles down to a steady rhythm. I place the lamb in front of his mother, who immediately begins to lick him, while I take another look inside the ewe. This lamb is probably a single, his well started horn buds testify to that, but I always check every ewe that I lamb to make sure she is empty. More than once I have been surprised by another lamb.

The ewe is exhausted from her prolonged effort. She will soon recover though. Hardy sheep these Blackfaces. I give her a shot of penicillin in case any infection has gained entry during the assisted lambing, and a couple of mls of multi-vitamins injected under the skin to give her a bit of a boost. In a few moments, she is on her feet again, busy mothering her lamb. Soon the lamb, too, is on his feet, taking his first feed. Before I leave, I trim up his umbilical cord and dress the navel with antiseptic powder. A hill shepherd should be able to save a lamb a day during his lambing time. I reckon that I can count this as one.

On the far side of the glen, the female eagle is sitting tight on her eyrie, close-brooding her downy eaglet. By the time I make my way round to her side, she has left her nest and has taken up position on her favourite look-out perch, a large protruding rock further up the hillside. As I pass directly below the watchful bird, she sweeps majestically off into space, her great wings needing to flap only twice to give her all the lift she requires. She curves away across the glen until she finds an invisible thermal which sends her spiralling up and up into the heavens. Even with the aid of my telescope, she is no more than a dark speck by the time her mate joins her, high above Ben Ducteach.

I work my way towards home, across the lower slopes of the Ben and onto Eves Road. Every pool and puddle along the length of the road contains a multitude of wriggling black tadpoles. The sheep are beginning to graze their way back up the face of the hill. The call of male cuckoos reverberates across the glen.

Near the West Park the hill cows are picking at the rank vegetation which the sheep find too tough and unpalatable. As soon as they hear me coming down the glen, they stop grazing and bellow at me impatiently. They assemble at the feeding place outside the gate and mill around while I fetch their hay and cobs from under the hap inside the park. I don't think they like being made to wait so long for their food, but now lambing is under way, the cattle definitely have to take second place. Once I am satisfied that all is well with the cows and calves, I step out the last half-mile to home.

I take a look at the keb and her twinned-on lamb in the calf pen. Both were lying side by side in the straw before my presence brought them to their feet. The lamb immediately makes for the ewe's udder and in a jiffy she is suckling strongly. The ewe, for her part, seems content with her acquisition. I decide to try them in the small paddock at the back of the byre. I open the gates and let them out onto the grass, running the ewe out first to see if she will come back to look for her lamb. This is always a positive sign that a firm bond has been established between them. She does. Tomorrow it ought to be safe to take the loose skin off the lamb.

After a welcome meal, I have a potter around the garden, before taking Tansy and her calves their supper. The pets also get a troughful of feed. Susie was due to lamb today and, right on schedule, produced a good pair of cross-Suffolk tup lambs. Penny is next on the list, the day after tomorrow. Finally the dogs are fed, and while Maggi and I are in the kennel, we count 133 pipistrelle bats leaving their roosting place under the tiles of the barn roof opposite.

I return to my comfy old armchair to listen to the radio, and read and sleep. Mostly sleep. After the ten o'clock news on Radio 4, I hit the hay. And so ends my first day's lambing of the new season, not bad as they go. I lie in bed thinking of it all happening out there on the hill, and wondering what tomorrow holds in store for me. Jupiter twinkles through my bedroom window.

I wonder how many maidens, young and not so young, will be leaving their beds as early as me, secretly to wash their faces in the magical morning dew. The first of May had long been held to be a day of enchantment, old customs and fairy beliefs. Only the May blossom finds some difficulty in fulfilling its role of flowering on this day. The poor hawthorn tree has had a hard time keeping up to date since 1751 when the calendar was altered by 12 days. In Scotland, this is the day of the Beltain fire festival. The word is derived from the old Gaelic word for sun, which in turn comes directly from the ancient deity of Baal.

The chill, early Mayday light finds me making my way past the remains of a ruined shieling, on my way to the tops of Glengyle. It was to these upland shielings and their summer pastures that the farm animals were brought at Beltain, keeping them at a safe distance from the precious crops growing on the in-bye land below. The day started with every household fire being extinguished and a new fire kindled by friction from a sacred tree, usually in the form of a beam. (Until recently, there was one such beam in the roof of an old dwelling in Glen Finglas where the marks of centuries of fire-raising could be plainly seen. Unfortunately, the building was destroyed during the construction of Finglas reservoir.) The new fire was taken to each farm in turn and set to a prepared pile of wood and dried peat. The cattle, which had been housed throughout the long winter months together with the sheep and goats, were all driven through the billowing reek from the fire on their way to the shielings. Each household then re-lit their own hearth fire from the one outside. This new fire would be carefully tended until the next fire festival, Samhain, come November.

Even when a ewe has safely lambed, problems can still arise. One ewe I come across, near the Square Rocks, has a large, fleshy mass hanging from her back end. She has pushed out her uterus, known as casting her lamb bed; this happens when a ewe continues to strain for some time after giving birth. Mona eyes-up the mother for me while I pick up her lamb and tie its four legs securely together, and then get near enough to the ewe to catch her around the neck with my crook. I lay my shepherd's smock on the ground behind the sheep, to prevent dirt getting onto the uterus, before gently turning her right over on her back. I take a long piece of twine from my pocket and tie one end to each of her back legs. Then, by hooking the twine over the back of my neck I can keep her rear end up off the ground, while still having both hands free to work with. I split one of the glycerin suppositories to act as an antiseptic and lubricant, and carefully work the womb back into place. There is always a distinct possibility that she will evert it again, so I tie a couple of twisted locks of wool across the vaginal opening in an attempt to hold everything in place. If this doesn't work, I shall have to put in a couple of stitches. I give her a precautionary penicillin injection and put a red mark on the back of her head to enable me to find her again at a distance. After checking her udder to make sure all is well, I turn the ewe and lamb loose on the hillside.

Far up on the high-end of Glengyle, I find myself at the Fairy Hill, on this of all days. According to legend, if I were to walk sunwise around the fairy mound seven times, I would vanish into Fairyland. But the only thing that does a disappearing act today is a herd of red deer which I surprise as they peacefully browse in this well sheltered suntrap. The deer troop away over the brow of the hill and by the time I look down into the Balquhidder glen after them, they seem to have simply vanished off the face of the earth. The mundane explanation for the disappearance of the deer lies in the excellent camouflage properties in their shabby, partly-moulted, old coats which blend in so well with the rather bleached-looking hillsides. As yet, there is no obvious new summer greenness, but the deer and sheep are adept in seeking out whatever fresh shoots there are in sheltered places and on south-facing slopes. Soon I expect to see both the red deer and Glengyle hills clothed in fine summer vestments.

Gail finds a young lamb trapped in a deep peat tunnel. If it had not been for the bitch's good nose for this sort of thing, the poor wee beast probably would never have been found. Just as fortunately for the lamb, not much water is running in the drain so, apart from being rather muddy and very hungry, it appears to be quite unharmed. After a good bath in the Glengyle Burn, I dry her off with wisps of dead grass. Then, being extremely careful not to choke her, I pour a little lamb tonic into her mouth as she sucks my finger. I follow that with a small feed of glucose water from a bottle warmed in my inside pocket. The navel is dressed with powder and the lamb, certainly looking and I hope feeling a good bit better, is popped into my lambing bag. After unsuccessfully casting around for the deserting mother, I reckon that, unless the fairies have got her, she probably had twins and has happily wandered away with the other half of her family. There is nothing else for me to do except take this orphan home and bottle-feed it until I get a keb to twin her on to.

The early morning bees are busy on the wing and tending their underground nests. I usually notice them visiting willow catkins in April. The members of the Andrena bee family in Britain number about three score, all of which excavate their nests in dry, sandy slopes, often in colonies. Strangely, they seem to favour well-trodden paths, the hard crust probably affording extra protection to the single, subterranean shafts. The pollen collected from the spring flowers is mixed with only a little honey, so that the paste provided for the larvae has a dry consistency.

My orphan lamb lies snugly curled up in a cardboard box next to the Rayburn while Maggi thaws out a small bottle of frozen goat's colostrum from the freezer. Colostrum is a thick, yellow and rather creamy liquid which takes the place of true milk for the first three or four days of the lactation, and is vital if the lamb is to have even a fair chance of surviving. First of all, colostrum is very nutritious because it contains special proteins in a form readily available to the lamb. Secondly, it is fortified with a high vitamin content to give the young lamb a good start in life. The third attribute is its protective quality, owing to the presence of ready-made antibodies against ailments such as scour. Finally, it acts as a laxative, having a high fat content which encourages the expulsion of the first faecal matter, called meconium. The failure of meconium emission is a primary cause of the high death rate amongst orphan lambs. Not until the foetal faeces have been passed can the lamb make use of important reserves stored in the liver. I insert a glycerin suppository into the anal canal to make sure that this is never a problem with lambs which I bring home.

Making my way through the uncurling, pale green bracken shoots on my way once more to the high ground, I pause for a few moments to watch a tree wasp at work. She is busy building a round, multicelled paper home beneath a low-hanging branch of a large lime tree. It is not a good choice of site: Brock Badger will soon discover this tasty morsel. A grey squirrel chatters angrily at me, and in turn is mobbed by an asortment of small songbirds as he high-tails it back to his drey in the form of a nearby elm. Continuing on my way, I climb up through a small defile at the back of the Castle Rock and pass close to the vixen's den. I wonder how long it will be before the keeper finds them; to him a fox is no more than vermin and must be exterminated in any way possible.

With the arrival of springtime and the start of lambing, all the old arguments against the fox are resurrected. Accusations of wholesale slaughter and enormous losses of young lambs are once more brought out and bandied about by farmers and flockmasters alike. One hears wild stories of 30, 50 and even more lambs killed in order to raise a litter of cubs. The cubs are weaned at around five weeks old, that is about now, the middle of May. At this stage, each cub requires roughly 4 oz of meat per day, so an average litter of five cubs would only need 8–10 lbs per week – the equivalent of one small lamb. In another fortnight, the danger period appears to be past and if the cubs had been fed entirely on lamb, which they certainly never are, the claim that even 30 lambs would be taken is obviously well wide of the mark. Tales of foxes killing for enjoyment or vengeance are simply untrue. It is Man himself who is most guilty of these charges; animals do not have such human attributes. Many shepherds believe that a lamb is often killed only for its tail to be bitten off and carried away to the den for the cubs to play with. Tails are indeed removed but from lambs which are already lying dead from some other cause. It is on dubious claims such as these that myths about foxes are based.

Foxes can and do kill but mostly small mammals and birds, and only for food. The principal prey in this area is the short-tailed vole, and a pair of resident foxes will account for some 9,000 of these small rodents in a year. A single, tiny vole will munch its way through 50 lbs of grass in 12 months; therefore, it can be seen that these foxes help to save an extra 200 tons of grazing for the sheep, quite a valuable contribution to the well-being of my flock. Carrion also features high on the menu and I firmly believe that almost all the lamb consumed by foxes comes from this plentiful source. Extensive studies over recent years by various organisations have established that 17 per cent of all lambs born to Scottish hill ewes are either dead at birth or die within 24 hours. This unfortunate state of affairs is directly due to the poor nutrition of the ewe during pregnancy. My own figures tally with this frighteningly high number of lamb losses, and much work needs to be done to improve the situation. Killing foxes is not the answer, however.

My eye lights on a newly-born lamb standing next to its proud mother. All is not well with this wee beastie; it is looking rather hungry, all hunched with its tummy tucked up. I settle the dogs down and seat myself on a convenient boulder to see if I can identify the trouble. It could simply be a lack of milk on the ewe; blind or blocked teats, or perhaps the lamb just cannot find its way to the proper place. I sit and observe. Every time the lamb attempts to suckle, the ewe turns keenly to mother it and inadvertently knocks the poor creature over in the process. This is repeated time after time again. I realise that this ewe is a gimmer and this will be her first lamb; the problem is one of inexperience on both sides. If I try to handle this sheep on the open hillside, she will probably bolt so I quietly work her down to one of the hill lambing pens. Once she and the lamb are securely inside the fence, I use Boot to face her up. The gimmer, alarmed for the safety of her lamb, stands her ground and stamps her front foot defiantly at the dog. His mother's attention elsewhere, the lamb makes contact with his food supply in no time at all and his tail waggles away in sheer pleasure.

Beautiful flowers of many kinds brighten up hill and glen. In particular, May is the month of the worts: milkwort, lousewort, stitchwort, woundwort, butterwort, and water starwort can all be found in Glengyle. I have a special liking for the milkworts which appear on the slopes almost as soon as I do. To a shepherd, the significance of milkwort (milk herb) if it lives up to its name is that it assures him that his ewes will have abundant milk. The delicate flowers, said to be used as soap by the fairies, vary from blue, through purple and pink, to a pure white. It is possible to find all these colours growing together.

The dark-fingered trees are in leaf and become more verdant by the day, slowly blending into the lower slopes of the glen. Only the stubborn oak and ash still resist the charms of the sun. The rowan and horse chestnut are heavy with blossom, but my own hive bees prefer to make their honey from the lime tree flowers. There is an old country belief that a swarm of bees in May is worth a load of hay. It also brings me a load of honey.

The bracken is growing in leaps and bounds, sometimes by as much as eight inches in a day. This is possibly one of the best known ferns but it is also the one with the most nuisance value. In the past 50 years, bracken has taken over countless acres of good upland grazing land. It is poisonous to livestock and is normally avoided by sheep, cattle, deer and rabbits, and so it spreads unhindered. The far-reaching underground rhizomes make eradication difficult, but modern herbicides have been developed to help landowners in its control. In the last century, long before the days of artificial weed killers, farmers controlled bracken simply and effectively by a system of drains. These hand-dug, stone-filled drains could be closed in the springtime to raise the underground water level. Bracken only likes well-drained soil and would not colonise the wet areas. In the autumn, before the time of highest rainfall, the drains were opened and the water-table dropped appreciably.

Partly hidden amongst the bracken on the lower slopes of the Wee Hill, I find a ewe couped over onto her back and quite unable to regain her feet. Sheep in this position quickly die, but luckily this one is still in the land of the living. The lamb, it seems, is stuck inside her. I make my usual examination and find two forelegs and a head which is exactly as it should be. Something else must be wrong. My gently probing fingers soon discover that the head and one leg belongs to one body and the second leg belongs to a different lamb altogether. I ease the spare limb back inside the womb, before reaching in to search for the missing leg. I locate it lying back against the rib cage and bring it forward alongside its partner. The lamb is soon out, blinking and sneezing in the daylight. I manoeuvre the second lamb into the proper lambing position and leave it to make its own way into the world. The first lamb had been cleaned up and has had her first feed before the twin puts in an appearance.

Strathard Gala day dawns fair and full of promise. The whole family is looking forward to an afternoon in Aberfoyle under a sunny, swift-filled sky, with stirring pipe-band music, colourful floats and fancy dresses. We come down from the hills in time to see a pretty Stronachlachar lass, Marietta Little, crowned Gala

Queen. The people from the length of the strath take part in a full programme of races, athletics and five-a-side football. Jamie and Victoria compete for and win a few of the coveted ribbons in the children's events. Maggi is a member of the winning women's tug-of-war team as the Stronachlachar ladies out-pull their heavier Aberfoyle counterparts. They are prettier too. Even I manage to take time out from my duties as MC to retain my 100 metre and 800 metre titles. The night is danced and reeled away at the Inversnaid Hotel.

The sun spends the greater part of the day above the horizon, a fact much appreciated by shepherd and sheep. Beneath the oak trees in the Boathouse Wood, the woodcock, coloured like a bundle of dead leaves, hatches the first of her two summer broods. As soon as the down dries into a warm, yellow fluff, she carries them one at a time, clasped in between her long toes, to a safe place near the loch shore. Above the open hillside, clouds of strange black flies flit and dance through the warm air, long legs dangling down. These are March flies and, as always, they appear in May to court and mate on the wing. The eggs are laid in the soil and the emergent larvae feed on grass shoots, holding the tips of the leaves below ground so that the leaf, as it grows, forms a loop with both ends in the soil. If I dig the soil out with my knife, I will find a legless, soft-bodied grub similar to a leather-jacket.

The ewes nibble the fresh grass as parties of baby-faced lambs scamper and leap around in the summery sunshine. Most of my ewes have lambed and the pace slackens a little. But there is still some lambing left to be done and not every story has a happy ending. My greatest problem in herding sheep over four square miles of rugged upland pasture is the chance against my being in the right place at the right time. It saddens me to come across a ewe which has died simply because I was not there to help her when she needed me. Sometimes the lamb has been stuck, and both have perished in that awful state. Even more harrowing is the sight of a small lamb curled up against its mother, together in death: the lamb born alive but the ewe dying in giving birth, denying it any food and succour. Many a disaster could have been averted, if only...

I try hard to reduce the odds. Over the years I have added

The woodcock coloured like a bundle of dead leaves

different items to my lambing equipment, and now I hope to carry everything I am likely to need in an emergency. But even with the right tackle at hand, things can still go wrong. Here I have a ewe stuck fast with a large tup lamb. The lamb's head is big in itself, but this one is carrying sizeable horn buds as single tup lambs are prone to do. I use the lambing cords; one looped around the back of the lamb's head and another with an end tied to each of the forelegs. This gives me the maximum possible pull, but unfortunately the lamb is already dead. I will give the ewe a while to recover her strength before taking her home and twinning her on one of the bottle-fed orphans.

Kebs and orphan lambs between them probably take up more of my time than any other single thing. Most of my orphans go onto a keb, and most of my kebs go back to the hill with a lamb following at foot. I like to get my kebs away as quickly as I can because I believe a ewe is happier on her own heft than anywhere else. The old skin coat is taken off on the second day once the ewe's own milk has had time to pass through the lamb and give it an acceptable smell. Then, if the ewe is still quite sure that the lamb belongs to her, they are free to go.

Occasionally things go unexpectedly in my favour. From the north side of Glengyle, on what will be my last full day on the hill this season, I watch a ewe lambing on Ben Ducteach. My heart is in my mouth. She is very close to the edge of a precipice. And, sure enough, she drops her lamb, literally, over a 60-foot drop. My heart falls with it. I make tracks across the glen and climb up the face of the Ben towards the keb ewe. However, when I reach the lamb, intending to remove its skin, I find her very much alive, lying apparently unharmed in a patch of soft moss. I successfully reintroduce the lamb to the distraught ewe before moving them away to a safer place.

On my way home, I see that a cross-Swale ewe, which I call Mary, has produced triplets for the second year running. Triplets are most unusual in hill-bred Blackfaces, that is why I am familiar with this lady and have given her a name of her own. I lift one of

An orphaned lamb

her lambs as she only just managed to rear the three last year when she was aged four and at the peak of her milk yield. This will be Mary's last year on the hill and I will be sorry to see her go to the sales in the autumn. As I carry home what must surely be my last orphan lamb of the year, the sun blazes down on my magnificent glen. I pause to take a drink of pure, clear, thirst-quenching water from the Glengyle Burn. For a while I relax and sit back on the soft grassy bank in the shade of the leafy alders with my dogs about me; I feel so close to the earth that I can feel it moving.

The wily hill fox

Counting the Tails

THE LONG HOURS OF SUNSHINE seem to lull the voices of our song birds. Some, like the mistle thrush, have almost stopped singing altogether although the closely-related song thrush can still be heard threading a few monotonous notes together. Now it is the constant hum of insects which is the very note of summer.

Dun mayflies, which may have spent three years as water nymphs, emerge to pass but a few brief hours as winged adults. Countless newly-hatched swarms flit over the sun-reflecting surface of Loch Katrine, while voracious trout rise to take any that stray too close to the water. During a period of a large hatch, many dead and drowning mayflies will litter the surface, attracting fish and fishermen alike. This is the time an angler will require all his craft and cunning to tempt his intended prey into taking his copy of rising nymph, emerging dun or egg-laying spinner. Archaeologists have found evidence that this ancient art of tying artificial flies goes back at least to 200 BC.

Mayflies exhibit a unique feature in their life-cycle. Not only do they moult throughout successive larval stages, but also once more after they have taken to the wing. In this final moult, the plain, brown dun metamorphose into a more colourful, longer tailed, sexually mature form, known as the spinner. The short-lived spinners do not eat, in fact they have no means of feeding as their mouth parts were pretty well lost during the final moult. Most spinners mate and die within a day but, given the right conditions and a lot of luck, may survive for four whole days.

Flowers everywhere are at their very best, gladdening the eye and reawakening an awareness of delicate perfumes far beyond the scope and ability of any cosmetic chemist to reproduce. All over the hill the white, tiny-flowered bedstraw and the yellow, five-petalled tormentil mingle amongst the summer grasses. At this time of year, when overexposure to the hot sun can catch the unwary, painful sunburn can be treated with a cooled lotion of tormentil steeped in boiling water.

Wild orchids abound on the moist, acid heathland, mostly of the Heath spotted variety. This exquisite flower can range in colour from deepest purple to purest white. The reproductive mechanism of plants is often rather specialised and the orchids are no exception. A foraging bee alights and pokes her head deep into the flower to reach the pollen and nectar. The male and female parts are not separate as in most other flowers, but are fused together with the male, pollen-bearing stamens a little above the female, pollen-receiving stigma. Orchid pollen is a little different from the usual fine dust, being made up into small sticky lumps. Some of the pollen rubs off on the head of the visiting insect, and as the insect wings away, the pollen mass shifts slightly so that when it arrives at another flower of the same species the pollen will come into contact with the stigma and pollenation takes place.

I sometimes tease a flower into releasing a little of its pollen on to a piece of hand-held cotton grass, mimicking a bumble bee. When held up, the shift of pollen on the cotton grass bud can be clearly observed.

Evening time brings to the fore what, without doubt, is my favourite flower: the fragrant honeysuckle. Simply to catch the slightest undercurrent on the breeze reminds me of the summer night, many years ago, when Maggi and I first met. We were picking dew-hung honeysuckle from a hedgerow in the wilds of Aberdeenshire – at six o'clock in the morning.

The Glengyle cows have been rather pushed into the background during lambing; out of sight for much of the time but never out of mind. They were fed and checked over each day; returning from grazing further and further out in the glen as the fingers of the growing season reached along the bottom ground and slowly up the slopes. One day they failed to show up, no matter how long and loudly I called to them. They were getting plenty elsewhere.

My Hereford bull, a gentle giant of a beast, dubbed Fray Bentos because of his massive horned head, returned from his winter quarters at Milngavie and was turned out with the herd in mid-May. If he is working as well as in previous years, some of the cows will already be back in calf and due sometime around the third week of next February.

The time has come round to disturb their peace and bring them home. Tomorrow the vet will be coming to castrate the bull calves and test the cows to make sure that they are free from both bovine tuberculosis and contagious abortion. With Bo, Gail and Dust at heel, Maggi and I head away to the far end of Glengyle in search of the summering herd.

It is only a couple of weeks before the end of the school term and the long summer holidays, so Maggi enjoys this chance to have a day on the hill with me. We will be home well before the school bus returns with Jamie and Victoria. We follow the Glengyle Water, keeping to the welcome shade beneath the burnside alders, stopping for a dip and a splash in the deepest pool, eventually leaving the water at the site of the nunnery and climbing to the shieling halfway up Ben Ducteach.

This shieling is in a good state of preservation. The stone-work is largely still standing, the doorway and two tiny windows in the front wall overlooking the glen, loch and distant Ben Venue. The roof, long since gone, would have been of turf laid over wooden poles. The origin of caber tossing is found in this style of roofing, with the young men of the community vying with each other to toss stouter, thus stronger and longer-lasting, timbers on the roof. Every caber was required to come to rest in a straight position. This is the basic rule of present day caber competitions.

Close at hand, in front of the main building, is a stone-built larder where food was kept cool and secure from thieving animals. Nearby is a small round sheep-pen or stell, where the sheep were kept each night. Later, when the large flocks of Blackfaces had replaced entire farming settlements, these same stells were used by shepherds to grow kale. The soil was rich from years of accumulated sheep droppings, but this time the stout walls would be keeping the sheep out.

Above the shieling is an outcrop of alkaline rock together with some of its characteristic accompanying plants. Conspicuous among them is a profusion of pink-flowered cranesbill.

We move on, round the face of the Ben, and find the cattle

lying deep in the lush grass on Ducteach's flat shoulder. They chew their cud contentedly in the noonday heat; no truth in the old town dweller's saying that lying cows are a sign of impending rain … not today, anyway. They are all present and correct but we leave them for a while, passing above them to take a look at the five-week-old eagle. If the cows have seen us, they give absolutely no indication of doing so. It is too hot even to twitch their tails at the biting flies.

From a vantage point to the left of the eyrie, we can clearly see the young down-covered bird, with the first feathers showing darkly on the top of its head. A sudden shadow passes across us as the female drops out of the sky onto the eyrie. She begins to tear up a red grouse which she has brought in. Only the female rips up food in this manner, the male simply carries his contribution to the nest and leaves it to await the attention of his partner. Herein lies a tale of good and misfortune concerning a shepherd, his cat and a family of golden eagles…

Not far from here, as the eagle flies, in the adjoining county of Argyllshire, a shepherd watched in amazement as an eagle swooped down and snatched up his cat. Fortunately, being a house cat and used to being handled, the mog did not struggle, which was undoubtedly the reason that her life was not crushed out by the powerful talons there and then. A short while later, the cat was left on the eyrie, a little bruised and somewhat breathless. The fact that she had been abducted by the male bird proved to be the salvation of several of her nine lives, and the undoing of the two small eaglets. Before the female could return to render the cat into strips of bird food, the cat had recovered her wits and turned the chicks into cat food.

Two days later, the shepherd was astonished to see his cat back on her favourite fireside seat as though she had never been away. On hearing the story, the local gamekeeper, knowing the location of the eyrie, accompanied the shepherd to the site. The few bloody remains of the young birds volubly filled in the details of this shaggy, but true cat saga.

Dust and Gail bring the cows to their feet and start them towards home, while Bo goes to retrieve the bull and three cows

The sparrowhawk patrols the edge of the wood

and their calves which were grazing a little way off. My dogs are expected to work cattle as well as sheep. The technique required in each case is a little different and some good sheepdogs can't work cattle, whilst some cattle dogs are unable to control sheep. A really good dog, like Gran, should, on command, be able to work almost anything that moves. Apart from sheep and cattle, the old bitch has in her time worked on pigs and poultry, flanked red deer so that they could be photographed, rounded up a party of university students missing amongst sand dunes and even apprehended a gang of house-breakers.

We were checking on a friend's house on the outskirts of Aberdeen while they were away for a few days' holiday. On arriving, I found that the house had been broken into and several juveniles were making a hasty exit via a ground floor window. My request for them to return was greeted with a few choice suggestions as to what I could do. Not many moments later, however, half a dozen rather bemused boys were herded back to me out of the gloom. After the incident had been appropriately dealth with, I left guard dog Gran in residence, just in case.

On the way down the glen, each one of my dogs takes turns in starting the ewes and lambs up the hillsides towards the higher ground. By the time shepherd, wife, bull, cows, calves and panting, tongue-lolling dogs get back to Glengyle, the sun is moving to the West.

Early next morning, Glengyle takes on the air of a Wild West cattle town, all trails leading to the Glengyle corral. First to arrive is the Dhu herd, bellowing loudly and steaming gently, followed a short while later by the Portnellan and Coilachra herds coming in from the opposite direction. Each group is kept in its separate lot, although there are a few moments of drama as the Dhu and Coilachra bulls threaten to utterly demolish the fence which separates their respective harems. The stretched, tortured wire squeals under the pressure, and staples catapult free from the larch posts. The problem is quickly solved as Alec McLellan and I shut the Coilachra bull inside the stout, stone-walled sheep fank, from where he continues to bellow his defiance to all and sundry.

Mr Watt, our vet, arrives in his car, after making his first call on the Water Board cows over at Corriearklet on the shore of nearby Loch Arklet. Close behind him comes a Land Rover filled with the otherside shepherds, Bob Morgan and his men, to see to their Dhu beasts.

With much shouting and stick-waving, each group of cows is put through the cattle crush where they are securely held, one at a time, in a head yoke. Bill Watt takes a sample of blood from the neck of each cow which is carefully labelled and will be sent away to a laboratory and checked for the presence or otherwise of brucella, contagious abortion. Next, he gives the cow two small injections on the side of her neck, about eight inches apart; the skin thickness at the injection sites is measured and recorded. In three days' time, Mr Watt will return and remeasure the skin to see if there has been any marked increase, indicating the presence of tuberculosis in the animal. Finally, the cows are dosed against liver fluke and stomach worms.

The calves, waiting in a side pen, come to their turn. Each calf is given a worm dose, then the heifer calves are let out alongside their mothers before the vet turns his attention to the bull calves. One by one, the victims are held against a wall by two men, one at the animal's head, the other at the hindquarters. Two incisions are made in the back of the scrotum, and both testicles are drawn out and removed. Maggi waits, bowl in hand, to collect these delicacies for our evening meal. (For those who are interested, Maggi blanches the sweetbreads in a pan of boiling salted water before removing the tough outer skin and frying these small, very tasty meat balls in a little butter.)

With the Glengyle rodeo over for today, Bob Morgan's posse drives off back to Corriearklet, while the rest of us hit the trail down the lochside to Edra. Here the bottom-end cattle receive exactly the same treatment.

Another hot day. This is flaming June, indeed. Iain summons all hands back down to Edra to set to and clip the tups. A dozen or so tups at a time are run from a large holding pen into a small handling pen and given a dose against liverfluke and worms. These tups are then run out through a few pens in a circle until they are back where they started. The small pen is filled up again, the engines started up and we are ready to go.

We all pile into the pen and each pounce upon the handiest tup, negotiate our way out through the gate and walk our charges over to our clipping stances, deftly turning them up into a sitting position. This is known as crogging. For all other sheep, we have a labourer to crog for us, but as tups are heavy and extremely well-armed, it is probably better to let the experienced shepherds handle them themselves. Starting with the hand-piece in my right hand, I open up the neck, clearing down the right-hand side, over the shoulder, across the ribs and belly, down the back leg as far as the tail. And then a little past it, to the left hip. Changing hands, I work down the near side until the fleece comes free. I release the naked animal, pointing him in the direction of a couple of his companions already standing in a back pen. He scrambles to his feet and takes off. Next please. And the next.

Until fairly recent times, sheep-shearing was a far more leisurely and social activity than it is today. Much gossip, or crack, passed back and forth over the constant snicking of handshears. Every man took a pride in turning out tidy, well-clipped sheep with no double cutting of the wool or injury to the skin. Then came new methods which required the expenditure of much less sweat than traditional techniques, and this meant greater numbers of sheep being clipped in a given time and with the advent of machines, the pace accelerated even more. Of course, there are still people who can shear to perfection, and do it quickly too. But, I am afraid to say that, in many cases, the striving for speed results in crude work and cut sheep.

In the old days, even the slightest nick in the sheep's skin would be treated with a special healing tar – giving rise to a maxim 'to spoil a ship [sheep] for a ha'peth of tar', meaning that if a cut went untended, blowflies might well lay eggs in the wound and the ensuing flesh-eating maggots would badly damage, even cause the death of the poor animal. It is no excuse to sacrifice the well-being of the sheep to the cause of greater speed. Every wound, however minor, ought to be dressed; it only takes a moment.

Alec, in the role of woolman, folds each fleece weathered side out, and rolls it up towards the neck end, twisting the neck wool into a thick rope for tying the wrapped wool. Wool merchants prefer to handle well-rolled and securely-tied fleeces. One fleece follows another and, in no time at all, the last tup scurries into the pen of clippies. In this heat they must be glad to lose their winter coats.

It is a very satisfying sight to see a batch of fresh, evenly-shorn sheep although we are not looking at them simply to admire our handiwork. A tup will often have what we call tight horns, the horn growing close to, or even cutting into, his lower jaw. This makes eating and cudding difficult, if not downright painful. Any such horns are sawn off just clear of the jaw, allowing most of the horn to be left in place. The process is no more painful than the cutting of your own toenails, being quite dead and nerveless. Before letting them back to their park, the tups' feet get the once over too, and overgrown hooves are neatly trimmed with a sharp knife.

Next, we take a pleasant run down country, towards Glasgow, to clip the rest of our tups, summering on Water Board land at Milngavie. From the Land Rover, the passing arable ground looks at its summer best, with fields of rippling hay alternating with green-growing cereals and meadows of fat, shining cattle. The largest of the lowland lambs must almost be able to detect the hint of mint sauce on the warm breeze. Mile after mile of hedgerows are highlighted by clusters of pink and white, delicately-petalled wild roses. A mousing kestrel hangs in the air, as if nailed to the clear blue sky.

The sun blazes down beautifully on bare bent backs, as shepherds as well as sheep discard outer garments. Someone is sure to need tormentil solution tonight, but for now it is lovely to soak up the sunshine. A picnic lunch, sitting deep in daisies, washing the sandwiches down with mouthfuls of strong, dry cider. Only aeroplanes seem to share the sky with the big sun; there is not a cloud, not a bird, not even a fly.

On the way home to the distant blue hills, I call in at the garden nursery to buy some young plants for the Glengyle garden.

Bill Watts returns to Glengyle to examine the cows' reaction to the TB tests, running his hand carefully over the neck of each animal in turn. Finally he gives the all clear. Tuberculosis used to be the scourge of some 25 per cent of all British cattle before strong action by the post-war Ministry of Agriculture almost eradicated it. I say almost, because in a small area of south-west England, a major outbreak occurred during the '60s. Known carriers of tuberculosis include pigs, cats and, more seriously, man. An infected dairyman could play havoc with the health of his herd. Fortunately, there is no longer any danger of the disease being passed on to humans as all the milk for human consumption is treated before being sold.

After the outbreak, reactors discovered during regular routine testing were slaughtered, but the problem continued unabated. The Ministry failed to find any new lead towards a solution until the summer of 1971 when a road-casualty badger carcass was found to be infected with bovine TB. Perhaps clutching at a straw, in an attempt to be seen to be doing something, the men from the Ministry implemented badger eradication schemes in the problem area. Throughout the 1970s and early '80s, countless badgers have suffered agonising and lingering deaths, but to little avail. It appears that the Ministry guessed wrongly as the latest available data seems to indicate that the percentage of outbreaks in eradication areas has not been reduced and, maybe, more interestingly, in the neighbouring districts where gassing and snaring were not practised, the proportion of outbreaks is not significantly higher.

Badgers probably pick up the infection by feeding on worms and beetles from contaminated pastures. Surely then it is wrong to blame the badger for being the source of the trouble, any more than blaming the elm bark beetle or Anopheline mosquito for Dutch elm disease and malaria. Of course, they are all vectors, spreading their respective plagues, and nobody would argue otherwise. However, the present Ministry action is a bit like trying to prevent your bathroom being flooded by bailing out the bath with a bucket instead of turning off the taps. Not very effective.

Before I am overtaken by the main event of the month, marking the lambs and counting the tails, there are a few things to put in hand: sheds need cleaning, the fank requires attention, and the park fences must be carefully checked.

The buildings which held, until a few weeks ago, stocks of winter feed, will soon be pressed into service for the sheep shearing. Bits and bobs of hay and straw, broken bales, bundles of strings, empty paper bags, dust and cobwebs and moulted feathers, are swept up and burned on the midden. Only the mud cup nests of the Glengyle swallows, high up in the roof rafters, are immune from the big spring clean. All day long, the busy parent birds fly one sortie after another, returning each time to stuff beakfuls of squashed insects into bottomless, yellow gaping mouths.

The fank is quite often in need of minor repairs as age and hard wear take their toll. A few loose stones to be re-set here, a gate to deal with there; it is surprising what wonders can be wrought with a handful of nails, a few pieces of wood and some string. The smearing shed gets a tidy up, too. Empty keel tins, plastic worm-drench canisters and vaccine sachets simply accumulate in various dark corners. A pair of grey wagtails is in residence, or at least, the female is, sitting tight on her clutch of four mottled, buff-coloured eggs. The wool-lined nest is situated snugly on top of the wall plate, hard under the roof. The ubiquitous blue darting swallows are in here too.

Nesting grey wagtails

Finally, there are the fences to be looked at. Armed with a pocketful of staples, hammer, pliers, wire and a few pieces of bale string, Gran and I set out to see what can be done. White rabbit! No, it is not the first day of the month, only me catching a glimpse of the resident albino bolting down its hole beneath the East Park gorse bushes. My fences are generally in a state of good repair, most damage being found where the weight of winter snow, which lay long and heavy on the wires, overcame the hold of some staples. These I replace. Also those lost during the recent heavy-weight battle of the bulls. Gates always represent a potential weakness: draw-bolts, snecks or catches mysteriously become undrawn, unsnecked or uncaught. To make doubly sure, I tie each gate with a newly-plaited length of red polypropylene bale string. String cut from bales is useful for tying so many things around a farm that its use is known as a 'farmer's weld'. No shepherd should ever be caught without his piece. With the gates tied fast and the fences patched and tightened, I feel that, for now, I can guarantee my parks are stockproof.

Even before the last of my late lambs has come into the world, all we north shore shepherds are heading for the Letter hirsel to begin gathering. The lambs are a little older on the three bottom-end hirsels as they put out their tups earlier at tupping time.

Traditionally, on the Friday before the Monday nearest the tenth day of June, the Letter ewes and lambs are driven from the wooded ground and high slopes on the back of Ben An, through the forestry fence and onto the open hill. After dinner, all the Letter sheep are gathered into a park to await the weekend.

On my way through the trees, I pass close to the Lady's Rock, a lonely spot haunted by the ghostly apparition of a lady who was tragically killed when her horse stumbled over the precipice. A local worthy, who spent more than 50 years on the lochside, claimed that no man would pass two nights alone at the rock. Not so long ago, a woodman's horse, engaged in hauling tree trunks out of the plantation, was unaccountably spooked into bolting over the same long drop, dragging a full load of heavy timber behind it. Although I have seen nothing untoward, or even felt uneasy, it is a quiet place and my dogs show a definite reluctance to sweep round the rock when looking for sheep.

On Monday morning, anxious eyes peer out to survey the weather prospects. It looks well settled. The slate-grey sky lightens gradually, becoming tinged with pale, bleached blue. I take my weather forecast from Mother Nature rather than the Meteorological Office. There is a great deal of truth in the countryman's adage 'oak before ash, just get a splash; ash before oak, in for a soak'. This year, the brown buds on the oak burst open well in advance of the black buds of the ash.

I load five dogs, Mona, Bo, Gail, Boot and Dust, into the back of the Land Rover with Alec's dogs, and Alec drives us down the deserted loch shore road, stopping at Portnellan to pick up Charlie and his team. Charlie, true to form, is standing outside his byre, dogs at foot, waiting for us with his usual touch of good-humoured impatience. Charlie would have been waiting for us for hours, even supposing that he had only just got there. At Edra, we meet up with Iain, Jock and John, before setting out for the Letter park to bring the sheep in to the fank.

The grazing ewes and their lambs are quietly and carefully shed into six cuts, each shepherd taking one group. This way the young lambs ought to be able to stay close to their mothers and not get lost, which is exactly what would happen if the whole flock was stirred up and mixed about. It is difficult enough for dogs to control lambs that have not yet learned to respect and respond to the collie in the way that we want them to. Lambs that have become separated from their mothers pose a threat to law and order; they tend to panic and break from the pack. The problem is most noticeable at the gates. Ewes readily run through, as they are used to doing time and time again; lambs, on the other hand, tend to run into the fence either side of the gate and have no firm idea about where they are supposed to be going. Some are successfully steered through the gate; others bunch together, then try to make a break for it. Boot, Dust and Gail are extremely good at turning back lambs and preventing mass breakouts developing in the first place. But even they are sometimes caught wrong-footed or simply overwhelmed by the suddenness, direction or sheer volume of a break. It takes a really good dog with a lot of experience to regroup lambs, calm them down, and quietly but firmly bring them back to the flock. Mona and Bo are the two dogs I entrust this task to. They do it well.

One by one, each cut of sheep is herded into the Edra fank. When the gate finally closes behind the last cut, the dogs are shut up in the kennels and the sheds, and we adjourn to the house for a well-earned breakfast. Mrs McDougall has prepared the standard breakfast: porridge, followed by bacon, sausage, egg and fried bread. An enormous teapot, which follows the shepherds from one handling to another, sits steaming on the Rayburn. Cups are replenished time and again.

Leslie McLaren, our erstwhile gamekeeper, arrives in his little red Volkswagen to act as our woolman. Leslie gives us a hand at these and the next set of gathers to handle and sort out the sheep and, once we get down to the clipping, rolls up the fleeces.

The Letter sheep are gently worked through the fank in small cuts. The handling pen is filled with a couple of score of ewes and lambs. The lambs are shed off by the simple means of holding up the ewes in front of a large wool bag, held across the pen by three men, and drawing the lambs back. Then the leaping, bleating skipping lambs are shooed into the small pen next to the dipping tank, to be marked and dipped.

We have two labourers to catch the lambs, one lifting up the tup lambs, the other dealing with the ewe lambs. Davie Bainbridge and his son Tommy, our regular assistants, are here today, sitting the lambs on a long, narrow marking-table, fixed on top of a gate. The ewe lambs are earmarked and tailed by their own shepherd: two back nips in the right ear, a few inches off the end of the tail, and the lambs are popped into the dipper. The tails are dropped into a large pail to be counted later. The lambs, having swum the length of the tank, scramble out and stand, draining in the dripper pen. The head shepherd always sees to the tup lambs himself. Iain castrates each lamb as Davie presents it to him, before marking, tailing and dipping the unfortunate creature. Occasionally, a particularly fine specimen of a tup lamb comes forward who escapes the dreaded rubber ring and is kept as a young tup.

While all this gory activity is going on in the marking pen, we are still busy in the handling pen. The hoggs are shed off into one of the side pens, and the remaining ewes cornered with the wool bag. Every ewe is handled underneath to feel the udder, picking out the ones with no milk: no milk equals no lamb. These eild ewes are run into another side pen. This leaves us finally with a cut of milk ewes who will be sheared later and now only require dosing against some of the internal parasites: flukes in the liver and worms in their stomach. Then they are let out to join up with the newly-marked lambs as they are released from the dripper. Lambs mill around, looking for their mothers, and ewes search diligently amongst the damp lambs, trying to mother up with their offspring. The noise is quite something.

Time after time, the handling pen is refilled, and the whole process repeated. Eventually, the last lamb is marked and the shepherd begins counting tails to get a final tally. Finally, the hoggs and the eild ewes are counted, dosed and taken down to stand in the clipping shed.

A late lunch follows the marking, Alison McDougall serving up a piping hot three-course meal. With nine hungry men sitting down at table, it does not take long for the vast amount of food to disappear from sight. The usual chat is batted back and forth across the table. Who's dead; who's dying; aye, it's a grand day; oh, the cost of dog food, did you see ... ? did you hear ... ? One at a time, backsides gradually settle into more comfy seats. Some shepherds snooze, others rustle through newspapers or back issues of *The Scottish Farmer* until, forty winks later, it is time to stir ourselves and go back out into the bright afternoon sun.

Sharp shining combs and cutters are fixed onto hand-pieces, engines topped up with petrol, bearings oils, and the crogging pen is filled with hoggs. Engines one, two, three start up. Parent swallows beat a hasty retreat, to sit twittering anxiously on the outside wires, while the noise and foul exhaust fumes assail their young ones in the nests. Davie and Tommy begin crogging. It will be a long time before the last sheep passes under the shear and is let run up at Glengyle. The first clean, brilliant white hogg leaps through the outside door into the sunlight, followed by another and another. Leslie, ear-muffed against the din, rolls fleece after fleece, tossing each bundle of wrapped wool into a large, wood-lined pen. As the number of clippies, standing in the outside paddock, grows, so does the mound of wool. Shirts are stripped off and sweat flows freely.

After an hour, Iain calls a halt. The rattling machines are silenced. Swallows swoop in to their nests above the rafters to feed their hungry broods. For ten minutes, backs are straightened; time to allow sweat to be towelled off, breath regained, drinks quaffed, blunted cutters changed and hand-pieces cleaned. Leslie sweeps up the small pooks of wool that litter the floor like fallen snow. These small bits, together with the fouled and stained pieces from the back end of the fleeces, which the woolman removes before rolling the fleeces, are bagged separately and known as broke wool.

Ropes are pulled and the engines cough back into life. Away go the swallows. Out come the roughies, off comes their wool and away go more clippies. Another spell of back-bending sees another hundred or so sheep put through. The eild ewes follow on behind the hoggs. They are a quicker and easier clip. Bigger certainly, but with far less wool on the belly and around the crutch, the places it takes time and care to clear. Ewes that have been clipped before are also inclined to sit more quietly than the hyperactive hoggs.

Even though we are finished inside three hours, and will undoubtedly speed up a bit as we move up the lochside, I don't think that
we will get anywhere near the British record of 610 sheep clipped
by two men in nine hours.

Shearing records are to be regarded with care, if not downright
suspicion. Some speed records are achieved by using lambs that have
already had their belly, crutch and tail wool removed. High figures,
such as G. Philips' total of 694 lambs in nine hours, look impressive
on paper but are not really relevant to our situation. Leslie Ramsden
sheared 390 sheep, also in nine hours, way back in 1961, and I have
not heard of a better individual tally. However, the above record of
610 sheep, set in July 1970, by Roger Poyntz-Roberts and John
Savery was done under similar conditions to the ones we work under.
The sheep were crogged for them. The following summer, the same
pair, this time crogging their own sheep, clipped a total of 555. The
fastest time for a single sheep is 46 seconds, established at the Royal
Highland Show in June 1957 by the famous Godfrey Bowen, after
whom the Bowen style of shearing is named.

No records for us today. Bits of wool and layers of grease are
cleaned off the hand-pieces. Combs and cutters are removed and
boxed, ready to be taken to the work-shop at Stronachlachar for
regrinding. A small flockmaster will usually send his combs and
cutters away to be sharpened, but we have so many to do throughout the season that it pays us to have our own special machine and
do the job ourselves.

The sheep are put back into Letter park. The ewes and lambs
are given plenty of chance to mother-up properly, before being let
out onto the hill again. Inevitably, a few lambs, for one reason or
another, fail to find their mother and have to make do with a
motherless existence for the rest of the summer. They will usually
survive, but seldom thrive.

Mrs McDougall sends us home full to the brim with another
excellent cooked meal. Plates of temping cakes and mouth-watering
scones are provided to fill up even the smallest hole. I know that I
am unable to eat another single thing. Back to Glengyle, and it is
the dogs' turn; I give them food and fresh drinking water. I clean
out and wash down their concrete runs before leaving them to a

well-earned, if brief, rest. Maggi has the hosepipe and sprinkler going in the sunscorched garden. We water everything in sight, and weed a bit here and there. We get eaten alive by the midges, obviously out and about for their supper. The bats leave their dark roosts with the same thought on their minds and begin feeding voraciously on the midges. Nature works in wondrous ways. I just wish that these bats would eat even more of the midges, then life would be a little more pleasant for the highland holiday-maker and gardening shepherd alike.

I slip in to a steaming hot bath to which I have added a splash of the sphagnum moss solution that Maggi has made up. It has no special name but is every bit as good and refreshing as any proprietary brand of bath additive. Sphagnum has several other uses. It naturally breaks down and forms peat and this system can be short-circuited by using the moss directly as a garden compost. Dried, it is also useful as an absorbent wound dressing.

And so to bed. I will need no rocking tonight.

Waking-up time comes round in a blink of an eye. Today, we are at Edra. The same men with the same dogs in the same fank, only the sheep will be different. The Edra hirsel rises gently to twin tops of 1,981 feet and 2,242 feet respectively. My beat takes me via the fank, opening the gates on the way, and up through the Edra park. I open the gate to the hill, before walking the length of the drystone dyke, replacing any top stones that have become dislodged. Near the west end of the dyke is a wee bowlie hole, a small hole built into the foot of the wall to allow the sheep to come and go between the park and the hill. I close the bowlie hole by building up stones across the entrance. Sheep appear on the skyline to my right, as Jock with John, Alec and Charlie make their way out along the east march of the hirsel, in front of the approaching sun. Iain, having left from his own house, has already made his way some distance along the Strone Burn, the Edra west march.

With my dogs at heel, I head away over the lush grazing that adorns the lower slopes of the hill. I need to keep moving this morning to keep warm. The air has a distinct chill as the eastern sky begins to turn a pale shade of cadmium yellow. Venus, low to

the east-northeast, twinkles coldly in the early light. I pick my way
carefully through the summer shallows of the Cross Burn, and step
up over an ancient, ruined stone dyke into the remnants of a farming system long since vanished from these parts.

In the age of the clans, before the Highland Clearances, a large
farming community, involving several closely-related families, would
have lived here. This old head-dyke would have divided their
lower, more fertile, infield ground from the rough, open hillside
pastures. A peculiarity of the Scots farming system was that cultivated land was treated in two ways. The better land, that close by
the homesteads and known as the infield, was under a constant
succession of crops. Onto this ground was spread all the available
manure in order to maintain soil fertility. The poorer outfield
land, beyond the headdyke, would have only a small area brought
under cultivation and cropped continuously until the soil became
exhausted. That patch would then be abandoned and another
piece of land taken in hand. Sometimes an attempt was made to
improve the outfield by the laborious practice of tathing, that is by
confining stock inside temporary folds built from turf divots.

A little further on, the dogs and I pass the huddles and heaps
of loose stones that once made up the walls of primitive houses
that comprised the old ferm-toun. As we progress along the glen,
my dogs gently turn the Edra sheep up the hillside from where we
will gather them up on our way back in. Round about me, the thin
call of nesting wheatears protests at this early-morning intrusion
of their summer territory. The nests are built in spaces under loose
rocks and stones; clutches vary between four and eight small, pale
blue, unmarked eggs which lie in shallow cups lined with fine
grasses, wool and hair. Incubation is largely by the female. Now
and again, one of the birds takes to the wing with an angry, grat-
ing chack-chack-chack. Wheatear is a corruption of 'white arse',
and the white rump, from which it gets its name, is clearly visible.

Rays from the rising sun strike the tops of the surrounding
hills. I arrive at the march fence which separates Edra from
Blaircreich, and settle down on a large boulder to wait for Iain to
return from more distant parts. I watch the shadow of the Edra hill,
Meall Gaothach, slip down the side of the Strone hill opposite. Bo

Wheatears nest on rocky ground

and Mona come nosing up, looking for a pat and a cuddle. Perhaps they are feeling the cold; I know that I am quite chilled, sitting here in the albeit diminishing shade, watching the sunshine approaching.

At long last, the rising sun peeks over the hill at me. I shiver involuntarily as my body accepts the welcome warmth. Sheep appear, moving steadily in front of Iain; we are off towards home. Things are likely to warm up quite rapidly now. The ewes and lambs in front of me begin the long trek back to the Edra fank. About 300 yards in, Dust suddenly points to something lying in the long grass. Treading softly, I draw close to the dog. Lying in a form is a beautiful, dappled, red deer calf, not many hours old. I wave the dogs back and tip-toe away as quietly as I can. It is very easy to imprint a very young calf like this, even by accident, and become its surrogate mother. If this happens, the calf will follow you to the ends of the earth. That can be fun for a while, an interesting experience but, after a short time, it becomes tying and very demanding. The young animal requires constant attention and regular feeding and, eventually, repays you by skipping over fences and demolishing everything in the garden. Any garden. Every garden.

As the beast has absolutely no fear of humans, the problem can be serious. In this respect, they are far worse than goats, and many a pet deer has ended up being shot by an irate gardener.

Everything with the sheep goes smoothly at first. One attempted break towards Strone, as we come to the Cross Burn, is rapidly brought under control by Mona and Gail. There is a bridge across the burn but the water is so low that it is safe for the sheep to cross almost anywhere. Outside the park gate, we have a few anxious moments as a couple of lamb-breaks develop and threaten to get out of hand. Eventually, after missing a heart-beat or two, the gate is shut and secured behind the excited lambs. Jock and John take the first cut of sheep, and get almost to the fank before a break of lambs escape back up the hill, and join the rest of the sheep. Alec and I take the second cut. But try as we may, we too end up losing lambs. Iain and Charlie come down with the last cut. All hands stand to, but still they break. Time and again, which is quite usual at Edra, lambs go belting back up the park. The dogs have their tongues hanging down to their knees. Breakfast still seems a long way off. Jock and John shed off a couple of score of milk ewes and let them out into the park to draw the lambs back. With a great deal of perseverance, we get the last of the lambs inside the fank. I have seen this operation take longer; in fact, one year it took over four hours.

The Edra lambs are marked and the eild stock clipped out, without any problems. Except, that is, for the presence of a 'Jenny Willox', a lamb with two complete sets of genitalia, one male and one female. Jennys are quite rare, but I imagine every shepherd gets one now and then. The most interesting one that I have seen had not one but two of everything.

The time of the full moon has passed by the time we have completed the handlings at Strone, Coilachra and Portnellan, and arrive back at Glengyle. The moon has been seen wearing a halo and, typically for Glengyle, the weather has taken a turn for the worse. A couple of days of soft rain and mountain mist refresh both hill and garden, and give the dogs a chance of a wee rest. The level of the loch is well down, the lagoon is completely dry. Tansy takes advantage of the extra grazing and spends her days, heavy-bellied, deep in lush herbage. It will not be many days before she calves again.

The wet spell passes over and the anti-cyclone cycles back, restoring the fine weather. These long days of little night are a time of strong enchantment. Anyone afraid of the mid-summer power of the Little People should wear a garland of yarrow. I prefer to utilise this particular plant for other purposes – yarrow tea for treating colds and a lotion for the healing of cuts and scratches.

We gather the low-end of Glengyle first thing in the morning, going out long before the sun gets up. The ewes and the lambs are left to mother up while we are at our breakfast; there will be stragglers from Portnellan and the Braes to look out for. Every strange milk ewe has to be secured, along with her lamb or lambs, in order that none of my neighbour's stock is marked for Glengyle by mistake. This is a time-consuming but very necessary job which must be completed before marking can commence. There always seems to be at least one straggler ewe that simply cannot pick up her lamb for ages. At last we have accounted for them all, and Iain and I can get on with marking and dipping my lambs. The eild ewes and hoggs are run into the East Park to wait there until the high-end has been gathered. I count the low-end tails and write the total into my note-book.

After Maggi has served up dinner, we set out to gather in the high-end sheep. Small, pale, eyebright flowers get pressed underfoot. The sheep come together at Bealach nan Corp and are taken the long road home in three cuts. Alec and I are left to take home the last cut, along Eves Road. When the lambs break, they quickly disappear amongst the tall bracken which flourishes on the top side of the road. This, however, impedes their headlong dash for freedom and gives the dogs a better chance to turn them back to the flock.

On the way home, we pass by the side of an ancient bloomery, a place where iron ore was smelted by a smelter and three or four men. When Messrs. Eves put in this road, they cut right through the layer of slag and charcoal which marks this site; eight inches of top soil had accumulated above the remains, indicating an age of some 400 years. Aberfoyle, at one time in receipt of a Royal Charter, was one of the principal iron markets in Europe during the 14th century. Iron masters used to come or send their agents from all over to buy the top-quality bloom bars. Andrea Ferrera, a Venetian sword-smith, who had more smithies than Queen Elizabeth I had beds, actually lived and worked for a while on the Achray Water, at the far end of Loch Katrine. A claymore, authenticated as a genuine Ferrara with a map showing the location of his smithy damascened on the blade, came to light some years ago.

The iron ore, usually bog iron, was brought in by horse-back to be smelted close to where the trees grew to provide charcoal. Sixteen hundredweight of ore produced two hundredweight of iron although in theory, the ratio should have been close to six to one. Each bloomery produced about three tons of iron per year, and consumed over 100 acres of standing trees in doing so. Oak, hazel and birch were considered to be the best wood. The ore was washed to remove extraneous dirt, heated gently to dry off the water, and finally pounded up into small fragments. Alternate layers of burning charcoal and powdered iron ore were built up in a small hollow dug into the ground, until a heaped mound was visible. The top sealing layer of charcoal was kept saturated with water to prevent it burning.

A ring of hearth-stones surrounded the matrix with two gaps, called tuyeres, at two o'clock and four o'clock in the circle. Through one tuyere, the ore and incandescent charcoal were stirred with an iron bar, bringing them into close contact with each other. Particles of iron united and formed a conglomerate at the bottom of the pit. Slag collected and solidified in the cooler air at the second tuyere and was either expelled or pushed back in again for further smelting. Sometimes, more slag and cinders from previous workings were added to improve the temper of the iron.

The temperature of the matrix never rose much above 1,200°C, and as the true melting point of iron is 300°C above this, the ore was never fully liquefied. The low temperature avoided the fusion of damaging impurities such as phosphorous and sulphur. As the iron was extracted from the pit, it was sprinkled with water and beaten with hammers, to facilitate the removal of any remaining slag. Each bar, or bloom, measured six by six by eight inches and weighed about 11½ lbs. Before each bloom cooled too much, the smelter would split the bar open with an axe, forming it into a 'V'-shape. In this way, he could inspect the quality of the wrought iron just produced.

By the time Alec and I get the sheep safely into the West Park, the lambs have become quite civil. The lovely scent of crushed bog myrtle leaves fills the air around us as we drive the tired animals the last stretch to the fank. There are a few straggler ewes here, too. I hope that by tomorrow morning they will have sorted themselves out and mothered up their own lambs.

After first spending almost two hours catching my neighbour's sheep, Iain and I can get on with the rest of my marking. All too soon the last lamb is lifted up, marked and pushed into the dipper. At this time of year, there never seems to be enough of them; however, the tail count is fairly satisfactory, well past the 500 mark and, no doubt, there will be more whole-luggers to come in at the next gathering. My neighbours, too, are likely to find a few of my sheep coming in when they gather.

Dinner precedes the afternoon clipping. Mid-way through, just as the last hogg is being shorn, Maggi comes in with the news that Tansy has calved a black heifer. Mother and child are doing well. The final shearing session sees us put through 155 eild ewes in well under an hour. Quite an improvement on the early efforts down at Letter.

The handlings may be over for now, but there is still the wool to pack. One of the large wool bags is suspended by ropes from the rafters, and while one man throws up the rolled wool, the other jumps into the bag to tramp in as many fleeces as possible. Alec and I take turn about at tramping and throwing. Bag after bag is filled, sewn up and labelled, until 22 wool bags later, the last fleece has been packed. Now there is only the broke wool to deal with. One of the bags that the woolman has been stuffing with sweepings is hung up and well tramped. The other bags of broke are tipped into the hanging bag and with much stamping it eventually all disappears inside. Full bags of broke wool are always very heavy. All the bags are carefully stacked, the bottom ones kept off the concrete floor by wooden planks. Wool in contact with stone or cement will draw the damp and become spoiled.

While I have been busy with the wool, Maggi has been to Stirling to buy a second calf to put on to Tansy. She arrived home with a nice, strong bull calf, in the back of the Land Rover. Tansy will have plenty of milk, not only for two calves but enough for the house as well. Grandfather Barrington always maintained that a single calf suckling a Hereford cow was the easiest way to turn a pound into ten shillings.

After being left in peace for a few days in the West Park, my lambs seem to be well mothered-up again. I open the gates and let them all away to the hill.

Numerous young birds are on the wing. Although some adult birds still have their beaks full with domestic cares, others are moulting into new plumage after the completion of their nesting season. During this period of extreme vulnerability, the birds keep very quiet. Butterflies are abundant and provide some birds with a plentiful source of food; small heaps of butterfly wings found under branches or fence posts testify to the feast.

One of the Water Board lorries turns up at Glengyle to be loaded with the wool, and then proceeds down the loch to Coilachra and Edra. By the time we heave up the last of the wool bags, we have a very big load on board. The load is sheeted over and securely tied before the lorry starts on the long run to our wool merchants at Paisley.

Fresh flowers add new splashes of colour to the countryside. Along the loch shore, yellow flagged irises wave in the afternoon wind. The roadsides near the house are adorned with beautiful, if transient, rhododendron flowers in various shades of pinks and purple. On the lower slopes of the hill, particularly on the areas where, a few years ago, the bracken was sprayed, foxgloves add their fingertips of colour. I have a soft spot for the less common, white-flowered variety. High summer is here, and I find it absolutely enchanting.

Sheep Shearing

DOUNE AND DUNBLANE AGRICULTURAL SHOW, one of the biggest one-day farming events in Scotland, is held on the first Saturday in July. Sheep, goats, cattle and horseflesh come from far and near, to be exhibited on the showground which is within view of Stirling Castle, and to compete for a tentful of silver trophies. The rivalry between the entrants, for possession of class, breed, inter-breed and supreme championships, is intense. On arrival, each animal is washed, brushed, oiled and polished until the face-reflecting results are satisfactory to the stockmen.

Row upon row of canvas-tented tradestands surround the main ring, and are backed by serried ranks of gleaming farm machinery of all descriptions. Nevertheless, with Maggi and children, the first port of call is at the lines of fat, shining beef cattle and sleek, big-bagged dairy cows. The judges have completed their work and departed, leaving red, blue, yellow and green rosettes in their wake, pinned to the animals of their choice. For the remainder of the day, other eyes will reappraise the orders of merit and, if nothing else, the ensuing discussions will be animated.

The same is certainly true at the sheep pens. Exhibits are handled, poked and prodded to find the exact length, breadth and depth of body hidden beneath the wool. It is here, around the sheep buchts, that well ken't faces begin to appear in large numbers. Progress is slow. It takes time to talk our way past huddles of sheep-men, leaning easily on their best horn-handled sticks, discussing everything under the sun. From here, people disperse to various parts of the show field. Some, of course, adjourn at once to the beer tent – which happens to overlook the main ring; others wander at random amongst friends and pageantry.

Maggi and I make a bee-line for the Rotary Club stand to treat Jamie and Victoria, and ourselves, to a feed of strawberries and cream. As all the money raised goes to numerous good causes, we

The Trials

have double helpings all round. The afternoon passes, dodging falling parachutists, watching a masterly demonstration of sheep-dog handling, buying icecream, cheering on the antics of the Young Farmers, and collecting the inevitable armfuls of assorted leaflets – never to be read later. We readily accept the hospitality offered at the TSB; their local bank manager, Willie Miller, is currently president of Stirling County Rugby Club. There is coffee and biscuits for Maggi and me, orange juice for Jamie and Victoria, but soon, President William discreetly proffers something a wee bit stronger. Before you can say malt whisky, the sober TSB stand takes on the appearance of an outside extension of the Rugby Club. It is surprising how many County members have agricultural roots.

In the gymkhana ring, horses and ponies have spent the afternoon jumping over an array of four-fault fences. The spectators groan and sigh, whether at the fortune of the horse and rider in the ring, or at the commentary of the Men's Wimbledon tennis final on hand-held transistors. I know not. I do know that the Bank of Scotland is doing exceptional business as people pack into their caravan to watch the tennis live on their television. Two sets each, I hear, and five games all.

Time for the Grand Parade. All the prize-winning animals will enter the ring first, followed by every conceivable piece of mobile machinery from the display stands. The cattle lead the livestock with a magnificent turn-out of our principal breeds. Goats and ponies follow on, then some larger horses in hand, before the enormous Clydesdales heave into sight, decorative harnesses shimmering in the sunshine. Horse-drawn rigs precede the display of tractors: new, old, older, vintage and veteran. There is even a steam-driven machine in pristine condition puffing its way around the ring. Large lorries and monster harvesters complete the great spectacle.

From now on, the show begins, very gradually, to run down. Most of the livestock leave immediately after the parade, loaded into floats and onto trailers for the return journey. Some have a long road to go home, and once there, hands have to turn to the usual tasks: cows to milk, beasts to be seen to, and so on, even on a Saturday afternoon. In the background, the loudspeakers announce that someone has won Wimbledon and everyone seems happy. We cast long afternoon shadows on the grass as we make our way back to the Land Rover, now standing in a space that earlier in the day was a sea of parked cars. By this time, the queue of vehicles making for the road is not very long, and we are soon on our way home.

The Coilachra hirsel is divided into two parts by the Cross Fence which sweeps down from the Strone boundary, across the Heather Ground and runs away to meet the Portnellan march. Three-quarters of the hirsel is outside the Cross Fence, including the massif of Stob a'Choin (the Dog's Fang). The remaining quarter, between the fence and the loch shore, contains some of the very best sheep grazing – a mixture of fine grasses, herbs and short heather. It is from this ground that Alec and I have come to help Charlie drive his sheep. Since the Coilachra marking a couple of weeks ago, the ewes and lambs have been living well, shut in below the Cross Fence. Now, it is time to put them out.

Charlie goes along the high ground, next to Strone, on my righthand side. Alec starts at the road side, away to my left. My duties begin at the east end of the Barn Park, just above the so-called Hanging Tree, a solitary Scots Pine which stands tall amongst the birch, hazel and alder. A prince among beggars. Next to the tree are the ruins of a small house from where Dorothy and William Wordsworth, in company with their friend Sam. Coleridge, embarked to cross Katrine's clear water. The party had spent the previous evening, in that summer of 1803, at Glengyle House and had been, of course, hospitably entertained. The three travellers were deeply impressed by their experiences and it was here that William found both his 'Sweet Highland Girl' and 'Solitary Reaper'.

I send Mona and Max struggling down through the high bracken to flush out the hidden sheep. Gail starts barking to let the sheep know that we are here and mean business. Gran watches the proceedings, stretches and yawns. The sheep run well forward in front of the dogs, up under the oak trees and out onto the clear ground between the Coilachra Barns. These substantial, old stone-built buildings are marked on the earliest maps of this area. One is still in use, even though it now possesses a galvanised zinc-sheeted roof. I walk under the oak trees, looking this way and that, making sure no cunning old ewes are lurking with their lambs in the undergrowth. The trees themselves have been severely defoliated by a plague of looper caterpillars. Many caterpillars can be seen suspended from the twigs by gossamer threads. Some drop on my head as I pass below.

In this large group of moths, known as Geometers, the caterpillars appear to measure their own length as they move. Their name means earth measurer. They are compelled to loop along because they have no legs on the middle segments of their body, only three pairs of true legs at the front and a pair of claspers at the rear, and it is this peculiar mode of locomotion which has given them their common name. Loopers appear every year, although not in these numbers or anything like it. Needless to say, the woodland birds are making the most of this abundant supply of food.

Britain has only two true, native hawks. One of them, the sparrowhawk, is to be found nesting at Glengyle, living amongst the conifer trees. Now and again, I catch a glimpse of one flitting through the branches. The round-winged hawks are true birds of the forest. They are somewhat slower than the sickle-winged falcons, but are better equipped for sudden twists and turns when hunting around the trees. The male patrols the edge of the wood, looking out for suitable prey. Once it has discovered an unwary group of small birds, it will dart down. Terrified birds scatter in all directions trying to escape, but for one of them it is usually too late. Twisting and turning sharply in flight, the sparrowhawk grabs its victim with its strong, steel-sprung talons, and kills it instantly.

The hen sparrowhawk lays her clutch of three to seven eggs early in June. She incubates them herself until they hatch, about now, some 40 days later. By delaying their breeding season, the sparrowhawks ensure themselves a rich supply of small birds to feed their hungry brood. Both parents are involved in bringing up

Wheatears nest on rocky ground

their young ones, but only the female actually feeds the chicks. The prey has to be picked over very carefully so the youngsters are able to swallow it. Only the hen knows how to do this; if she were to die, then the chicks would perish too.

The ewes and lambs still in the park beat a hasty retreat out through the gate, across the road, and draw away up the hillside. More sheep, hunted along by Charlie's dogs, appear out of the bracken. I send Bo out on an away run, to get in behind them and keep them moving along. The net steadily tightens, the sheep come together at the Cross Fence and begin to funnel out through the gateways onto the open hill.

As we descend to the road and the Land Rover, the SS *Sir Walter Scott* steams into view, making for Stronachlachar pier opposite. That means it must be almost a quarter to twelve. The *Sir Walter* on Loch Katrine, and the paddle-steamer *Maid of the Loch* on Loch Lomond are the last relics of the 19th-century Scottish Steamboat Age. All the larger lochs had a resident steamer, Loch Awe, Loch Eck, Loch Maree, Loch Shiel and Loch Tay amongst others. Prior to 1843, clients were transported the length of Loch Katrine on the *Water Witch*, an eightoared galley manned by local gillies. The first steamer, named *Gypsy*, arrived to threaten this idyll in the summer of 1843. The oarsmen stood to lose a sizeable part of their income so one dark night, not long after, *Gypsy* was taken out and scuttled. When the foul deed came under investigation, the authorities ran into a language barrier. Suddenly the Erse-speaking gillies seemed to forget any of the English tongue that they may have had. Interpreters always came away with the same answer, no matter what the question – the Gaelic equivalent of letting sleeping dogs lie, Sir.

The Loch Katrine Steamboat Company, not to be outdone, launched a second steamer two years later, the *Rob Roy*. Maybe the name of the vessel had something to do with it, but this time the Highlanders admitted defeat and allowed her to steam unhindered for more than ten years. By now, the first phase of the Glasgow Water Works was underway, and the *Rob Roy* was much used for the carrying of men and materials. A successor, in the impressive shape of a larger and more up-to-date *Rob Roy* II, entered service in time for Queen Victoria to sail up the loch on her, as far as Royal Cottage, and declare the reservoir open. This propitious event took place on Friday, 14 October 1859, the day that Glasgow received its first supply of pure Loch Katrine water.

On 20 February 1899, the order for a fourth ship was placed at the yard of William Denny at Dumbarton. It was a sub-contract from M. Paul and Co who were to build her triple expansion steam plant. The new ship was named the *Sir Walter Scott* and was launched on the last day of October, the same year. She was sailed up Loch Lomond as far as Inversnaid, and then dismantled prior to being transported the four miles overland to Loch Katrine in a knock-down state. Someone obviously had been reminded of the enormous problems faced by the fully-rigged *Gypsy* between Callander and the loch. The ten-mile journey had taken 11, desperate, mud-soaked days. At Stronachlachar, the ss *Sir Walter Scott* once again took shape, all 110 feet of her, and she was ready for service early in 1900.

Since the beginning of this century, the *Sir Walter* has plied her trade between the piers of Stronachlachar and the Trossachs. She carries a complement of seven, and is allowed a maximum of 416 passengers. The Water Board took over ownership of the

Steamboat Company in 1954 in order to exercise stricter control over potential sources of pollution. Being coal-fired, there is no danger of oil contamination, and the deck hands try to ensure that nothing or nobody drops into the country's purest drinking water, either accidentally or otherwise. The only pollution I have seen on the loch are the floating rafts of yellow pollen which drifts down from the trees and settles on the water throughout the month of June.

The steam whistle blows and *Sir Walter* steams away from Stronachlachar. It is 12 noon.

All the north- and south-shore tups are now on their summer pasture at Milngavie. The superintendent there makes sure that someone checks them regularly to see that none is looking sick or lying dead, but now and again they need a more experienced eye cast over them; a shepherd will notice things that a layman may well miss. If a problem can be treated early enough, it might be prevented from becoming serious. Bob Morgan and Iain Campbell alternately send somebody down to look things over. Iain has detailed Jock and me to take a turn today.

The early-morning road to Glasgow is fairly quiet, mainly light commuter traffic into the city, and we make good time. The tups are grazing in three groups, in four parks. Our aged tups are held in a separate field from our shearlings, while Bob's tups all run together over two adjoining parks. Jock and I make a start on our older tups, gathering them into a handy corner. Bo and Jock's dog, Roy, hold the sheep while we scrutinise them carefully, looking out for tight horns, dirty tails, bad feet, split heads or festering shear wounds. Their horns appear to be all right: it is only a month since we gave them a thorough going-over. There are a couple of dirty tails, an indication that all is not well with the digestive system. We give these tups a dose for worms, which usually does the trick. Any limping sheep are turned up, their feet pared with a sharp knife, and foot-rot paste, containing copper sulphate, is liberally applied. Split heads and other breaks in the skin are checked to make sure that nothing nasty is lurking in there, and then bathed with wound-dressing oil. This oil not only promotes fast healing but also helps to keep away the insidious, blood-sucking flies.

Jock and I go through the other side's tups before moving on to see our shearlings. Once again Gran and Roy bring up and hold the sheep for us. These younger tups have more vigorously-growing horns and we find a couple that need a bit of attention. I use my small-necked, iron cleek to catch the animal by its back leg. There are a few feet to trim too, and some heads to splash with oil. Before leaving, Jock and I check the water troughs to make sure that the water is running. It would never do for stock to go thirsty while summering at the Water Works.

The road home is crowded with convoys of holiday traffic: coaches full of neck-craning tourists; motors piled high with suitcases, ragged polythene sheet flapping in the slipstream; caravans of cars towing caravans.

Recently, a caravanning couple were driving up Loch Lomondside, late at night. The wife began to nod off and, at her husband's suggestion, went to bed in the caravan. A while later, the driver stopped the car in a lay-by to stretch his legs for a few minutes. The wife, probably woken by the sudden tranquillity, also decided to take a little walk. Just as she closed the door behind her, the car started up and away went her mobile bedroom, leaving the lady shivering in her flimsy nightdress, and the rest of her clothes fast disappearing into the distance. She had no idea what to do next.

Eventually, after what must have seemed like an age, she saw headlights coming along the road. To hide, or not to hide, that was the question. Taking her courage in both numbed hands, she flagged down the approaching driver, who turned out to be a rather surprised motorcyclist. Nevertheless, the intrepid and, no doubt desperate damsel, mounted the pillion, and the pair set off in pursuit of the runaway husband. In no time at all, the young Sir Galahad, on his high-powered charger, roared past the startled spouse, nearly causing a nasty accident.

The moral surely is: if you are going out at night in Scotland, put on something warm.

The Letter sheep are gathered together as we begin the job of milk clipping – shearing the milk ewes. Below us, in the mirror calm water, the wooded island, known both as Eilean Molach (Shaggy Island) or Ellen's Isle, stands as a silent tribute to its colourful past. In times of danger, the MacGregor women and children took refuge there. For extra safety, every boat on the loch was beached there too.

However, boat or no boat, one of Cromwell's English soldiers, having been away from his home comforts for a long time, decided upon getting himself a woman, a MacGregor woman. Came dusk, he swam surreptitiously across to the island; gliding quietly in between the moored boats, he laid his hand stealthily on a gunwale and poked his head up to take a look around. It turned out to be his last. Helen Stewart leapt upon him and cut off his head with a single blow of her dirk. The ravisher's headless body fell back into the water and floated slowly to the shore where it was recovered by his comrades. The body was buried in one of the secluded hollows close at hand, at a spot thereafter known as The Place of the Man. There is only bird song above the tiptoeing, browsing animals to disturb his slumbers, and the occasional shepherd's footfall to remind him of the land of the living. After that fateful event, the Shaggy Island was rechristened to perpetuate the name of the savage heroine.

The Letter milk ewes are drawn off as the sheep pass up the shedder and are taken away to the clipping shed. While the rest of us get down to the clipping, the shepherd of the hirsel and Charlie, assisted by a host of small but very willing boys, deal with the lambs. The school holidays have started. Any whole-lugged lambs are marked, and the whole lot dosed for worms and put through the dipper. Ewe after rough ewe is crogged to the shears; and clippie follows clippie out into the afternoon sunshine. By the time the engines are shut down for the last time, I have sweated and clipped my way through 96 milk ewes. The sheep are put back into the Letter park to mother up before we have our tea and go away home.

The warm evening air is thick with flying ants, slanting sunlight flashing from their beating wings. Sun-warmed stones and boulders seethe with swarms of black-bodied ants, about to launch themselves into the nuptial flight. Some hitch a lift on Tansy's back as I take her in for milking. It is always the winged males which appear first, closely followed by the females. During mating, the queen stores her mate's sperm in a sac inside her body, and she can then do without a male for up to 12 years. Perish the thought. After mating, the males drop to the ground and, as they cannot feed themselves, they soon starve. The females, however, come down stronger than ever, shake off their wings, and retire underground to begin a round of continuous egg laying.

A snipe drums

In the distance, on the far side of the loch, a snipe drums, an unusual but not unknown sound so late in the season. Up above, in the deepening sky, Jupiter and Saturn become clear evening stars. The mornings of the milk-clippings do not start as early as the marking gathers. Anyway, the nights are already becoming noticeably longer. Edra, the farm which provided the Earl of Perth with his standard-bearer during the 1745 campaign, is the next hirsel to be clipped out. The sheep are improving all the time, getting a better rise in their wool, and I manage to push my tally up to 119 ewes. By the end of the day, there is not a lot of cider left at the bottom of my gallon flagon.

Strone, the head-shepherd's home ground, is the largest of the

northshore hirsels. The ground slopes up from the lochside, forming a wide, wet, partly-wooded basin between the tops of Cruinn
Bheinn (Crune evan) and Meall Mór. At 1,200 feet, the 1½-mile
long back-lip of the basin turns steeply down into the Strone glen.
To the north of this stands the separate heft of Ben Vane, marked
on the map as Beinn Mheadhonach.

An avalanche of dogs pours out as soon as I open the back
door of the motor. Alec and Charlie head away west, towards the
higher ground of Cruinn Bheinn, dogs bounding around their feet.
I start the day by driving the plantation with my team: Bo, Mona,
Gail, Dust and Boot. Good, noisy hunting dogs are necessary to
flush sheep out of this dark, dense stand of mature conifers. These
artificial forests are not as rich in bird life as native woodland, and
their dense cover quickly suppresses ground plant growth. Roe and
red deer take full advantage of the undisturbed conditions. The
plantation edges and transecting rides provide valuable habitats
for several species of birds and animals, including the exclusively
Scottish wild cat.

A barking roe deer and her month-old twin fawns turn back
between the dogs and dash away into the heart of the sanctuary.
A drove of red deer and several packets of sheep, however, break
cover and head out over the boggy moorland. The Scottish bog is
not a popular place for exploring: the difficult terrain deters most
people from venturing too far from the beaten tracks. Yet to me
these bogs hold a particular fascination. They form in areas where
hard, impervious rock and high rainfall combine to provide a wet,
acid soil. These conditions prevent vegetation from decomposing
and new plant growth takes place on top of the remnants of previous seasons' turf. In this manner, peat develops and contains
within itself its own history. Peat workings have provided a great
deal of evidence in relation to the vegetational, climatic and historical changes that have taken place in Scotland, in some cases as
far back as the last Ice Age.

As we pass the prominent rock outcrop known as the Hawk's
Perch, my sheep are taken up by Alec while I swing in the opposite direction to try to make contact with Jock. On the higher,
drier ground, bell heather and ling have replaced some of the

cross-leaved heather and cotton grass of the bog. Coveys of young red grouse whirr out from under my feet, babbling their disapproval. I see Jock in the distance, approaching along the shoulder of Meall Mór, with John somewhere below him, and we gradually turn the sheep between us down to the floor of the glen. Then there is a long wait until Alec and Charlie meet up with Iain and they bring their sheep sweeping down towards Strone.

The sheep are cut and each lot herded off the hill, through the parks and into the Strone fank. Breakfast beckons. Margaret Campbell cheerfully serves up the usual fortifying meal before we start the handling. The lambs are dosed and dipped with the aid of the squad of young lads, while the roughies are walked over to the clipping shed at Edra. It is simpler to take the sheep to the machines than the other way about. One hundred and twenty-three milk ewes pass through my hands today.

Throughout the summer months, many sheepmen participate in the increasingly popular pastime of sheepdog trialling. The very first trials were held in 1873 near Bala in North Wales to promote, of all things, the sale of Welsh whisky. Alas, that particular distilled elixir failed to become established, but the novel idea of one man and his dog competing against others caught on. Ten dogs took the field on that auspicious afternoon, competing in front of a crowd of 300 people. The winner that day was James Thompson, an exiled Scot, with his Scottish-bred dog, Tweed.

A trial course is designed to present the dog with the different tasks it will be faced with on the normal daily round. The course is divided into six basic sections and pointed according to the degree of difficulty presented to the dogs, usually a total of 50 points.

Outrun (worth ten points): the run taken by a dog going out to get in behind the sheep. Ideally it should be pear-shaped, with the dog wide at the far end so as not to disturb the waiting sheep.

Lift (five): this is the action of starting the sheep moving in the intended direction. The lift, although only worth five points, is important because it gives the sheep their first feel of the dog.

Fetch (ten): bringing the sheep to the feet of the handler, keeping the line of approach as straight as possible.

Drive (ten): herding the sheep away from the handler on a triangular course, taking in two sets of gates with the emphasis still on directness.

Pen (ten): the dog works its charges into a small pen.

Shed or *Single* (five): the dog either has to divide the flock into two or take out a single sheep. Again only worth five points, but often it is the quality of work at this stage which finally separates the top dogs on the day.

Each part of the trial is judged separately. Dogs start with full points and deductions are made for errors. There is always a time limit set for a course, after which a dog must retire. Such a dog is allowed to keep the points for each completed section of the trial. Any dog taking a grip of a sheep is instantly disqualified. The points system on the popular television programme 'One Man and His Dog' is done rather differently, and the pen ends each trial.

On the third Saturday of this month, the local trials are held at the Garrison of Inversnaid. I have entered with Mona, and we have been drawn to run somewhere around mid-afternoon, the order of trial having been decided by ballot. We arrive *en famille* at the trial field soon after lunch. I report my presence to the secretary and enquire after the leading points of the dogs already run. My next port of call is to the very heart of the proceedings – the bar. It is here that all that might have been is relived and all that might be is meticulously planned. Voices rise and fall as, later in the day, will the men themselves. Drinks are bought and elbows raised. Friends are met and supplied with more drink. And so it goes on until the sudden word goes around that a certain dog is on. Many of the country's top dogs are here, including the current Scottish champion. The bar empties and if the run is promising it remains this way. The number of people who drift back to the bar is a fair indication of how well Stuart or Alister or Charlie is doing out there.

I watch how the sheep are behaving. The recently clipped hoggs seem to be very flighty and need treating with the utmost respect. Two runs before my own turn, I let Mona out of the Land Rover and take her to spend a penny or two. I like us both to watch the end of one run and the whole of another before we go on. This time there is no hurry because a fresh lot of sheep have to be taken to the pen, up at the start, before the pair in front of me can get started. These sheep could be of a quite different nature. But the run goes well, at least the sheep seem more inclined to stay together.

On the way to the post, I stop at the judge's box, a horse trailer in this case, and pass the time of day with Mr Shanks and his time-keeper. The course director waves his flag to signal for my packet of sheep to be released. At my post, I position Mona on my left-hand side, the side I intend to run her. As soon as my sheep are in a good position I send Mona on her way. She runs rather wide at the start, skirting a dense stand of bracken, and no doubt the judge will have a bit off for that. Mona moves in nicely behind her sheep and lies down. The sheep stand still. I whistle her up to lift them. And again. Jimmy Shanks will have pencilled off another point or two.

The fetch could not be much straighter, the bare hoggs coming on smoothly. As they approach my post, I back away a little so that Mona can keep her charges in as direct a line as possible. She turns them round the post in a clockwise direction and begins her drive. Here we meet our first real problem. The ground between me and the first set of drive gates is extremely soggy. Rather than take a drier detour and lose points, we persevere on the direct path, and lose a lot of precious time. At long last we get out of the bog and through the gate. I give a bye command to turn the sheep onto the cross drive, and we are underway once more. A slight waver at the second set of hurdles allows one hogg to slip past on the wrong side. More points gone. Mona brings the sheep around towards the pen.

I can leave my post now, and go over to the pen. With the gate wide open, Mona comes up on her sheep: close… closer, the sheep shuffle about nervously. One breaks away. Mona flanks in a flash of black and white, turns the beast back to the rest. Up again, steady … and they are in. I shut the gate and heave a sigh of relief. Out again, quickly. Time must be getting short. But before we can steady the flying hoggs and attempt a shed, the dreaded whistle sounds out for time up. Nevertheless, I am well pleased. That was a good enough run to put us well up in the prize list – at the moment. Whether I stay there depends upon the work that follows.

Back in the bar I talk about the time lost in the swamp and all the places around the course where points could have been saved. But that is just what a beer tent is for. At the end of the day, Mona takes the fifth-place prize money.

The weather upon Saint Swithin's Day, 15 July, is of the greatest interest to all countrymen. The saying 'If it rains upon this day it shall rain for the following forty days and forty nights' is so ingrained in folklore that a single drop of rain is sufficient to strike fear into the heart of the stoutest farmer, even if he professes not to believe in such things. The innocent saint passed away in the year 862, and for the next 109 years he lay in peace, causing not so much as a cloud to pass over the face of the sun. However, in 971, someone had the wet idea of digging up the venerable body and reburying the sanctified relics elsewhere. Upon which the heavens promptly opened and did not close again until it had rained for the proverbial period of forty whole days.

This Saint Swithin's Day, it rains.

The mist rolls in along the top of the Portnellan hill that we are trying to get gathered, engulfing everything, so everyone stops. The sheep become cloaked in a foggy mantle and vanish. There is only one thing to do: find a sheltered spot and sit tight until it lifts. In no time at all, everything is bedecked with tiny beads of moisture. My dogs curl up and settle, lying soft and comfy, the black on their coats becoming veiled with silver droplets. Every time one of them moves a muscle, it receives a deluge from the drooping, water-laden, overhanging grasses. It is so quiet. All sound is muffled. Listen. You can almost hear the imperceptible creep of dampness as it permeates into every nook and cranny. Clothes hang heavy; hair and beard gather the water and drip... drip... drip.

The mist swirls and eddies amongst the humps and hillocks, creating illusions and teasing time and again before eventually evaporating as suddenly and silently as it came. The whole world comes back to life.

The Coilachra and Portnellan handlings have been hampered a bit by the catchy weather. Being able to get the sheep dry enough

Roe deer court, encircling an old oak

to clip is our biggest problem. The Coilachra fank is covered by a roof, but there just is not the room underneath it to put all the roughies inside at the same time. The Portnellan sheep are clipped at Glengyle where there is ample room to put them in under cover – if you can get them dry in the first place. It is a fact of shepherding life, however, that no matter how unhelpful St Swithin is, we always manage to finish the job, some time.

Mars is the morning star as all our shepherds set out to gather in the low-end of my hill. A pair of roe deer play ring-a-roses around an old oak, forming a perfect fairy-ring in the grass. Rings such as these are a common sight at this time of year. The courting roe buck, who does not collect a harem like red deer, selects one female and pursues her through the glades until they end up circling a tree, bush or rock. This chase continues until the buck gets his way, having worn a distinct roering on the ground. The buck may then go in search of another mate or quite happily stay with his first partner.

It is warm work, battling uphill through the jungle of bracken. The fronds, tall, green and waving in the wind, have clusters of ripening spore-producing sacs on the underside of their serrated leaves. The spores are produced without any sexual activity on the part of this plant. When the spore sacs, called sori, release their contents onto the damp soil, masses of tiny plants known as prothalli form a thin, green film over the ground. These prothalli contain the male and female reproductive parts. The mobile male cells swim, via the surface water adhering to the plant, to reach the female receptacles. From this sexual stage of the bracken's life cycle, new plants as we know them will grow up to plague us further. Thirty years ago, squads of Irish labourers were hired to scythe down the bracken twice every summer. What wouldn't I give to have such a squad here now?

On the way in with the Glengyle sheep, we tangle with the bracken again. Some of the ewes and lambs take full advantage of the dense cover in an attempt to evade capture. The men up above make use of their bird's-eye-view to shout down directions and advice to those toiling in the depths below. In places, the bracken is more than head height. Men and dogs disappear and appear through the foliage, flushing out recalcitrant animals and sending them sprackling down the hillside to join their companions standing at the fank below.

While the other shepherds are slaving away in the clipping shed, Alec and I see to the lambs. Once more the laddies give us invaluable assistance, dosing and dipping pen after pen of wriggling, jumping fidgets of sharp-horned lambs. The unmarked lambs are sorted out. Most of them belong to Glengyle, and are marked accordingly before being dosed and dipped. The addition of these lambs to my lamb count makes the total even more respectable. Alec makes sure that all the newly-marked Portnellan lambs have their mothers, before chasing them along the road towards their own ground. Ewes and lambs that have come in from the Braes of Balquhidder are put into the East Park to await transport back to their home farm.

By the time Alec and I appear amongst the clippers, the last of the ewes are standing in the byre, being gradually worked forward into the crogging pen by the croggers. We have a pair of guest shearers today. The Dhu shepherd has got his back bent, and the other is one of the men from Stronachlachar who has his own collie and is sometimes called out to give the shepherds an extra hand.

The second ewe I am handed has gone wrong in the udder. Poor beast, she must have had an attack of mastitis which, instead of clearing up, became worse and worse until her whole vessel was inflamed. In extreme cases, the infected area turns blue and then goes crimson and may, ultimately, rot off. The damage is irreparable and I will need to cull her from the flock at the back-end handling. In order to remember her, and any other sheep who need to be drafted before their time, a red keel mark is slapped onto the back of her head. Before letting her go, I give her an injection of penicillin to combat the infection.

Maggi serves up chicken and celery broth, roast beef with gravy, new garden potatoes, cabbage and carrots, to 11 hungry men. This is followed by apple and blackberry pie with home-made ice cream. The enormous tea pot steams on the Rayburn, but by the time we set off to the high-end, it is virtually empty.

The Portnellan shepherd comes with me in the Land Rover as I drive out along Eves Road to Ben Ducteach. I am faced with my usual double outrun, first to the top of the Ben and down again, across the head of the glen, before climbing up to gather the top reaches of the Parlan Hill. The panorama from these heights is past description. Breathtaking is the adjective which comes to mind; after all, I am rather puffed by the time I reach the 2,175 foot summit. The hill is as dry as I have ever seen it; running water is scarce but the peat bogs are still wet enough. Butterworts and sundews, two insectivorous plants which compensate for the low nutrient level of the soil by catching and digesting unwary insects, flower in profusion on the damp conditions.

Butterworts, also called bog violets, have pale green, roll-edged leaves which trap not only insects but pollen and any bits of plants which come into contact with them. The flowers are solitary, nodding, violet-like structures on tall, bare stems. If I look around carefully, I can usually find a few of the smaller, pale-flowered variety. Butterworts have a strange overwintering stage, passing the ice-bound months by lying on top of the ground as a rootless rosette. The milky juice from butterwort leaves is said to protect newborn babies from unwelcome evil.

The more colourful sundew plants are another of nature's true wonders. The red-stalked, spoon-shaped green leaves are covered with sticky red hairs which can curve inwards to trap their prey. The six-petalled sundew flowers are encased in a series of buds at the top of a five or six-inch-long, leafless stalk, but are seldom seen open. A plant such as this must have a prominent place in country lore. It is believed that a liqueur distilled from the dewy leaves can cure all skin blemishes, including warts, corns, acne and freckles.

Sheep and shepherds assemble in Bealach nan Corp, disturbing underfoot legions of small, newly metamorphosed frogs. Iain and I herd the last cut while Alec brings the Land Rover behind us. Eves Road, normally wet for most of its length, is dry and dusty. The sheep head towards Glengyle under a grimy, yellow haze.

Although most of the puddle life has dispersed along with the water, nature has evolved some marvellous methods of preserving life, even under the most adverse conditions. Amongst the diverse life forms I have found in and around the pool-filled ruts is a very interesting microscopic wee beastie with eight legs called the water-bear. Most species of these tardigrades are land animals living in damp places, but some can live completely under water. When the water dries up, waterbears go into a dormant state, known as cryptobiosis. On the return of more favourable conditions, the tardigrades become reanimated and resume normal activity.

The high-end milk ewes are clipped out and the lambs given the routine treatment. Even before the very last clipped sheep has had time to dash outside, ring-pulls are pulled and cans of export and lager are thirstily thrown down welcoming throats. I slip away to open the gates and run the still damp lambs out of the fank into the Middle Park. The headlong stampede is met by full-bagged ewes anxious to find relief from the teat-tugging lambs. Some lambs are mothered up at once, others take longer.

Alec and I are faced with a veritable mountain of Portnellan and Glengyle wool to pack. Jamie and Colin, Alec's son, give us a hand, throwing up the fleeces as we get two bags hanging at a time. Victoria painstakingly writes out the labels and ties them onto the sewn and stacked bags.

We are careful to sew up our woolbags only with the special waxed twine provided by the merchant. The one thing that sometimes causes them problems is the chance of finding oddments of string in an otherwise good consignment of wool. Even worse is not finding them until they show up on a manufactured product that then has to be rejected. All the wrong types of string, baler twine, polypropylene, and even the special, previously approved, paper string, are virtually certain to cause contamination. The Wool Marketing Board cannot hope to persuade manufacturers to pay top prices for what may be regarded as suspect raw material.

It is mainly thanks to the Wool Board's sustained, world-wide promotional efforts that our increasingly heavier clips are finding a market. At the moment, our British flock of 32 million constitutes a half of all European sheep and three per cent of the world total, grows about 50,000 tons or 45 per cent of Europe's wool, two per cent of the world output. Most of the Blackface wool is sold abroad, largely for stuffing mattresses. Higher grade British wools are being used for an increasingly wide range of top-quality products. The woollen industry is doing what it can to bolster Britain's sagging economy.

For the best part of 300 years, from the 14th to the 16th century, the British economy was largely based on the wool trade. By the middle of the 16th century, wool production south of the border amounted to 8,500 tons, from about ten million sheep. The big monasteries were among the most important wool growers, specialising in the heavy-fleeced breeds, the ancestors of our modern Romney, Leicester and Down sheep. At that time, Scottish wool yield was about 2,750 tons from three million head, mostly Blackface and Cheviot. The big expansion of sheep farming in Scotland came much later, after the Highland Clearances of the 18th and 19th centuries. Wales, too, until more recent times, had relatively few sheep, apparently preferring to rear their famous black cattle.

The north shore wool is loaded onto a lorry and taken off to our merchant. Seventy-five large woolbags, each with between 30 and 40 fleeces tramped inside. On arrival in Paisley, each bag will be weighed and the producer's name, address and weight of wool noted. The bags are laid aside until their turn comes to be graded.

The grader stands at a large table and examines every single fleece as it comes out of the bag. By tradition, Blackfaces have their wool rolled with the outside out, although most other breeds have their weathered side turned in, which helps the grader to form a speedier opinion as to the quality of the fleece. If the initial cursory examination shows up no serious faults in colour, quality or presentation of the wool, the fleece is tossed into one of the long line of large, wheeled baskets standing in front of the grader. Each basket represents one grade of wool.

Wool is downgraded for many different reasons, and financial penalties are incurred. Black wool, extraneous matter and kemp are easily noticed even in the wrapped fleece. Kemp is a coarse, white hair fibre found amongst the wool; it will not take a dye. A few random fleeces are unrolled to check for any hidden faults; bits of loose wool packed inside, double shear cuts, soiled wool, excessive keel, any one of which can result in a reduction in the price paid for the entire consignment.

We avoid many grading problems by using the services of a reputable woolman. Other faults can be overcome by exercising greater care on the clipping boards. But the last word must lie with the tup breeders who can do so much more to improve wool quality and eliminate kemp.

One of my ewes and a ewe lamb belonging to her are brought home to Glengyle after wandering over the hills and far away. She came down at the Garrison of Inversnaid, the venue of the recent sheepdog trials, and the site of one of Rob Roy MacGregor's confrontations with the Hanoverian authorities. In a desperate attempt to subdue the wild Highland clan, it was decided to burn out the MacGregors at Inversnaid, and build a fort on the ashes. In 1713 the dastardly deed was done. Rob took to the hills with the vow that the planned fortifications would suffer the same fate as his farmstead.

In spite of a continuous watch while the stout walls were thrown up, never a Highlander was seen. On a bitterly cold day towards the end of December, wagons piled high with timbers for the bunks, tables and other fittings left Aberfoyle and rolled up the difficult track that was awash with mud and half-melted snow.

The same evening that the wagons arrived at the new fort, the MacGregors arrived, too – in force. The timbers were piled high in the middle of the building and set alight. The blazing inferno lit up Glen Arklet from end to end and warmed the Gregarach while the lowland troopers and the handful of workmen stumbled away through the bitter night.

The fort was repaired and garrisoned but the MacGregors still held sway and, over the years, proved that they could take it any time they chose. Eventually, a promising young English officer was entrusted with the job of bringing the warrior clan to heel. In this task he singularly failed and, in true British tradition, he was promoted and sent to the farthest-flung corner of the Empire – Canada. Once there, he overcame tremendous odds and, obviously having learned a lot from his dealings with the Gregarach, he took Quebec. The French never recovered from the results of this battle; neither did General Wolfe. He died from his wounds and became a national hero. It is a thought that if it had not been for the Clan MacGregor, Britain may never have taken Canada and the history of the British Empire, and of the world as we know it, would have been quite different.

The small paddocks in front of Glengyle House are badly in need of a trim. The lush summer growth has included the tough, unpalatable rushes and the inedible thistle, besides the good grasses and succulent clover that I would like to encourage further. I am able to borrow Alec Scott, one of the Water Board drivers, who spends a great deal of his summer sitting in his tractor, mowing miles of roadside verges. If I can get the rushes cut regularly, the grass and clover will prosper. Last year the tractor became bogged down in a wet patch and a lot of time was spent getting it out again. Consequently one of the paddocks was left uncut, and this season the rushes dominate that pasture.

Thistles, too, would soon become a problem if they were not kept in check. There is a country saying 'Cut thistles in June, you cut too soon. Cut thistles in July, they are sure to die'. The emblem of Scotland is, as everyone knows, a Scotch Thistle. The thistle was adopted as the national device after a barefooted Dane accidentally trod on one as his night-time raiding party was trying to sneak up on a slumbering Scottish camp near Dunkeld. The agonised cry alerted the sleeping Scots, who leapt to arms and promptly routed the invaders. The plant responsible for raising the alarm was, in fact, the common spear thistle but, at some point over the years, the Scots superseded this humble variety with the more noble-looking Scotch Thistle. The fact that this usurper is not native to Scotland did not seem to matter.

My honey bees have been busy flying to and fro past the house, going from their hives to the giant lime trees and back, all day, every day. It is an amazing sound, hundreds of thousands of bees swarming over the clusters of tiny yellow flowers, collecting an excellent run of lovely lime honey.

It is not only the bees that are laying in stores of winter feed. From now on, every fine day, the three Water Board lorries will journey down to the arable land around Stirling, and bring home load after load of hay until every available space has been crammed full of golden-green bales.

In the long grass around the house and steading, grasshoppers stridulate long into the night. I don't suppose they have ever heard of Aesop.

Blackface tup on his summer pasture

The Lamb Sales

ALTHOUGH FOXES ARE LARGELY silent outside their mating season, during the latter part of the summer vixens can be heard giving contact calls to their young. By this time of year, the cubs have left the den and taken up more independent existences on the hillside. The vixen goes from one cub to another, spending all the daylight hours teaching them to fend for themselves.

The cubs have grown rapidly into gawky, lean-looking animals, with short coats and large ears. From the moment when the cubs first pounced on the twitch of her tail, the vixen has encouraged the development of their basic instinct, procuring food. Through successive stages of leaf-stalking and butterfly-chasing, to the first hunting of beetles and small rodents, the training has been long and thorough. Young predators play at their hunting and killing games for a longer period than the young of potential prey spend at practising escape and evasion. The survival of each individual depends initially upon its ability to feed itself or avoid being eaten.

On the hill, the red deer hinds have moulted the last of their rough winter hair, and glimmer in their peak summer pelage. The calves, still beautifully dappled and growing fast, follow their mothers everywhere. At the back of Ben Ducteach, beyond the newly-vacated eagle eyrie, the stags have finished growing their new antlers, and spend hours rubbing off the dark velvet covering. As a result of this labour, strips of velvet adorn the march fence while the rest straggles down untidily from the beam and tines of the proud antlers.

In between stacking loads of sweet-smelling hay into the Glengyle steading, I take the opportunity to go a little way up the burnside and join the family, lying in the sun. Jamie and Toria are making the most of the last fortnight of their summer holiday. The water is pleasantly warm and, after working in the heat of the hay

Through the dipper

shed, it is very nice to sluice off all the dust and grime. Lying, drying off in the sun, the total lack of birdsong is distinctly audible. August is the one month when even skylarks stop singing. The sky is silent, and the burn has to sing solo as it ripples past, flowing over sun-warmed rocks.

The burn, besides a few bathing bodies, is full of interesting things. Shoals of tiny minnows feed on the myriad forms of invertebrate life found in the crystal-clear water. Minnows are good to eat but, as they seldom exceed four inches, a great many need to be netted in order to provide enough for a meal. Trout, pike, mergansers and leggy herons also hunt this stretch of water for these quicksilver fish. If a predator happens to puncture the skin of a hapless minnow, a warning agent is released which diffuses through the water and, as a starburst, the rest of the shoal disperses to safety.

Another hunter of the tiny minnow is the dipper. Dippers are conker-coloured birds, each with a dazzling white bib. They live along fast-flowing mountain burns, in narrow territories each about two miles long. Dippers first catch the eye by bobbing up and down on a conspicuous rock standing in or alongside the water. The bird will then dive into the water and walk along the stony bottom, searching out food. Mottled-grey chicks, the season's second brood, are already to be found in and under the water; learning to fly will come later.

Down on the Carse of Stirling, the early cereal harvest has begun on a handful of well-placed farms. As the combine and baler clear the first acres, leaving short, crisp stubble to be stocked with upland sheep, my thoughts turn toward the highlight of my hill shepherd's calendar, the lamb sales. It is not the number of lambs that I have marked which now concerns me, but how well they have grown through the summer, and the current prices being offered for store lambs. Because of their very geographical location, very few lambs are ever forward enough to be sold fat off hill farms, and my lambs are presented as stores at the annual Blackface lamb sales in Stirling.

Low ground flockmasters have been selling fat lambs since Easter time and, as the last of their in-bye lambs near readiness for

The dipper bobs up and down

the butcher, they will start buying store lambs off the upland sheepwalks. These stores will be fattened up, first on the stubble and hay aftermath, followed later by root crops and brassicas, and then supplied to the meat trade throughout the winter.

The news coming over on the early morning farm bulletin on Radio 4 is of falling prices. There are many factors affecting the laws of demand, not least the influence of the faceless bureaucrats in Brussels with their 'Common Agricultural Policy' or, as I prefer to call it, 'Non-Policy', and the ever intransigent French. France has the largest lamb consumption in mainland Europe but, unfortunately for us, only opens her market to other members when it suits her. At the moment, the frontier is effectively closed to our lamb; the latest consignment was turned back to Britain because the tyre pressures on the container lorries were incorrect. I can only hope that the situation will improve before the Glengyle lambs are brought forward.

The heather is coming into full flower and, slowly, the hills take on the magnificent purple hue so loved by highlanders and admired by the holiday makers. There are three varieties of heather on my hill. The cross-leaved heath, *Erica tetralix*, has already been flowering for a couple of months without making much visual impact;

now it is the mat of bell heather, *Erica cinerea*, and ling, *Calluna vulgaris*, which is so outstanding.

Heather has an unusual feature which helps it to flourish under difficult damp, upland conditions. It grows both on acid peat made up from compacted, partly decomposed vegetation, and on poor, thin mountain soil with practically no humus. In order to ensure adequate uptake of nutrients, heather roots form an association with a microscopic fungus, the underground network of fungal shoots serves the purpose of root hairs, which the heather lacks and the fungus also concentrates the principal plant foods, especially nitrogen, in a form suitable to the host plant.

Even though heathers are associated with wet soil conditions and high rainfall, they exhibit classic water-conserving characteristics. The leaves are typically evergreen, being short and narrow, with their margins rolled downwards to enclose the underside and thus reduce water loss. Food reserves are saved by the heather keeping its leaves, thus affording an invaluable source of feeding to the hill flock and a wide variety of wild life all the year round.

From dawn to dusk, fishermen try to outwit the Loch Katrine brown trout, each exercising his own degree of skill, endeavour and cunning. Many anglers go to any length of making their own flies. One such man, fishing with a couple of friends a fortnight ago, watched trout tantalisingly rising all around his boat but steadfastly refusing any lure that was offered. He noted that the fish were feeding on a hatch of brownmoths, dropping like confetti out of the lochside oak trees. Last weekend, the same party returned to the water, this time armed with their own copy, tied by the observant gent, built up from a Bryant and May match, a number eight hook and a duncoloured hackle. They took home 24 trout, weighing some 16 lbs.

Local children and shepherds pursue their ancient rights and cast worm-laden hooks out from the shore. The school stays shuttered and silent while the pupils idle the holidays away with other thoughts to occupy their minds. Unknown people, wearing gaudy unisex anoraks, burdened under huge rucksacks, can pop up almost anywhere. They always seem to be in a hurry to be somewhere else.

The level of the loch drops an inch every dry day as Glasgow swallows its enormous draught of one hundred million gallons. The water trickling into Loch Katrine from the numerous burns throughout the catchment area is just about what is required to be released over the dam at the Trossachs to keep the Achray Water in flow. The Glengyle boathouse is high and dry, and most of the ground in front of the house, land that would have been familiar to Rob Roy, is once again to be seen. It is on this land that the MacGregor clan would have mustered in response to the summons of the Fiery Cross.

The Fiery Cross was made from two pieces of wood, lashed together. One end of the horizontal spar would be burned and charred, and the other side hung with a blood-stained cloth. The warning was unmistakable; if you failed to obey, you would be punished by both fire and sword. The Cross would be carried by a relay of runners at a speed well in excess of ten miles an hour, even over the most difficult terrain.

The head shepherd sends out the Fiery Cross and the rest of us hurry down to Edra; handling time has come round again. This time, weather permitting, we will do two handlings each week, starting with Letter and Edra and the lambs will go to the sales the following week. There are two markets in Stirling, the Live Stock Marts Ltd at Kildean, and the Caledonian Mart (Stirling) Ltd at Millhall. We patronise both establishments.

Before making a start at gathering the Letter Woods, I spend a few moments gazing down into the low water, looking in vain for a glimpse of the fabled Silver Strand, a once-famous beach of pure white sand, but the underwater currents of the raised loch must have long since carried away the deposits of fine quartz silt.

The sheep are herded in off the Letter ground. The name Letter, quite common in the Highlands, literally means 'a place on a gentle slope'. Once we get inside the Edra fank, the lambs are shed from the ewes as the flock is worked through the narrow shedder. The lambs are then separated, ewe lambs into one pen, wedder lambs into another.

The ewe lambs are brought back into the handling pen first, a couple of score at a time. Small lambs are drawn off until the shepherd has reduced the number to that needed for flock replacements. These ewe lambs are now known as stock hoggs. They are given a worm/fluke dose, their initial Covexin 8 injection of 5 ml, keeled for the hirsel and dipped. Finally, the hoggs are returned to the company of ewes to spend another few weeks with their mothers. The Letter stock is taken back along the road to the usual park to finish mothering up.

The wedder lambs are next to be brought forward. Again, the smaller lambs are picked out. This time we have one pen for the medium-sized and a second pen for the smallest lambs, eventually leaving us with three groups known as tops, seconds and thirds. The top wedders have a neat, half-inch wide, red ring painted on their left horns; the seconds are painted on the right and the thirds get a wee spot of red keel on the back of the head. Finally, when the paint has had a chance to dry, all the wedders and small ewe lambs are chased through the dipper.

Each group of lambs is taken to stand in one of the various parks close to the Edra steading. Herding newly-speaned (say, spent – means weaned) lambs can be fun – if you have a twisted sense of humour. A large cut of lambs, with not a ewe in sight, can be quite a handful. Without recognised leaders, they tend to burl round and around in a circle like some giant Catherine wheel, and our dogs have to work hard to steer them in the right direction. Young dogs can easily become bemused by the whole thing. Sooner or later, a few of the lambs will see their way through the open gateway and then the rest pour into the park behind them.

The night of the full moon is clear and sharp, with just a touch of frost in the air. The long grasses are wringing wet and next day I need to don my waterproof leggings to keep myself dry. Mars is still a brilliant morning star at the other end of the sky from the setting moon as I trace my steps along the glen behind Edraleachdach – 'the farm between two stone-flagged burns'. Jock's Edra sheep are handled through the fank in exactly the same way as the Letter hirsel. The peculiar 'Jenny' lamb being neither one thing nor the other will be sold by his or herself.

Up goes five bob, bang goes a shilling, down comes a guinea. At least that used to be the costing of shooting grouse. The Glorious

Twelfth opens with shadowy, tweed-clad figures taking to grouse moors in the still dark of night. Battalions of beaters are marshalled into position by regimental gamekeepers. Almost as soon as it is light enough to read the print on an Ely cartridge, whistles shrill out and before the birds have time to wipe the sleep from their eyes, they are driven towards the waiting guns. Hardly have the first salvos died away than the race is on to deliver limp, bloody-feathered still warm carcasses to leading hotels and restaurants up and down the land. A more up-to-date costing would surely be: up goes a pound, bang goes twelve pence, down comes not much.

I don't care a great deal for the methods of these so-called sportsmen. Still, when all is said and done, grouse shooting together with deer stalking are economic necessities on many estates, and can mean the difference between making a profit or a loss. Hill farming has not always been in this sorry state. After the Second World War, government aid, together with improved technology, led to a great expansion in hill farming. This resulted in growth of the Highland population for the first time since the Highland Clearances. It did not last. During the 1950s, in the wake of cheap food imports, farming returns began to fall, bringing about a steady decline which continued unabated throughout the next two decades. In the mid-70s, with the economics looking worse than ever, the situation took a drastic downward turn, and we are still falling.

Over the last few years, costs have risen by almost 70 per cent while market prices have only gone up by about 25 per cent. Increased subsidies have helped to bridge the gap, but it is no existence depending on the vagaries of bureaucrats who, at a stroke, may reduce or wipe out your livelihood. I do not have to plead poverty on behalf of the hill farmer; the figures speak for themselves. In 1960, one Perthshire hill farm showed a return of £10,000 or 50 pence an acre. Last year, the profit on the same farm had fallen to £700, or a mere 3.7 pence for every acre. In between times, the number of families making a living on the farm had been halved, from ten to five. If this trend continues, the Highlands could again be cleared, leaving vast, empty tracts to forestry plantations, holiday development schemes and nature.

Throughout history, the delicate balance of nature has been frequently upset by man, but sometimes Nature tips the scales against herself. Last winter, our goldcrest population was absolutely decimated by the hard conditions which made their insect and spider food virtually impossible to find. Now, in what has been an extended breeding season, one of the few pairs of surviving adults are busy with their third brood of the summer. Under more normal circumstances, two broods of six to ten young is the usual run of things; this year, in the nest near the graveyard that I have been keeping an eye on, there have been about a dozen chicks in each clutch. It is not easy counting the young who are crammed into a tiny basket of moss, suspended beneath a spruce branch by strands of cobweb that hardly look strong enough to support the weight of such a large family. With more than thirty young birds taking to the wing from one nest alone, the goldcrest population is already well on the road to recovery.

Roe deer, on the other hand, have a longer-term problem to face. Their mating season is just coming to an end and, with the embryo taking about 27 weeks to develop, the fawns would be dropped into the world in February. Not exactly the best time to be born. So roe deer have evolved a system of delayed implantation whereby their

A young roebuck

gestation period has been extended to 40 weeks. The newly-fertilised ova lie dormant until November to December before beginning to grow. The young are then born the following May and June, the time of good weather and plenty food.

This practice of having a latent stage in the embryonic development is not restricted to roe deer. My somnolent badgers produce their offspring, deep in their setts, in April after extending their gestation period in a similar way. Stoats even go a stage further and leave their options wide open. If they mate in the spring, the subsequent pregnancy lasts two months. If they mate now, the period is eight months, the ova remaining quiescent for the first six months. In these, and other cases of delayed implantation, Nature is giving the young of the species the best possible chance of survival in what is, after all, a very hard world.

The lengthening August nights, full of midges and bats, bring the heavenly bodies back into focus. Tonight, spectacular meteor showers burst through the clear dark sky. The moon, not long past full, reduces the brilliance of some of the smaller shooting-stars but, nevertheless, it is worth getting a crick in the neck to watch for a while.

By dawn, Mars is the lone sentinel of the sky. While Jock, John and Iain are away to Stirling to sell the first of the Edra and Letter lambs, I take a stroll around the three Glengyle parks to have a look at the dykes, fences and gates. Newly-speaned lambs will spend the first day or two doing little else other than looking for a way back to the hill. I pay particular attention to the long-standing dykes because lambs can scramble up and over walls that would otherwise keep heavier sheep securely contained.

In my Middle Park, I find a section of wall which would best be rebuilt rather than simply patched. It takes a little time to dismantle the stones, layer by layer, piling them up in heaps according to their size and shape. Once the slip has been cleared back to a sounder structure, I can make a start on the rebuilding. Stone by stone, the hole in the wall is closed up. One of the secrets of dyking is to pack the interior spaces of the wall as solidly as possible with small stones.

I was taught the craft by an old Welsh dyker, Billy Cobb, who looked as old and weathered as the grey stones he worked with. He came to the farm where I worked as a boy and spent a week or two putting the walls back into shape. I used to watch him bend his rickety back and pick up a stone, lifting it as gently as if it were a sleeping creature, and lay it to continue its slumber in the wall. He taught me that there was a place for every stone and every stone had its place. I seldom saw him discard a stone once he had laid his horny hands upon it.

The turn of the Strone sheep comes around. On the ground beneath the trees of the Schoolhouse Wood where I start gathering, instantly recognisable ant hills are to be found. These heaps of soil and pine needles can be over three feet tall, and on a sunny day vast armies of worker ants can be seen out and about in a state of high activity. Wood ants eat a wide variety of things which they come across while on scavenging forays, often accounting for large numbers of insect pests. They also farm for a living, keeping herds of aphids in underground galleries, milking them of their sugary sap by stroking them with their antennae.

Below me, near the shore of the loch, is the site of the schoolhouse itself. Not much remains of the building today, although it was lived in within recent memory and there are people still living who actually came to school here. No school buses in those days, and very little in the way of a road; the children had to walk, summer and winter, some from as far as Glengyle. When the burns were in spate, long detours involving some steep climbs were required in order to reach a narrow crossing point. During the colder months, each pupil carried, apart from his or her daily victuals, a peat for the school fire. If the peat was forgotten, the defaulter had to sit shivering at the back of the class for that day.

At the Strone fank, we find that the grass growing inside the pens, usually lush, long and untouched between handlings, has been cropped short. Iain solves the mystery by revealing that three stags have been coming down off the hill at night and jumping in over the high stone walls to feed on this small area of verdant richness.

From Strone, we have moved on to the Coilachra hirsel. Charlie is already waiting for us at his fank when Alec and I arrive early in the morning, closely followed by Jock McDougall. We walk out to the cross fence, blethering about the price of lambs and this and that. The young dogs frolic and chase around, the older dogs follow quietly at heel. We linger a few minutes at our 'official rest point'. There are a good many of them around the hills, spots where shepherds take a breather.

We each take our dogs and go our separate ways. I have to walk along the glen towards the Hungry Loch, past another of the ruined fermtouns – the old Highland settlements – and the strips of ground long since gone out of cultivation. Given the implements of the day, the ploughing of this barren soil must have been a backbreaking job. A large two-man wooden plough would have been drawn by a team of four horses yoked abreast. A third man led the horses, walking backwards, all the while looking out for hidden rocks which might damage the precious iron ploughshare.

On the steeper slopes, where the horses could not work, or in places where the soil was simply too shallow for the big plough, the men resorted to the caschrom (literally, crooked foot). A caschrom was made from a single, curved piece of wood, about five feet long, fitted to a flat block tipped with an iron sock to act as the share. A peg was fixed near the bottom of the shaft, against which the ploughman pushed his foot as he thrust the share into the earth, and with a jerk turned the turf over. The man would work backwards, turning a succession of clods into a tidy furrow. If he walked from January until April he might have turned over five acres.

Although the caschrom is undoubtedly the earliest true plough, it is still to be found on some crofts of the outer isles and on the precipitous slopes of Wester Ross. It was said that land turned with a caschrom would yield five heads of corn for every three produced on a similar area worked with the old horse plough. In the warm air above the peaty morass of sphagnum, rush and cotton grass which surrounds the Hungry Loch, the crown jewels of the insect kingdom dart and hover in all their glory. Dragonflies are unlike any other insect, they can move each of their four wings independently or two at the same time in opposite directions. By doing this, the dragonfly can vary its speed from hover to 90 mph, and can even fly backwards.

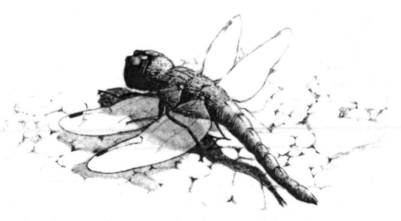

Dragonfly, the crown jewel of the insect kingdom

Each male patrols a particular stretch of bank, driving away other males of their own and other species. Females spend much of their time feeding away from the water, returning to be mated. Fertilisation takes place on the wing and some species remain bonded together while the female lays her eggs in the tissue of water plants, sometimes above but more frequently below the surface. A few species simply broadcast their eggs from the air. Female Aeshnas lay independent of male support, often immersing their bodies as far as the wings in the process.

Dragonflies spend most of their lives as aquatic larvae, growing through ten or 12 stages before metamorphosing into the winged adult. The nymphs or larvae are voracious hunters. The prey, whether it be insect, worm, water snail, tadpole or tiny fish, is seized by an extraordinary development of the lower lip which is formed into a pair of large pincers. This is called the mask. The nymph breathes through a set of gills in the stomach and has to continually pass water along the intestines. If threatened, the creature can expel more water and jet away from the danger.

Dragonflies originated in warmer climes and presumably arrived in Scotland after the last Ice Age. In order to survive the change in environmental conditions, they have adapted to a long larval, short flying life cycle from the long tropical flying season coupled with a short larval history. It is only during the brief Scottish summer that temperatures rise high enough for the adults to take to the wing.

All three pairs of legs on these fierce predators are directed forward, and are used not for walking but for catching their victims. Although in some places dragonflies are known as horse-stingers, they are perfectly harmless – except to other insects. Just imagine, though, fossilised dragonflies have been discovered with a wingspan exceeding a foot.

Mona and Gail take off on a wide sweeping run, catching all the sheep which Alec has turned below the Blue Rocks of Stob a'Choin (the Dog's Fang). Gran trundles along behind a handful that have come right down, almost to the burn of Allt a'Choin. I take the sheep forward while Alec takes a turn out the back of the Stob, looking down the Braes of Balquhidder and over the twin lochs of Doine and Voil. It was on Loch Voilside in 1306 that the newly-crowned King Robert Bruce made a last desperate stand after being defeated at the battle of Methven, before being spirited away by loyal clansmen into the safety of the surrounding mountains.

In March of that year Bruce, having slain Sir John Comyn in Greyfriars church, Dumfries, made his bid for the Golden Round of Scotland, thereafter riding swiffly through Glasgow where he raised many more supporters to his cause. He then made for Scone, to be crowned upon the true Stone of Destiny, not the sandstone counterfeit which Edward had ordered to be carried back to London.

When Edward learned of these events he despatched an army under Sir Aymer de Valence to burn and slay and raise the very devil if needs be; and the county of Fife was to be given to the man who could take the Bruce, dead or alive. The English force, aided and abetted by many Scottish knights who were still in service to Edward, set up their headquarters at Perth.

Bruce came in good battle order to St Johnstoun, the old name for Perth, and called out Sir Aymer to take the field against them. The English declined but offered to come out on the morrow. The Scots retired to their camp, near to Methven woods and broke ranks. Some had gone foraging for food and others had disarmed and were taking their ease, when the enemy fell upon the unsuspecting camp. The King himself raised the alarm and rallied his men to arms. The surprised Scots fought a bitter rearguard action but many brave and noble men fell before Bruce ordered his men to disperse as best they could. The retreating Scots were mercilessly pursued by the English knights.

It was thus that Robert the Bruce was brought to the shelter of Loch Katrineside. From here he later travelled a few miles to the north and was given sanctuary by the monks of St Fillan. It was during this sojourn that Bruce learned of the wondrous arm relic of St Fillan, an early 8th-century monk of Irish descent who came to live in Glendochart. In order that the saint could work at his writing in the darkened cell, he was blessed with a right hand and arm which glowed, illuminating his manuscripts even in the dead of night.

Before the ultimate battle, to come eight long years later at Bannockburn, Bruce summoned the saint's miraculous arm to be brought to his tent. The monk in charge of the sacred relic was in something of a dilemma; believing that the outnumbered Scots were about to be defeated, he hid the arm in a safe place and presented the empty casket to his monarch. Bruce asked to see the actual relic and, after a few moments' hesitation, the monk confessed to what he had done. However, when the box was opened the fluorescent arm was in its rightful place. That, surely, was the most auspicious omen anyone could wish for, and the following day the invaders were driven from Scottish soil.

The ewes and lambs come together below Stob a'Choin, and are divided down the middle; Alec and I take charge of the hindmost cut. Once we have the cross fence at our backs again, the sheep travel easily through the short, blooming heather, kicking up clouds of fine pollen which dusts over the boots and leaves a distinct honey taste at the back of the throat.

Huge, brown, hairy caterpillars of the Northern Eggar moth are busy feeding on the flowering heath. This variety is similar in many respects to the closely related Oak Eggar found south of the border, except that our caterpillars take a full two years before becoming winged adults. The first winter is spent as larvae, buried snugly amongst the heather roots, while the second is passed in the pupal state. The moths emerge in May and June and are sexually dimorphic, the males being smaller and darker than the females. The night-flying females attract their mates by means of a sex phero-mone, the scent of which is conveyed over an enormous area. The males respond to the call, flying by day as well as by night.

As we come down the hill towards the fank with the sheep, we are walking into the sun and I notice that a partial eclipse is taking place. The disc of the moon is silhouetted against the sun's solar face. No sooner is the gate shut on the last cut than we are away for our breakfast at Isa McLellan's. Charlie, being a bachelor, has Alec's wife to do the food for all his handlings.

The Coilachra sheep are worked a little differently from the other north-shore hirsels. Besides drawing the lambs for the sales, the hoggs and cast ewes are drawn out and taken away to wait in the Barn Park. A few lucky hoggs will find that they still have their mothers with them, the others will just have to eat grass. The Coilachra handlings are made a lot of fun by the presence of the shepherd's younger brother, Angy, a cheerful Down's Syndrome and usually full of high jinks when in the fank.

My local, the Altskeith at Kinlochard, has arranged a Sunday after-noon cricket match between our own Taverners XI and the Cross Keys from Kippen. The picturesque ground, beneath the wooded hills of Aberfoyle, is in marvellous condition; the triangular cucum-ber sandwiches are cut but, perhaps not surprisingly, it rains.

Long before trials were a twinkle in a sheepdog's eye, shep-herds were to be found whiling away summer evenings playing cricket, a game which they invented. Cricket originated on the sheep downs of England during the reign of Henry II, since when it has spread world-wide. Early sheep pens in the south of England were constructed from woven hurdles and a shepherd would defend one of these wicket gates with his upturned crook as a ball of wool was bowled at him, the object being to hit the wicket and dismiss the batsman. As late as the 18th century, cricket bats were still curved, an echo of their humble beginning.

I am wakened as a brace of floats come grumbling past Glengyle, headlights piercing the last of the night. Today, it is the turn of Iain and Charlie to sell their lambs at Stirling. The drivers will need to make two journeys in order to get the lambs from both sides of the loch into the sale. Outside my window, Tansy bellows through the dawning, calling for a bull, precluding any further sleep. It is two months since she calved-time to think about putting her in calf again. The hill cows ought to have been well covered by now, so I can pinch Fray Bentos from them for a while.

After breakfast Gran and I wander along the summery glen to look for the bull. The high-end lambs I get a look at seem to be doing well; in a couple of days I will be able to see them all. Angry, needle-sharp squeaks, followed by rapid rustles, betray the presence of bellicose shrews underfoot in the long grass. There is plenty of grass underfoot but already it is beginning to lose its colour, fading into a dozen softer shades. Of the many grasses growing on the hill, I am particularly interested in the sheep's fescues, of which I have two varieties.

Sheep's fescue is widely distributed throughout the British Isles, growing on a wide range of poorer soils, providing they have adequate drainage. On hills and mountains such as these, there are many places where it can be the dominant grass. It is a short, very hardy, drought-resistant plant which can withstand continuous close grazing. Although its total yield of foliage is low, what it produces is nutritious, and it provides valuable feeding for my sheep. There is an unusual variety, found only on mountains, which in place of seeds produces miniature plants from its flowers; they drop to the ground and take root, thus helping to maintain a densely-tufted sward.

We find the herd grazing the slopes of the Parlan Hill; they appear to be healthy enough, well fed and contented. There are still plenty of diseases which we must keep an eye out for, but no longer do we live in fear of the dreadful Murrain which, until eradicated in 1877, ravaged Europe for fifteen centuries. The last big outbreak in 1865–66 killed 324,000 cattle in Britain alone. Murrain, caused by a virus known as Rinderpest, was characterised by horrible ulcers of the mucous membranes. The animal stopped feeding and wasted away.

At the first signs of the cattle plague, which could well mean the death of nine out of ten valuable animals, two courses of action were taken. First of all, every fire in the glen was put out and not rekindled from the sacred bough, to give fresh life to any hearth, until the visitation had passed. Secondly, a man would be despatched posthaste to Ardvorlich, on Loch Earn, to fetch a jar of charmed water which would be sprinkled over the beasts. On the return journey, the jar was not to touch the ground as the charm would then be broken. Fortunately, present-day treatments are more readily available if not surer acting.

Fray Bentos walks home to Glengyle as if he knows what I have in store for him. He is such a gentle, well-mannered creature that it is a pleasure to be in his company. A young buzzard sits on the Big Devil and shouts skywards to be fed. Today he is lucky, tomorrow he may not be. Already the season of change is upon us. The sow badger will have gone dry, and her cubs will not be alone in having to learn how to fend for themselves. It is the time of year when rugby training has started and, tomorrow, the children go back to school.

A pleasant walk from the house, up past the Castle Rock and over the Wee Hill, takes me out to join in the Portnellan gather. The flock is brought together on the nose of the hill before being turned down towards the loch. Even though there is a sound fank in the Portnellan East Park, there is no dipper built into it, and for many years the sheep of this hirsel have been taken the mile along the narrow road to Glengyle.

In the days when it was the practice to bathe sheep, lifting each animal in turn onto a bath-stool, a swim tank was not necessary. It was a long and laborious process: every sheep was lifted onto a slatted stool, with its legs passed between the rungs, head towards the shepherd who was seated astride the narrow end. The shepherd parted the wool along the back, opening a shed with his hands. An assistant then poured a wash from a jug along the shed, following the shepherd's hands. Other sheds were made about three inches apart, until the whole back had been bathed. The sheep was then turned on its back so that all the underparts could be thoroughly washed too. This way, on a good day, about 40 sheep could be done.

Using up-to-date methods, we put Alec's lambs through the tank at a much faster rate. No sooner are they all standing dripping, shaking one after another and sending showers of dip rainbowing into the air, than Andy Donaldson arrives with the lorry. The lambs are loaded onto the three decks of the float and set off for the Edra parks. Alec takes his ewes and stock hoggs back along the road as far as his West Park. Holding them in will make the gathering of my low-end a little simpler, and any sheep spotted grazing out on Portnellan ground will be swept up and brought in with the Glengyle sheep. I give the pens a sweep out, ready for my big day. The harvest moon hangs new in the evening sky, pale and frail like a sickle of straw.

With my dogs and the twin morning stars for company, I set off to my hill before anyone else arrives at Glengyle, climbing up the steep, well-worn route up the Coireasach Burn. During the last few days, magnificent Mercury has been joined by an even brighter body, Jupiter. It is difficult to tell them apart with the naked eye.

I have plenty of time to go down, deep into the Braes, and bring out the Glengyle sheep grazing on the alpine-type pasture of the north-facing slopes. Soft-coloured, delicate flowers are noticeably more numerous on these summits than on the lower, peat-covered hefts. Alpine herbage is richer, too, which stimulates a high milk flow in ewes and hinds alike, growing as they do on free-draining soil consisting entirely of weathered particles of mineral-rich bedrock. The low profile adopted by these species keeps them from being harmed by the driving winds. The Ben Nevis observatory, over a 13-year period, recorded an average of only 104 days each year when the air speed did not reach 50 miles per hour.

The sheep and deer are only transient visitors to this territory of the ptarmigan and mountain hare. At times, I have even seen our smallest mammal, the pygmy shrew, running about between the scree stones. Turn over a few stones and you enter the domain of four or five kinds of spider. Such spiders only venture abroad when conditions are right, and therefore are not subjected to the wide range of conditions that have to be faced by web-dwelling types.

Apart from me, there are a few moths of the Cambus family and the mountain ringlet butterfly which seem disposed to visit the high tops today.

Away to the west, mist ominously rolls in over the Argyll hills. The low-end sheep are driven down through the frost-touched bracken into the paddock below the fank. Breakfast was booked for half past nine and Maggi has been keeping it warm for two hours since then. I don't know where the time goes. By the time we have cleared the last of the bacon, eggs and tomatoes and sunk the last cups of tea, the mist has arrived here, blanketing Ben Ducteach and covering the Square Rocks.

There is nothing to do except sit around and await further developments. It is surprising what shepherds can find to do to while away the time between meals on a day like this; yarn, yawn and whittle at sticks.

Iain and Alec recount, for what must be the hundredth time, the tale of a Glengyle gather, years ago, under the previous head shepherd, Murdo Bain. A sudden early morning mist had stopped the assembled herds going out to the hill so that they had dossed down under some empty woolbags and tried to catch some sleep – all except Murdo, who tramped impatiently back and forth across the wooden floor in his heavy, hob-nailed boots. Every few minutes he would stop, only to poke his head out of the door and assure his men that the mist was lifting and it was time to make a start. The shepherds, having gathered themselves together, went outside only to find that the mist was down as far as the back of the park dyke. Murdo's exhortation would be repeated every five minutes, sleep was impossible, but the mist stayed hugging the dyke.

Maggi breaks the monotony by serving dinner. Someone, at least, has been busy, preparing vegetable soup, steak pie with peas and potatoes, rhubarb crumble and gallons of custard. Apart from the meat, everything came out of the garden. We take a leisurely hour and a half over the meal and by four o'clock the head shepherd reckons it is clear enough to gather. And it really is.

If the mist stays off we should be back with the sheep before darkness overtakes us. As usual, I drive Alec and myself the length of Eves Road. Time is of the essence as I stride out for the top of the Ben, hunting my sheep on in front of me. Mist hangs on the higher hills to the north and west. Fleetingly, three golden eagles appear out of the cloud cover, take a look at the hurrying intruder and vanish whence they came. Ripe blaeberries sweeten my way along the Parlan Hill. I suddenly spot a gleaming sheep's skull, cracked like china, peeping at me out of the heather with empty egg-cup eyes. I find the rest of her skeleton in a nearby peat hole, surrounded by tufts of grey wool. She won't be coming in today.

The living sheep come together at Bealach nan Corp and are taken in hand, a cut at a time, before being turned towards home. The ruined nunnery of Kil-mi-Cailleach stands forlornly in the gathering gloom. The wise women of Glengyle were quite famous, not only for their ecclesiastical qualities but for their judicial edicts. If a court had difficulty or failed in reaching a verdict, the case would often be referred to the nuns. After praying and deliberating over the subject, it seems that the matter was always satisfactorily resolved. That is, until the celebrated case, reported by Ian Lone, a 17th-century Highland bard, which led to their judicatory downfall.

A man had accused his neighbour of stealing his new mare after a Sunday service at the kirk. The defendant stoutly maintained his innocence, claiming that he had done no more than sit up on the animal, just to get the feel of it. However, before he could dismount, the horse took fright and bolted, carrying him off. The local sheriff could make nothing of the case and put the matter into the hands of the wise women. In due course, they returned a double-edged verdict. The defendant, they decided, had been telling the truth and should be released forthwith. On the other hand, the horse was guilty of abducting the poor man, tantamount to kidnap, and they condemned the animal to be hanged.

The Glengyle sheep make it home before the last of the eternal light completely fades away in the west. Six weary shepherds sit down to one of Maggi's specials, mixed farmhouse grill. There is not much in the way of home baking left on the table by the time the other herds leave to go home, and I go out into the night to fetch Tansy into the byre and feed my tired dogs.

Morning comes on dreich and damp, typical Glengyle handling weather. Iain and Charlie are away selling the last of their lambs, and even though we have Davie and Tommy to make up the numbers, with the children back at their lessons, the fank seems strangely quiet. With an eight o'clock start, Maggi does not need to cook breakfast, simply provide us with a ten o'clock tea. That is an understatement. Ten o'clock tea is comprised of several plates piled high with piping hot, buttered toast, a dish of hard-boiled eggs, a mound of sliced cheese and a large pot of honey. Some of us must have drunk more than 200 cups of tea at the handlings since we started in March.

After the lambs have been shed off from their mothers and separated into their respective ewe and wedder pens, I begin to draw my replacement ewe hoggs. I like to keep any ewe lamb that obviously has Swale blood in her, providing of course that she does not have any disqualifying faults. I like to make sure that their mouths close properly, giving them a good bite, essential for efficient grazing. The most common fault in this department is a sheep with a sow-mouth, the lower jaw being noticeably too short. The opposite, sharngobbed, is rarely seen as it tends to be fatal at an early age. Good feet and legs are also necessary if the sheep is to get about these hills in order to find her food in the first place. Eventually, I decide on 210 hoggs which are then jagged, dosed and keeled before being turned out with their mothers.

Dinner is sharp at one. No excuses for being late today when we only have to walk down the fank. Mince and tatties is traditionally supposed to be one of shepherds' favourite meals. Maggi follows it up with a steaming rice pudding, as thick and creamy as a Chinese wedding cake.

Back in the fank, Alec helps me to draw the wedder lambs while the rest of the men paint the horns, tops on the left, seconds on the right. There are always a few riggs, male lambs that, for one reason or another, we are unable to castrate. They are marked with red keel on the tailhead. The same mark is put onto a tup lamb which is not good enough to keep for breeding. The third draw of wedders and the surplus ewe lambs are marked on the back of the head, and all the sale lambs are ready for the dipper.

Alec Scott arrives to float any lambs to Edra, to wait there until the Monday market. An extra pair of willing hands is always welcome, and when Jamie arrives back from school, he pushes the lambs under as they swim the length of the tank and the work is soon finished.

With Alec, there is another mouth to feed at tea. No problem though, the spaghetti bolognaise spreads around seven plates just as easily as six. One thing about Maggi's cooking, there is always plenty of it. After tea, the lambs are loaded onto the three decks of the float and set off down the road. They will spend a few days keeping up their condition on the lush Edra grass, in company with Alec McLellan's wild geese.

In the bird world, a complete moult usually follows the breeding season. Changing feathers puts them at greater risk from predators which explains why our birds are more secretive around this time. After a moult, the late summer plumages of many male birds is a dull copy of their beautiful spring finery. As the winter progresses, the plain tips and edges of the feathers wear away to reveal the dress plumage beneath. Birds lose their ability to fly when they drop a large number of wing and tail flight feathers at the same time. Dippers and mallard moult in this fashion, but are still able to feed themselves; other birds, who must be able to fly well in order to obtain food, shed their flight feathers a few at a time during a prolonged moult.

Our summer visitors have developed complex moult behaviour around their migratory lifestyles. They can simply moult rapidly before leaving us or, like the swallow, wait until they reach their winter quarters. Some cannot make up their mind and do half at each end of the journey; this is known as arrested moult. The willow warbler goes one better and changes all of its feathers twice, once in Britain and again in Africa.

It is not to Africa that I am going, but Stirling. The day of the sale becomes alive with activity. Early in the morning, Andy Donaldson stops at Glengyle and picks me up. Down at Edra, Iain, Jock and John have got the Portnellan and Glengyle lambs up from the park and are busy shedding them into their different classes. The painted horns and keel marks make this job comparatively straightforward.

The lorry is loaded up with Portnellan lambs and sets off for the first run to the market. It will be a couple of hours before Andy returns for my lambs. Time passes; listen. At long last the float roars into the close; a broken fan-belt caused the delay.

We arrive without further mishap and off-load the lambs, running them up alleys between pens of heavily breathing cattle to the sheep yard. Maggi has already arrived in our own Land Rover and she gives me a hand to put them into their designated pens. Then we wander down to the ring and watch the cross-bred lambs being sold. After the crosses, the first of the Blackfaces come into the ring. We meet a great many people that we already know and others whom we will get to know. Eventually, it is time to go back to my lambs, ready to bring them forward in their turn. Prospective buyers walk slowly past my lambs, look them over knowingly, exchange a few pleasantries, and move on along the long line of full pens.

Soon the Glengyle top lambs pour into the ring. Iain and I, crook in hand, stir them around like a big bowl of porridge. Tom Wallace, the auctioneer, extols their virtues, announcing that he has never seen them better. Gradually he wrings a few final bids from the ringside, before the hammer falls and my best lambs go to a new owner. The price could have been better, the French market being open again.

Fray Bentos, a gentle, well-mannered bull

Wild Harvest

FOR THE MOMENT SUMMER lingers on, but soon September will produce the first indication of the harder times which come with lengthening nights. Down on the arable ground, harvesting farmers compete against the wetness of western Scotland for the wind of September is predominantly from the south-west, bringing with it more than ten inches of soft warm rain. A few fields of unbaled hay, some of it cut many weeks ago, are now left mouldering to their fate as gigantic gleaming combines set to reaping the acres of heavy-headed corn. Ton after ton of newly-thrashed cereal pours forth from these monstrous machines into a shuttle of high-sided tractor-drawn trailers, each one racing alongside in order to catch the golden fountains of oats, wheat and barley.

Traditionally, oats was the predominant cereal, providing the staple food of the people and, together with oat straw, the principal winter stock-feed; oats, unlike wheat and barley, is native to Britain. Over the past 20 years, the pattern of grain growing has radically changed in this area, as in the rest of the country. During the 1950s, new varieties of barley became available which offered to the farmer a greater yield potential than the oats grown at the time. There is also greater stockfeeding value in barley than in oats and this, harnessed to the fact that tractors were rapidly replacing genuine horse power on the farm, meant a reduction in demand for both feeding oats and oat straw. Furthermore, coupled with the possibilities of selling their top quality barley to the distilling and brewing industries, farmers found barley economically far more attractive than oats. It is only in the west and on upland holdings that oats has maintained its age-old position, being most suited to the poorer soils and higher rainfall, and being able to ripen with the minimum of sunshine.

The effect of the new varieties of barley was spectacular. Even

Red deer stag

as late as 1963, twice as many acres of oats than barley were grown. But ten years later, the position had been completely reversed. The variety Ymer, which made the initial incursion into the oat acreage in Scotland, was of Swedish origin and particularly suited to Scottish conditions. Recently, Ymer has been replaced by the English-bred Golden Promise which now accounts for more than half of all Scottish-grown barley. Golden Promise is highly favoured by the whisky distillers. About one third of all barley is used for malting, the remainder of the crop being mostly used as stock-feed.

Wheat, introduced into Scotland from Scandinavia about 2,000 years ago, was to be found growing on strips all over the Highlands. It was a strong standing, bearded type, difficult to thrash but had the advantage of being bird proof. Now, fewer than two thousand acres of wheat – that amounts to less than six per cent of the total cereal acreage – is grown in this region, almost entirely in the drier rainshadow to the east of Stirling. Most of the wheat is used for bread, the rest for cakes, biscuits and stock-feed. Bread today is usually made from a mixture of home-grown wheat and the harder wheats which are ripened in the hot American summers. Hard wheat is acknowledged to be superior for baking than the soft ones resulting from our cool, moist climate.

With the onset of harvest, the Water Board lorries, their float bodies removed, yoke into the daily grind of carting home loads of newly-baled, golden straw. Straw makes up an important part of the diet for my outwintered hill cows, and although it has only about half the protein of good hay, it does have much more starch, and is a good deal cheaper too.

The first Saturday in September sees the colours of Stirling County Rugby Football Club taking to the field in earnest. Up and down the land, a new rugger season gets underway on firm, well-grassed pitches; last winter's scars are a long, healing summer away.

I have arrived now at the autumn of my playing career and find that I am being gently eased down through the club; 2nd xv last season, 3rd xv this year. At least I have been given the honour of leading out the thirds. It is, I believe, what is commonly known as promotion downwards! Stirling County have fixtures for seven sides and as long as I can get a game somewhere, I am not worried about which team I am playing in.

Most old County players just fade away; some, a chosen few, end up in the Stirling County Wolfhound xv. This is our 'social' side, and in order to qualify for selection, a member must be, first, old; secondly, sociable and, finally, able to play a wee bit of rugby. One such stalwart is Easton Roy, Club Captain way back in 1953–1954 and still propping with great gusto for the Wolfhounds in his 60th year. My ambition is, one day, to fulfil the necessary requirements to become a Wolfhound myself.

It is not only on the arable land that a bountiful harvest manifests itself: along every hedgerow and in every thicket hips, haws, nuts and berries are maturing into full colour and ripeness. This wild harvest is every bit as important as that of the farmer. It is this food which will sustain much of the wildlife throughout the coming winter and add extra succulence to the countryman's autumn fare. Any day now, Maggi will be serving up the first mouthwatering bramble crumble of the season, smothered with Tansy's smooth, rich cream. This same fruit, which above all others brings people with tins and bowls and polythene bags flocking into the country-side, also attracts a vast array of other visitors.

The gossamer thread of spiders, hung heavily with drops of early morning mist, shines amongst the tangled briars, trapping unwary flies drawn by the sweet, juicy berries. As the sun quickly warms the chill early autumn air, wasps and flies come to feed; butterflies flit delicately from fruit to fruit, daintily sucking up droplets of juice through their long, hollow tongues, all the while slowly opening and closing their wings. The red speckled ragged winged Herald moth may forsake the ivy blossom and be seen drinking at length from pierced brambles.

Many species of birds, some of which, like the thrush and robin, nested within the protection of the brambles in the spring-time, now return to feed on the berries or prey on the insects. I particularly enjoy watching the blackbirds which have a peculiar 'pip-spitting' action, wiping the stick blackberry seeds off their beaks onto the leaves. This is just one of nature's many ways of spreading seeds. Foxes and badgers too have a taste for blackberries and help to distribute the seed which, protected by a very tough seed-coat, passes safely through the digestive system. Seeds dispersed by birds and animals in this manner benefit from the action of digestive acids on their outer coat. Germination is made easier and the newly emerging seedling is able to feed from the surrounding deposit of rich plant food.

Blackberries are relatively late in this part of Scotland. Even so, after 29 September, Michaelmas Day, they become the sole property of the fairies and should be left to them.

Early touches of frost bring the first hues of yellow, orange and red to the foliage, highlighting the white tunnels of the Nepticular moth larvae and reminding me of the passing year. Other seasons seem to drift from one into the other somewhere around the expected time. Autumn, however, is the one which can normally be depended upon to begin on schedule. Warm, sunny days can, and most often do, continue well into September, but before the tenth of the month sharp nights and misty mornings are commonplace. This sudden change appears to prompt the last of the young cuckoos to up and leave the woodlands of Glengyle and head towards their winter quarters in tropical Africa. Even a visit to the shops in Aberfoyle has a different feel about it now; tourists still throng the village but high in the sky above Main Street, the noisy, twittering swifts are conspicuous by their absence.

As the summer wings away south in company with the departing swifts, my thoughts turn to the last gather of the year. With the August lamb sales safely past, my quarry this time is the surviving five-year-old ewes. Of the 210 originally kept as new hoggs for breeding stock, 40 or 50 will have succumbed to one of the many causes of death which afflict sheep. The profitable breeding life of a Glengyle ewe is governed by the conditions of the hirsel itself. I can only keep my ewes through four lambing seasons, that is until they are 5½ years old, before I have to sell them at the cast-ewe sales. On lower, more hospitable hills, old ewes may be kept for another 12 months before being sold off to end their days on in-bye, low-ground holdings.

The principal factor governing the ability of a ewe to eke out a living on Glengyle, or anywhere else, is the condition of her mouth. Sheep, like deer and cattle, have a peculiar arrangement of teeth. They have no top teeth at the front of the mouth, only a pad of hard gum. Below this, if all is correct, are set eight sharp incisor teeth which are of the utmost importance to the animal. Plants are grazed by being pulled across the incisors by the tongue. At the back of the mouth, a sheep is equipped, top and bottom, with broad-topped grinding molars, between which the tough fibrous food is loudly munched.

Lambs are born with eight milk incisor teeth. They are replaced by permanent 'hard' teeth two at a time, starting with the centre pair which come through at about 15 months of age. The next two erupt at 21 months, pushing up either side of the first pair. The third change occurs around 27 months, followed, finally, by the last pair which appear at three years old. This stage is known as 'full-mouthed'. Although low-ground lambs may change their first teeth up to three months sooner because of the higher level of nutrition, the intervals thereafter are just the same: six months, six months and nine months. This makes telling the age of a sheep a simple task up to three years old. Beyond this, the incisors gradually grow longer, become looser and, depending on the health and condition of the animal, eventually start dropping out.

A sheep with missing teeth is called 'broken-mouthed' and has become, by virtue of her condition, a much less efficient feeder. A broken-mouthed sheep would find it almost impossible to survive on Glengyle, especially in a hard winter. I sell my old ewes before this problem arises in more than a handful of sheep.

They say that all good things must come to an end, and now the sands of time appear to be fast running out for my old Welsh bitch. Gran, all of a sudden, has become very frail and looks an extremely old dog which, of course, she is. Since losing her dominant position in the kennel earlier in the year, I have had to stop her mixing socially with the rest of the pack. While out at work there is no problem: I call the tune and can keep order, but back in the kennel even the pup will bully her. A sorry state of affairs for the once proud matriarch.

Several times a day for the past fortnight, I have had to lift her from her bed and sometimes carry the old girl outside so that she could attend to her business. Until yesterday she was eating and drinking well. Her eyes were so bright and alert that I am sure she was not suffering at all, simply fading away before my very eyes. Now she has stopped eating and has only been persuaded to drink a little warm milk and honey. Her eyes are asking for help and I am very much afraid that the time has come.

With a heavy heart I ask my neighbour for a loan of his gun.

The sun is shining through the canopy of leaves, dappling the ground with soft light as I carry my faithful friend towards her last resting place. I lay her on the ground, directly in a shaft of warm autumn sunshine alongside the MacGregor burial ground. I fondle her head before stepping back a few paces. The gun feels unusually heavy. Gran looks me full in the eye for a long moment and then turns her head away. She knows.

The immediate silence which follows is more deafening than the gunshot. Then I hear an alarmed pigeon wing away noisily through the foliage, perhaps carrying her spirit into the Great Beyond. In the distance, high on the hill, a couple of crows raucously bid her farewell.

I wrap her soft, peaceful body in a thick, white fleece and bury her beneath an old, red-berried rowan tree where she will forever lie safe, warm and comfy. Tear drops mix with the earth as I cover her up. Sixteen years was a long time.

The frosty first light of dawn is heralded by the first geese of autumn. A skein of pink-foots, already heading south from their Icelandic breeding haunts, pass down Glengyle, wink-winking their way towards the stubble fields of Stirling. This is only the spearhead of vast flocks of greylag and pink-foot which, after their long sea crossing, will descend upon the Carse to feed on the spilled grain and crop valuable grazing.

Strone is the first hirsel to be gathered this time. The Strone hoggs go away to their wintering a little earlier than any of the others. It feels very strange not to be able to bring Gran out with me.

Her bed is empty. Strips of clear water on the otherwise rucked surface is Loch Katrine's way of foretelling rain.

At the Schoolhouse Wood, the secret, underground lives of the fungi are exposed by the sudden profusion of their fruiting bodies. On the ground, the brightly coloured yellow and red toadstools of the Russula family grow in the company of the deliciously edible, slatey-mauve variety. Inside the wood, on dead or moribund birches, I can easily find razor-strop fungi. This bracket fungus, with its brown top-side and white ventral surface, has more than one use for the practical countryman. As the name suggests, it was once used for honing razors and, so I am told, it is good for making your own corn plasters. As I have no foot problems, I have found only one use for it, kindling fires. Another tree parasite is the honey-tuft fungus. Close examination of an infected trunk will reveal black, bootlace-type strands, called rhizomorphs, together with the white, thread-like mycelium which actually glow in the dark.

No sooner do we begin handling the Strone sheep than it starts to rain. And how it rains. In no time at all I can feel water running down my neck, down my arms, down my back and even down the sheuch of my arse. My boots begin to fill from the inside. A spring erupts inside the first handling pen and a small burn begins to flow the entire length of the fank.

Spate waters from the lochans, burns, and black, mysterious, allegedly bottomless high mountain pools pour in their hundreds over cataracts and through rocky defiles into the glens below. This place is, surely, well named. Strone is the diminutive of the Gaelic *Strongalvaltrie* – 'headland of the rapid burn'. The rain rips down on the teeth of the strengthening winds. The Strone burns boils out, white, far into the dark, storm-lashed loch.

We do all we can with the sodden sheep, before hurrying home to a hot bath, dry clothes and warm hearth.

In the comfort of Glengyle, Maggi and I have a hand of canasta. I am no great shakes as a card player although, in the old days, shepherds were known to have walked prodigious distances to pit their wits against their neighbours. One card in particular intrigues me, the nine of diamonds, otherwise known as 'The Curse of Scotland' – and not without good reason.

During the reign of Queen Mary (1542–67), one George Campbell attempted to steal the crown from Edinburgh Castle. He failed but did manage to abstract and make off with nine valuable diamonds. Such a crippling tax was imposed upon the people in order to try and replace them that the nine diamonds became known as the nation's curse. Even today in some parts of Scotland, the card is still called George Campbell. The curse did not end there, and strangely the Campbells were once again involved. The order for the Massacre of Glencoe carried out on 13 February 1692, when men from the Campbell clan slaughtered practically every Macdonald, man, woman and child in that snow-mantled glen, was signed by the Secretary of State for Scotland, the Earl of Stair, whose coat of arms bore nine diamonds. Fifty-four years on, in the bloody wake of the Battle of Culloden, the Duke of Cumberland wrote his victory despatch on the nine of diamonds. The butcher was obviously fully aware of the significance of this card.

I seem to have drawn too many nines of diamonds. No wonder I lose yet again.

The weather moderates somewhat and we are able to finish the work in hand at Strone. The stock ewes, hoggs and cast ewes are all efficiently dealt with before men and dogs move on in turn to tackle the Letter and Edra hirsels.

We wage a continuous campaign against the elements. Autumnal mists and squally showers hamper our progress. A mantle of mist over the hilltops makes gathering Edra impossible for the moment. Iain decides to send me to Milngavie to bring home the 180 tups for dipping. We will need to make two runs. Andy Donaldson drives the float down the winding road, and soon we emerge from the highland mists and enjoy a nice, sunny day. A typical pattern of contrasting weather on either side of the highland boundary fault, especially at this time of year. Mona and Gail sleep away the miles, curled up on the floor at my feet.

The fully-laden journey back to the hills takes ages; the lorry finally grinds up the Duke's Pass, returning us to the realm of mirk, mist and fog. At Edra, Iain, Charlie, Alec, Jock and John handle this lot while Andy and I set off for the second load.

Any horns that have grown too tight to the head will be cut

back to make room for the animal to chew his food in comfort. Overgrown toes will be neatly trimmed. Finally, teeth will be checked for soundness and the whole batch dosed and dipped. Then it is back to the rich grass of Milngavie for another couple of months of the easy life.

When Andy and I return with the rest of the tups, we somehow manage to bring the fine weather back with us. These sudden clearances are very welcome, and those which come after dark are often accompanied by frost. Already the bracken is turning to its winter hue.

The Edra sheep are duly gathered in, handled and then the stock ewes returned to the hill. Their season is over. The Edra fank is tidied up and swept clean for the last time this summer; the dipper is drained and left empty. We move on up the loch.

True to its name, the lower slopes of Coilachra abound with groves of plump, ripening hazel nuts. But, with the Coilachra hoggs and cast ewes securely held below the cross fence since the last handling, there is no need for us to stop here and now we come directly to Portnellan.

It was from this place, 'the port for the island', that boats set off for the nearby Black Island. As the summer growth on the conifers darkens into its winter, frost-hardy state, the island takes on the much deeper tone which is responsible for the name.

The island is practically uninhabited. A few small mammals, including a family of moles, and the usual assortment of birds enjoy the peace and tranquillity. The absence of sheep is testified to by the lush vegetation and the presence of tustan, a small shrub belonging to the St John's wort family. I have no evidence of anyone ever living on the Black Isle, but I do know that for eleven days in November 1716 it was the rather uncomfortable home of John Graham, Lord of Killearn, who was marooned there by Rob Roy MacGregor.

Graham, second cousin and factor to the Duke of Montrose, had, four years earlier almost to the day, been responsible for the brutal multiple rape and total degradation of Rob's wife, Mary, during her eviction from Craigroyston. When Rob returned home some time later, he found his house and steading nothing more than a smouldering ruin. Mary had fled. Rob followed and eventually found her amongst kin in Argyllshire. Mary, in her distraught state, refused to return to him; she felt sullied and could no longer live as his wife.

MacGregor swore vengeance like he had never sworn before. Killearn would pay dearly – probably with his life. The factor, fully aware of his peril, made sure that he was well protected. He only ventured forth in the midst of a well-armed body and never went near any place where the wild Highland men might have pounced. Rob, however, was nothing if not a patient man; besides, he had other problems. Following the collapse of the '15 rebellion, Jacobites everywhere were having a tough time. Glengyle House itself had been put to the torch. About this time, Graham began to relax his vigilance; after all, rumour had it that MacGregor had fled to Ireland.

On 19 November, the factor was engaged in collecting the farm rents in the small inn of Chapellaroch, near Gartmore. The door crashed open. Rob strode into the room, closely followed by a large number of clansmen.

Some years before, in this same room, Rob had relieved the factor of the Duke's rents by the simple expedient of pretending to be at the head of a strong raiding party. In fact, he had but one faithful retainer with him. That evening, after tarrying a while, treating the tenants to food and drink, the outlaw pair had ridden off laughing and loudly enjoying the jest at the factor's expense.

Tonight, Rob was in deadly earnest. Not one of Graham's men even contemplated drawing a weapon. Rob made sure that every tenant had in his possession a valid receipt; then checked the monies before sweeping the whole lot into a leather satchel with his broad hand. It was at this point that John Graham's blood must have run cold. As MacGregor sat to write a letter to the Duke of Montrose asking a ransom for his factor's safe return, it suddenly became clear that this was to be no simple robbery. By now the hapless man was terrified.

The innkeeper's son was despatched to His Grace with the demand, on the factor's own horse, while Graham was bound hand and foot, bundled onto a sure-footed Highland pony and carried off to the vastness of Loch Katrine, there to be incarcerated on the Black Isle. Rob immediately sent for Mary. After four long years, revenge would be hers.

Day in and day out, north-westerly November gales lashed the island. For the Laird of Killearn, the only shelter would be that built by his own hand; his food only what he could forage for himself. Escape was impossible – being a gentleman, John Graham could not swim.

It was 11 days before Mary arrived at Portnellan, the family home while Glengyle was being rebuilt, 11 days and nights in which Graham must have bitterly regretted that fateful day at Craigroyston as he contemplated what might now be in store for him. A boat with two men was sent to the island. When they returned, they brought with them a dishevelled, bedraggled, half-starved, snivelling wretch, the sight of which melted away whatever hardness there was in Mary's heart. As she looked down at the wreck of humanity shivering at her feet, who can tell what thoughts, what awful pictures were going through her mind.

When MacGregor asked what was to be done, Mary could only whisper four barely audible words, 'Let him go, Rob.' MacGregor could not believe his own ears. He surely would have killed the factor in cold blood, but Mary prevailed by quietly pointing out that in that case Rob would be no better than this dog, Graham. Anyway there was the ransom. Having received no word from Montrose, MacGregor opened up the satchel and again counted out the money. The total came to £3,227 2s 8d scots (£286 18s 6d sterling), exactly the sum demanded in the note. Rob deemed the ransom paid in full; gave Graham a meal, a receipt, and sent him packing.

Rob and Mary were fully reconciled. Nine months later, a fourth son, Robin Og, was born.

Alec, Jock and I prepare to gather the west side of Portnellan. Alec heads away fully half an hour before I need to go out from Glengyle. He has to go right over into the Braes of Balquhidder to bring out any of his sheep foraging down the back of the hill. On my way out, I make sure that any Portnellan ewes lingering on Glengyle are hunted homewards. After 20 minutes or so, I reach the top of the Wee Hill and, looking down, I can see Jock McDougall fighting his way up through the vast stand of bracken. He looks as though he is swimming the breast-stroke, uphill.

On the other side of Portnellan, Iain, Charlie and young John will be making their way out towards the Hungry Loch. Overhead, the 'tsip' calls from a loose flock of meadow pipits tell me they are on their erratic way south.

A cut of Portnellan sheep runs in around the shoulder of Stob an Duibhe and heads straight for Glengyle. I have been expecting them and Dust and Gail are already in position. The leading ewe spots the dogs and stops, uncertain about what to do next. The long line of sheep bunches and mills about before the leader decides to retrace her steps. The others follow. Alec hoves into view and at his shout the sheep once again alter course, this time going the way we intend.

With everyone at the right spot, three men on either side of the hill, the net begins to tighten. Just as the sheep begin to think that they are getting away from us, Jock appears and uses his dogs to turn them down a sheuch in the rocks and on downwards towards Loch Katrine. Alec waits behind to hold the sheep coming forward from the other cut. Jock and I drive our sheep off the hill and along the road to the Glengyle fank. The rest of the flock will come down close behind us.

As Jock and I wait for the others to come in, I notice a few owl pellets in the long grass beneath one of the old beech trees. These pellets are made up from the indigestible parts of the owl's food. From the fur, feathers, bone, teeth and the like, it is possible to deduce exactly what the main ingredients of the owl's last meal were. These pellets, from our resident tawny owls, consist mainly of the remains of short-tailed voles, with a good sprinkling of purple pieces of elytra from ground beetles. Some of them even contain living moth larvae. In nature, nothing goes to waste.

We work the Portnellan sheep steadily through the fank, stopping now and then, at the appointed hour, to be fed at Isa McLellan's table. I would not say that there was any element of competition between the wives on the lochside, but wherever we draw in our chairs, we are faced with a veritable feast.

The Department of Agriculture has decided that it is time to take a check on the number of breeding sheep kept on the Loch Katrine hirsels. Mr Hope is the man sent out from Stirling to make an official count of the stock ewes before they are returned to the hill. This is to make sure that we are not claiming hill sheep subsidy on sheep we do not have.

Alec Scott's float stands waiting, backed up to the loading pen of the Edra shed. The Strone hoggs are about to embark for their winter pasture. They were dosed and dipped at the Strone handling but, that day, they were far too wet to innoculate. Now their wool is all fluffed up and the skins are dry and clean which makes it easier to maintain aseptic standards. A 2 ml booster vaccination of Covexine 8 is given subcutaneously behind one shoulder and 1 ml of Louping-ill vaccine behind the other.

Only the Strone, Letter and Edra hirsels are troubled by Louping-ill, a virus disease mainly affecting sheep. It is transmitted by ticks and, throughout the country, is responsible for many more sheep losses than foxes and dogs put together. The virus is introduced by an infected tick sucking blood. After a period of one to three weeks, the virus may invade and damage the nervous system of the sheep, resulting in the spectacular symptoms associated with Louping-ill or 'trembling' as it is sometimes called. Violent muscular spasms are followed by a period of excitability, uncertain gait and, finally, inability to stand. Death rapidly follows. Louping-ill can also affect cattle, goats, dogs, grouse and man. I am lucky that Glengyle is free of this nasty disease.

We take a spell from the sheep. It is cattle round-up time. Maggi takes a stroll up the glen with me, to bring in the herd from the slopes of Ben Ducteach. Beside a small tributary, running down into the Lag a'Chuirn ('hollow of the cairn'), are the ruins of a few small buildings, one of which is said to bear the name of Tigh na Cuirte, the courthouse. It was here that cattle thieves were tried. The Lag a'Chuirn was on the line of an important drove-road out of Argyll and, judging by the need for a courthouse, much of the trade passing this way must have been of the illicit kind.

A kestrel hovers, head to the wind. Kestrels, along with other birds of prey, suffered a dramatic decline in population during the two decades following 1950. This was due to harmful chemicals being widely used in agriculture. Today the situation has been greatly improved by better ecological understanding all round, and the kestrel population of the British Isles is put at more than 100,000 pairs.

Maggi and I watch this reddish-brown female, her back and tail darkly barred. Kestrels regularly hover when hunting, although sometimes they will hunt from a branch or fence post. In the strong breeze, the wings are almost motionless, the tail feathers fanned out. The body may move but the head remains absolutely still.

The kestrel glides down, silently. Prey has been sighted in the grass below. Suddenly her wings come together above her back, her talons extend and she drops onto her victim.

Maggi finds a toad with a neat hole in the top of its head. It is still very much alive, although it is walking in a slow and unsure manner. It looks for all the world as though it has been shot. On closer examination, it becomes apparent that this is the result of nasal botfly infestation, the larvae having bored their way to freedom through the skull. Sadly, it will die quite soon.

Dust forces the cows into the cattle pens. Charlie has walked his cows to Glengyle, too. Both lots of calves are separated from their mothers and are floated down the road to Edra. We leave the sloe-eyed cows bawling for their lost children.

Inside the big Edra shed, the Strone and Edra calves are already penned. The animals are first divided into stirks and heifers before being drawn into smaller lots, matched according to colour and size. Every calf is then given a numbered metal ear-tag, with the herd number on the reverse side. These numbers are carefully recorded and written into the Livestock Movement Book together with each animal's destination, in this case, Stirling market. In the event of an outbreak of one of the virulent, 'notifiable' diseases anywhere in the land, all possible contacts can quickly be traced through the movement books.

The calves are bedded down with plenty of straw to keep them clean. Hay, too, is provided in great abundance; they must look plump and full at the sale tomorrow.

The night air over the loch echoes with plaintive cow-calls.

Next morning, all three floats are on the move early, as calves are ferried the long road from Corriearklet and Edra into Stirling. The noise inside the market is incredible: 3,000 calves are calling incessantly for their milky mothers now far away. I hope the roof is on securely. We off-load the calves and herd them to our allotted pens. Conversation is impossible. All around us, stockmen are busy brushing and grooming and spraying and polishing. Gleaming, smart beasts catch the eye at every turn.

With our calves settled in their pens, we take refuge in the relative calm of the dairy shed where there is a show taking place for the handpicked calves. Most of these beasts have been receiving special treatment for quite a while. In here the trimming, washing and brushing is augmented by oiling and powdering. No effort is spared in order to show off their animals to their greatest advantage.

Judging can never be easy. Eventually the prize tickets are handed out. Bob Morgan, the head shepherd at Corriearklet, has a red card, first place in the Shepherds' Class.

The bells ring, adding to the clamour, to announce the start of the sale. The calves in the first row of pens are turned out into the passage, and the long, long, procession to the ring gets underway. The Loch Katrine shepherds crowd into the ringside seats to watch the early lots go under the hammer. The price pattern is soon established. Our calves are halfway down the catalogue so we have time to go and get a cup of tea. Probably time for several cups of tea. Days at the market can seem very long, especially if you are drawn at the end of a big sale.

Eventually the gates are opened and our calves start up the long passages towards the ring. I can see two Glengyle calves amongst the top draw of stirks and my big roan heifer has made the top heifer draw too. The rest of my calves are all mixed through the other lots.

In the ring, under the bright lights, the calves are walked around. The auctioneer takes bids from all sides. The hammer falls and out they go, on their way to a new home. Lot after lot comes in, stirks first, then heifers, then it is all over for us. Time to relax and go for a good meal in the market restaurant before heading back to the hills.

The late broods of swallows have left Glengyle in response to the invisible signal that tells them it is time to begin their perilous six thousand mile journey to South Africa. Solitary jays rustle amongst the dense, browning oak foliage, searching for any acorns missed by the grey squirrels, and flying away to bury their prize in a place they are quite likely to forget – an ideal method of seed dispersal.

The *Sir Walter Scott* has steamed her way down the loch for the last time this summer and the fishing boats have been taken out of the water for the closed season. There are still a few tourists about, but there is a definite feel of autumn in the air. The rowan trees are hung about with scarlet and gold pennants. Beneath the lime and birches, a few fallen leaves are stirred into life by the wind.

Autumn is the main time of year when I feed my bees, to ensure that they have sufficient reserves to see them through the winter months. The weather and general nectar-gathering conditions of late have been so poor that the bees are rather short of stores. A hive with about 20 lbs of honey on the combs will require an additional 20 lbs of sugar, given as a syrup before the beginning of October. At this time, I also insulate my hives, using a thick layer of oven-dried sphagnum moss sandwiched between wire mesh below and plywood above. The moss will absorb any condensation produced during the winter, keeping my bees snug and dry. We reach the last Glengyle gather of the year. Iain has already been on the telephone to enquire about the weather at this end of the loch. The sky is overcast and there is a touch of mist playing around the Square Rocks, but I am pretty sure it will clear away. The sheep themselves usually prove good guides. Today they are grazing with their heads to the wind. If they were the other way round, with their tails to the wind, it would soon be raining. I tell Iain that it looks fair and that I am heading away. Collecting my dogs about me, I make for the Coireasach Burn.

The bracken is collapsing. The sheep tracks are almost impassable, criss-crossed by gigantic, legless pteridophytes which grab you round your ankles. Heavy overnight dew makes it absolutely essential to wear a complete set of waterproofs, but even so the dampness permeates through my protective clothing. My dogs look as though they have been through a cloud-burst. At last I beat my way free of the saturated vegetation. The dogs shake themselves all over me, shower after shower cascading into the air. That over, it is safe for me to peel off my sweaty over-garments. The cool mountain air prickles my skin as I get my breath back.

Climbing on, I quickly warm up again. Iain, Alec and John arrive at the foot of the burn, and begin battling their way through the tangled undergrowth behind me. I know just how they are feeling. Jock will be faced with the same problem around the Castle Rock but Charlie, walking out from his house, will be able to keep on clean ground all the way to the top of the Wee Hill.

The Glengyle stags have striking, clean heads, the velvet having been completely rubbed from their new set of antlers. As September gives way to October, they begin to get restless. The occasional distant roaring heralds the approach of the rutting season.

I have to go deep down into the Braes of Balquhidder to take some of my own sheep in hand. One of them is a cunning old roughie with a whole-lugged tup lamb at foot. She had not been in all summer, and has no intention of coming home this time if she can help it. Having made straight for her hiding place under a bank in a steep-sided burn, she stands defying Mona. I go down and give the dog a bit of assistance. Once the ewe and lamb start moving again, I allow them plenty of time. Gradually we regain our own ground. From here on, it is no time at all before the low-end sheep are being steered through the dreaded bracken, leaving a well trampled swath for the shepherds to follow, and turned into the fank.

Maggie has the venison and vegetable soup on the table as soon as we walk in the door. This is followed by roast lamb with mint sauce, creamed potatoes and cabbage. Steaming bread and butter pudding, tea and biscuits finish off the meal.

Replete, we return to the fank and shed the hoggs from the ewes. I think we all need a little time to let our food settle before going out to tackle the high-end of Glengyle.

Alec and I take the Land Rover out Eves Road to Ben Ducteach. The day has improved, the sun begins to break through the cloud cover. I toil my way up to the top of the Ben and tell myself that it is keeping me fit for my rugby. Alec and I turn the Ben Ducteach sheep out the way, before sweeping them around the head of the glen and working the whole lot back along the north side. I am enjoying a blink of warm sunshine. Gail is in particularly good voice. She runs out fine and wide up the Parlan Hill, barking all the way to hunt the sheep down off the top. I have never heard her better.

I meet up with Iain at the Fairy Hill. Below me is the Fairies Meadow where some long-forgotten battle took place. The imposing Beinn Chabhair ('hill of help'), on the opposite side of my neighbour's glen, must have been from where timely assistance arrived. Iain and I turn the sheep down into Bealach nan Corp. The first cut of sheep are already on their way down Eves Road. Iain and I follow homeward with our lot while Alec brings up the rear with the Land Rover. The sun has been swallowed by the clouds. The afternoon has turned quite cool.

With the high-end sheep standing safely in the paddock below the fank, we hurry down to the house to see what Maggi has cooked up for our tea, but there is no need for anyone to tell us. Before we open the door, the delicious aroma of frying ham assails our senses. The top of the Rayburn is covered with pans of sizzling sausages, eggs, bacon, black pudding and crisp fried bread. Home-baked cake and gallons of tea complete the proceedings.

After breakfast at home, the team the next morning assembles in the Glengyle fank. The high-end hoggs are shed off and joined up with their neighbours off the low-end. The whole group are vaccinated, dosed and fitted with a yellow plastic ear-tag. Finally, the hoggs are dipped. Almost before they have stopped dripping, Andy Donaldson arrives to float them away to their wintering at Harthill but they will need to be a good bit drier before we can safely load them up.

Anyway, it is time for tea. So while we wait, we can all adjourn to the house for cups of tea and hot buttered toast with honey or marmalade. Six shepherds, a labourer, a lorry driver and Mr Hope, who has come to count my stock ewes. The place is full.

We load Andy and send him on his way to distant Lanarkshire. Then we turn our attention to the ewes. The five-year-old cast ewes, those with the green tags, are drawn out. So are any ewes with a red keel mark on the back of their heads, a sign that some-one had found a broken mouth or damaged vessel. The remaining stock ewes are carefully scrutinised in case there are any that for one reason or another are unsuitable for breeding.

Finally, the stock ewes are dosed, keeled (scarlet on the left hip) and dipped. Mr Hope, in his official capacity, counts the damp sheep out of the dripper pens.

Then, using Mona, Gail and Boot, I put my ewes back to the hill for the winter.

We are rather late going in for lunch. Maggi does not actually say anything but it cannot be easy keeping food for eight people hot enough to serve, without the risk of it spoiling. It is just that we wanted to finish the dipping before coming in. A herd's wife of bygone days used to serve the meal at the precise time it had been ordered. If the men were not there, it was too bad. Many a time, when they eventually deigned to appear, they had to break through the grease on the surface of their soup. Maggi's carrot and rice soup, thankfully, is scalding hot. This is followed up with the shepherd's favourite – mince, tatties and chopped neeps. For dessert there is blackberry and apple crumble with thick, yellow custard. And, of course, tea, more tea and biscuits.

Later, whilst going the rounds to check that my parks holding in the cast ewes are secure, I accidentally disturb a somewhat som-nolent snake nestling amongst the tumbled down stones of an old dyke. The early hibernating habit of the adder, Scotland's only species, is good news for all small rodents. If bitten, the diaphragm of a mouse goes into immediate spasm and the animal dies from asphyxia within ten seconds.

Alec and Maggi are on hand to help me sort out my cast ewes and prepare them for the sale which takes place next Monday. From a total of 147, I draw out 34 second-quality sheep and eight red-headed 'feeders'. This leaves me with a top draw of 105 select ewes.

A heavy curtain of rain moves menacingly down the glen

towards us. Smartly we move inside, under cover of the smearing shed where we can handle the sheep in the dry. Alec and I each catch one ewe at a time, carefully dressing their heads and tails with a pair of handshears. While we are holding them, Maggi doses them, and then paints a bright band around one of the horns; tops on the left, seconds on the right.

By the time we have worked through them all, the rain has passed over. Alec keeps the sheep coming forward and I heave them, unceremoniously, into the dipper. Maggi plunges every ewe beneath the surface with a dipping-pole. Then it is back to the parks with them until Monday morning.

The old smearing shed is very handy in an emergency, not that we use it very often these days. Before the introduction of protective dips, sheep had their coats smeared in order to keep out the winter weather. Smearing was done in a similar manner to bathing, by the shepherd sitting with a sheep on a slatted stool, but with a thicker mixture of tar and butter made from excess ewes' milk which was worked into the wool. The fleece was parted into sheds along the body, each shed being about an inch from the next. In this laborious manner, the entire body was covered. A good man may have managed a score of sheep in a day.

By about 1885 dipping had all but superseded smearing, although upland flockmasters persisted in the old ways much longer.

Alec Scott arrives at Glengyle with his headlights still on. He backs his three-decked float to the entrance of the loading pen, and drops the tailgate. The ewes are run on, 16 or 17 to each compartment. The morning is quite dry so the sheep up on the open top deck should arrive in Stirling looking their best, dry skinned and well fluffed up.

The sale at Stirling's Kildean Market is vast. Pen after pen of cast ewes stretch away into the distance. Last year, there were 10,269 ewes sold, and judging from what I can see, there will be as many again today.

Every ewe here is guaranteed as being 'uncrossed', a rather quaint custom which surprisingly still persists. It used to be

believed that once a pure-bred ewe, or cow or bitch for that matter, had been mated with a sire of a different breed, any future
progeny would be tainted by that crossing. Perhaps some people
still believe in it.

My top ewes are looking very good and have been attracting
a lot of interest. Iain and I stir them around the sawdust-littered
ring, showing them off to their best advantage. The bidding goes
on and on: past £20... on past £22... arrives at £23... and the
hammer cracks down at £23.10. Top price of the year for the
entire lochside. They were sold to Mr Maitland from Comrie who
also bought my old ewes last year. A man obviously well pleased
with the Glengyle stock, he will breed from them for one or two
more seasons.

After the first really hard frost, the scarlet rowan berries,
which are hanging heavy on the boughs, are ready to be picked
and turned into jars of jelly. At this time of year, it is often a race
as to which comes first, the necessary night of frost or the marauding flocks of fieldfares and redwings. If Maggi gets first chance,

A fieldfare on his favourite rowan

she always leaves masses for the birds, but if the voracious hordes wing their way from the north in front of her, then there is nothing left for us bar the stalks.

The Coilachra cast ewes and hoggs, like the hazel nuts, have gone. But the shepherds have not quite come to the end of the road; we still have the stock to attend to. This is the last gather of the season. Charlie is in jovial form in the fank as we work through his ewes. All day long, the sky overhead is busy with formations of flying geese. Below, the first whooper swans of winter have settled on the loch.

The handlings come to an end. Our own particular harvest of lambs and wool has been gathered in. At the end of the day, each shepherd makes his way quietly back to his own fireside for the winter. Things were rather different in the old days when the end of the harvest was a time of great festivity.

The Highland harvest was always late. Because of this, it was often found that the early ripening of the top grains on the stalk meant that cometh the reaper those fat grains were awanting. The common belief was that they had been claimed by the fairies. The relief felt when the last of the remaining grain was safely harvested must have been enormous. The survival of the community through the impending winter had almost been assured. However, certain rituals had to be performed in order to make sure that the 'charm of plenty' bestowed on them by the little people would not be broken. The very last stand of corn was ceremoniously cut by the youngest girl on the field, and this sheaf was tied into a 'Maiden' and adorned with blue ribbons. The Maiden would then be given to the youngest boy to be carried home; he would have to take care never to let it touch the ground or the spell would be lost.

The Maiden was hung on the wall inside the farmhouse, and a harvest supper followed. A special cup, containing a mixture of oatmeal, ale, whisky and a silver ring would be shared among the company. Whoever got the silver ring, if single, would be the next person to be married. At the mid-winter rejoicing for the return of the sun, the Maiden was taken down from the wall and ceremoniously fed to the livestock.

Our own harvest at Glengyle continues unabated. In this time of plenty, Maggi lays in supplies ready for the hard months to come. Kitchen cupboards conceal jars of dried herbs, honey, fruit preserves and assorted pickles. Amongst the lamb, venison and trout in the freezer, there are containers of glaciated fruit, vegetables and fungi. Supper tonight is a large plate, piled high and a mouth-watering mountain of freshly picked, fried holatus toadstools with onions.

It is not only food that Maggi has gathered in. Any day now, the house will slowly fill up with steam, cauldrons will bubble and plop on the stove and Rayburn, and windows will cry down the inside as Maggi pokes, prods and stirs in the natural dyes for her wool. Fleeces will magically change from natural white into various shades of red, yellow, gold and brown, depending upon which lichen, leaf, root, bark or berry has been added to the brew.

It is interesting to note that the ancient setts of Scottish tartan were all woven in a limited range of dark toned colours. After the introduction of synthetic dyes, things brightened up and the more gaudy dress tartans appeared on the scene.

The craft of wool dying is as old as history, maybe even older. The domestication of sheep goes back twelve thousand years to the times of presettled, Mesolithic agriculture. Dogs, too, would have developed from the purely hunting strains into herding strains at this juncture. Five thousand years later, sheep had become fully domesticated, and the quality of the meat and wool gradually increased. The invading Romans introduced us to long-tailed, white woolled sheep and spinning and weaving became widespread. These sheep have almost entirely swamped our older, smaller, darker, short-tailed stock now only found on the Hebridean and Shetland Islands.

Soft organ music drifts on the sunlit evening air, across the glen and back again. It is our Harvest Thanksgiving service at Inversnaid church. The building was erected in 1895 and is dedicated to St Kentigerna, the daughter of one of the Kings of Ireland who came to spread the word of God amongst the heathen Picts. The Scots were always Christian but, at that time, were restricted to lands in the far south-west of the country. Apart from her contribution to missionary work, St Kentigerna is revered as the mother of St Fillan, the monk of the glowing arm and the miracle of Bannockburn.

Each of us listens to the words of our minister. I truly give thanks to God for his bounteousness, and raise the song of Harvest-home.

Inkcaps and a wee mouse

Red Sky at Night

THE FIRST SNOW of winter has crept in overnight and morning finds the hill tops surrounding Glengyle capped in soft white. Ptarmigan, in their half-changed plumage, sit invisible to all. The ewes, however, are keeping to the higher ground, not minding the ephemeral arctic conditions, foraging upon the yellowing pastures before the hard frosts burn them off completely. Icy fingers have already touched the bilberry leaves amongst the grasses to shades of fiery red. Now that the last of the lambs are off the hill and the milk dried off, putting on body condition as quickly as possible is of paramount importance to each ewe; they must be prepared for the hard times to come.

At the end of each gather, I am left with a number of stragglers belonging to various neighbours. Once everybody has finished gathering his own ground, arrangements are put in hand to exchange prisoners. I have already sent sheep home to Ardleish, Beinglas, Keilator and the Braes o' Balquhidder, and received a load of Glengyle wanderers in return. All that I have left in the straggler pen now is a handful of ewes which belong across the glen, on the Dhu. I set off to walk these five sheep the short distance home, the way all stragglers used to be taken. I use Gail and the newest addition to my kennel, her great granddaughter Finn. At five months old, this pup is showing a great deal of promise.

Having crossed the bridge over our march burn, onto the Dhu ground, I see Chick Campbell coincidentally heading my way with seven Glengyle sheep. We meet at Eves Road-end and have a crack about things in general, as shepherds tend to do. The dogs look to the sheep. Chick has his old Craig with him, a dog that has won him a trial or two recently. Perhaps Finn, in the fullness of time, will be as good. We swap sheep and return homeward with our own charges. A few lying leaves from the limes and birches along the road are stirred into life by a quiet breeze.

The nights are noticeably drawing in now that we are on the dark side of the September equinox. A hunter's moon, full in the sky, floodlights the landscape and unrolls a moonwalk carpet right across the ink black depths of Loch Katrine. On the hillside, rutting stags, antlers glinting, roar into the night to warn us usurpers away from their harems of hinds. Around the house, bats are on the wing, swooping and feeding up on the last of the summer midges and any other winged insect that their high-frequency, echo-location signals pick up. They are laying down enough fat reserves to see them safely through their long winter sleep. For exactly the same reason, below, on the ground, hedgehogs are hunting, snuffling amongst the dying vegetation, preying voraciously upon a wide variety of insects and small animals. Although fat black slugs appear to be their favourite food, they will sometimes tackle something much more enterprising.

A few weeks ago, a local shepherd and his wife were rudely awakened from their slumbers by the alarm of a brooding hen below their window. On investigation, they discovered the mother hen doing her utmost to drive away a hedgehog which was trying to get at her young chicks. The shepherd, a kindly man, removed the hedgehog from the coop and set it free some distance away. Satisfied that all was well again, the good people returned to bed. Hardly had their heads touched the pillow when pandemonium broke out once more. The hedgehog it seems was determined to have chicken for his supper. This time, before help could arrive, it had succeeded in seizing a small chick and was making off with his victim. The robber was promptly dispatched to continue his hunting in the Great Hunting Ground in the sky while the injured chick was taken inside for immediate first aid. I saw the unfortunate creature before it died. It had been quite badly mauled.

Although one of the common causes of sheep mortality at this time of year is now easily controlled by one of the components of the Covexine 8 vaccine, it was not always so. In the early winter, it was not unknown for shepherds in certain districts to lose a number of sheep, often yearlings, always in seemingly good condition. Such losses are still associated with the onset of frosty nights and are caused by 'braxy', a bacterial disease which attacks the fourth stomach of the sheep. The infected animal dies very quickly, sometimes in a matter of hours. A tell-tale sign is blood-flecked froth around the nose and mouth of the dead sheep. Shepherds used to cure the mutton from braxied ewes in barrels of salt.

October is the time of tup sales. All over the country, farmers, flockmasters and shepherds journey to market places big and small, the all-important task of finding replacement tups foremost in their mind. Stirling's opening Show and Sale of Blackface shearling tups and tup lambs is held at Kildean on the first Saturday of the month. I arrive early at the mart and while Maggi takes Jamie and Toria on to their minirugby training, I spend the morning meeting people and looking over the tups that have been brought out for the sale. There are over a thousand shearlings and more than 700 tup lambs entered in the catalogue.

The official judging took place yesterday afternoon and although the prize money is not large, the kudos is considerable and the competition keen. The owner of an animal lifting one of the first-place trophies pockets a mere £2.10, while a red card for the best pen of five makes their owner richer by a breathtaking £5.25.

Every man here has his own idea as to exactly the type of animal he is looking for to improve his stock. Often they will back their judgement with hard cash; the record price for a Blackface tup is £21,000. Some men prefer the short-woolled, Newton Stewart type of tup; others, including myself, tend towards the heavier-coated Perth strain. From here on opinions as to the merit of this or that particular point can diverge considerably.

Personally, I like my Blackface tup to be well set on his legs and have sound feet. This should enable him to travel long distances both in search of food and ewes that have come into season. His head, that all-important factor which denotes Breed Character, must be strongly horned, broad between the eyes and completely free of wool, being covered with short, glossy black hair; however, I do like to see a bold white flash on his forehead, either pure white or containing a small number of distinct black dots. Colours must be distinct and not run into each other. The mouth is to be wide, with the teeth squarely meeting the upper pad. His neck must be strong and at least as long as the span of my hand. The back should be broad and level, with a good spring of rib. If he fulfills all these qualifications and also gives an impression of character, alertness and strength, then he is the tup for me.

Every year, we keep a small number of home-bred tup lambs for our own use although, for obvious reasons, they can never go back onto their own ground. The rest of our replacements are bought in by John Young who is engaged in an advisory capacity by my employers. As the Glengyle shepherd, unfortunately I have no say in the matter. Still, I always enjoy looking at good quality livestock.

Maggi returns to pick me up in time for me to get to the rugby club for lunch, a hot pie washed down with cold Guinness. My team looks like making its usual last minute mad dash to our away fixture. While I prop up the bar, I detail my tight-head prop to tick off the names on the team sheet and collect the £1 match fee which will finance our après game refreshments. Eventually 15 able bodies and one lone supporter are crammed into a number of cars and we speed off in the general direction of Greenock, to the west of Glasgow.

The pitch of Greenock Wanderers 3rd XV is down on the windswept waterfront, and here we suffer our first defeat of the season, six points to ten. And how we suffer. As our blood slowly thickens, we see a promising six-point lead whittled away by the north wind and an equally determined, and obviously well-acclimatised opposition. At half-time, I suspect that the referee is going down with hypothermia. But it is late in the game when their hooker fails to catch the six-figure line-out code, called into the face of the wind by his pack-leader, and asks for a repeat that something finally snaps. The man with the whistle lets out a numbed cry about being damned cold and getting a damn sight colder, and awards us a kickable penalty on the grounds that Wanderers have delayed the throw-in. Needless to say, the wind carries the kick and our hopes well away from the target.

Back in the blood-tingling warmth of the Wanderers' club house, the supporter – who disappeared from the scene after sharing our half-time oranges – seems to think the final score is six-nil to County; he has even telephoned our result back to Stirling. He assures me that he had watched the entire second half from the window seat of the bar. I put him right and he explains that Wanderers must have kicked their two penalties and scored a try while he was at the bar ordering the one drink that had lasted until the final whistle. I certainly don't know what game he was watching.

The dark road home to the hills is alive with migrating frogs and toads as they make their way to their winter retreats. I take care to avoid as many as possible and hope it is only beech mast which crunches under the wheels of the Land Rover.

The two big wedders which I intend to put into my freezer to tide us over the winter are about as well fleshed as they are going to be on the grass that is left. They are certainly fit to kill and I reckon that they ought to be passed by the meat grader and qualify for the subsidy paid on graded sheep. The idea behind this subsidy, known as the Sheep Variable Premium Scheme, is to encourage a steady flow of lamb onto the market, especially early in the season. The lower sale ring price paid for young lambs is compensated for by a proportionately higher subsidy per unit body weight. I expect my wedders to weigh in at about 40 lbs each, dead weight. In order to claim the subsidy, I do not kill my own sheep, but take them to the abattoir at Dunblane where they are slaughtered and graded. Alasdair Beaton, a local butcher, collects my carcases for me, cuts them up and freezes the meat. The payment I will receive will more than cover the costs of this service and leave me a little in hand to buy some extra winter feed for my sheep.

As usual, I collect the skins and take them home for curing. I use an old recipe, given to me by a Shetland shepherd: steep for two weeks in a solution containing salt, saltpetre and alum. This is followed by a couple of weeks stretched tightly on a frame, to enable the skin to dry naturally. Finally, the skin side is dressed with a wire brush and the fleece combed into fluffiness. This pair of skins, one black, one white, are twins from our black ewe, Sunday, and will add extra comfort to my old armchair this winter.

The foliage on our deciduous trees has become an arresting

display of pyrotechnics. The coloration on the wind-stirred beeches varies from lemon to russet to deepest foxy-red. Beneath the shedding chestnut tree, at the back of the house, the children throw up sticks to knock down conkers; the yellow, multi-fingered leaves lie deep under their feet. Each gentle breath of wind brings a cascade of golden guineas off the birch branches.

It is time to dust off and sharpen my power saw, ready to begin laying in a stockpile of logs for the winter ahead. So many people own power saws that we could soon revert to the conditions of the Middle Ages where, as one bishop writing to a European colleague commented, trees were as scarce as hens' teeth.

Every winter I power my way through vast amounts of wind-felled timber, clearing up a great deal of ground. Come the following backend, I am always surprised to find so much freshly blown wood lying about, mostly birch, pine and oak. I don't even have to go far from the house to get my firewood, and use either the Land Rover or wheel barrow to get it home.

Jamie is busy gathering up all the smaller branches, which I would normally burn, to fuel his Guy Fawkes bonfire which is growing by the day. This is a good time of year for a general clean-up campaign. Fank, steading, house and surrounding grounds are all scoured for combustible rubbish for the coming conflagration.

As I take Tansy to the byre, I notice that the polecat hutch is empty. Maggi must have gone a-rabbitting. She uses her very amenable polecat jill, called Buidhe (say Boo-ee), meaning 'golden coloured'. Buidhe is an efficient little hunter. When introduced into a burrow, she will always try to bring her victim to the surface, in true polecat fashion, inching her way out backwards.

I prefer polecats to the more common ferret which I have found too prone to lying up deep in the ground with its kill. I never dig them out though; I use a simple ploy taught me by my grandfather. I take off my sweater and tie the top, bottom and one sleeve closed. Then I shove the other sleeve down the hole and leave it for 24 hours. Next day, the ferret is invariably found to be curled up, fast asleep, inside the sweater.

I have seen Buidhe sometimes when Maggi has not been quite quick enough to seize the struggling prey before Buidhe releases her hold. The polecat fixes her handler with a beady stare, twitches her mouth and disappears into the dark again after the rabbit that has promptly bolted back down its hole. In no time at all, Maggi will have killed and gutted three or four plump rabbits. She always lets the small ones go free, to grow into bigger ones – if nothing else eats them first. The local foxes don't bother much with rabbit, but our resident buzzards eat little else. The huntresses return home. There will be casseroled rabbit for supper tonight.

A slip of a new moon hangs in the clear sky. A new moon often brings a change in the weather. The glass is steadily rising while the thermometer is falling. A distinct tang of woodsmoke is borne on the crisp night air. Our tawny owls have come out to hunt and a large number of the so-called winter moths are on the wing. At least the males of the species are, the tree-dwelling females being quite flightless. These are the same moths whose plague caterpillars defoliate the oak trees during the early part of the summer.

Brown trout, seeking suitable places to spawn, are running up the burns which feed Loch Katrine. The hens will lay their tiny eggs in fine gravel where they are immediately covered by the white milt from the attendant cock fishes. At a constant water temperature of 6°C, the eggs will take somewhere in the region of 77 days to hatch. Meanwhile, the fallen leaves from the alder trees which line the course of even very small waterways for much of their length, provide excellent food and cover for a multitude of invertebrates upon which the trout fry will feed.

For this, All Hallow's Eve, instead of the usual youth club Friday night of games and bedlam, I have organised something different. Assorted turnip lanterns grin grotesquely in a lighted row, the whole length of the great mantelpiece in Stronachlachar Lodge. Most of the children have come garbed in appropriate costume: witches, warlocks, wizards, ghosts and spectres abound. After the prize giving, there is dookin' for apples; stories in the dark, of the supernatural and things that go bump in the night; and a gruesome game of body-snatchers and dissectors. The children's evening is rounded off by giving everyone a toffee apple to take home.

For Maggi and me, though, the night is still young and we motor into Stirling for the rugby club annual fancy-dress dance. The children are put to bed at Walter and Margaret Kennedy's house, a very handy stone's throw from the club, and Maggi and I will gratefully crash-out here in a few hours' time. We turn up dressed as a couple of aged and decrepit Stirling County Wolfhounds. Maggi has done such a tremendous transformation on herself that it is absolutely ages before anyone tumbles her. I hope someone in selection takes the hint, although, knowing my luck, they will probably select Maggi for the Wolfhounds before me.

I thought the best costume by far was that worn by John 'Sammy' Tucker. I first noticed him sitting quietly in a corner, sipping his pint, dressed in an evening suit. Perhaps not the most original idea for fancy-dress. Then, after about 20 minutes, he got up and walked the length of the room, going towards the gents'. The effect was devastating and I, for one, nearly choked on my Guinness. The back of the suit was neatly cut away to reveal the naughtiest set of ladies red underwear I have seen in my life. Sammy even had fun buying the lingerie. When he had explained that he wanted everything in his size, for the fancy dress, of course, the shop assistant muttered something about them all saying that, Sir.

These modern-day hallowe'en frolics have completely clouded the much older Samhain (pronounced, Sar-whin) festival. Samhain was the winter counterpart of the springtime Beltain, and celebrated the ritual return of the goats, sheep and cattle from their summer haunts, high on the hills, to the ferm-toun. Fires were kindled from four sacred boughs and the animals driven through the thick smoke, so they could breathe the magical properties into their bodies. The cattle would then be housed at one end of the family home, not to see the light of day again until turned out, or perhaps carried out, next Beltain, 1 May.

At the end of a long summer on the hill, teaching her cubs the difficult art of survival, the vixen gathers her well-scattered offspring around her once more at the family den. She has spent every available moment daily honing their hunting instincts, and she has also made them aware of every danger that can possibly cross their path.

I once witnessed the instant learning effect of a maternal warning. For several evenings one summer, I had been watching a litter of young cubs playing outside their earth after the vixen had gone out to hunt. One day she must have picked up my scent because within minutes of my arrival, the vixen reappeared, 'hic-upped' a warning to the cubs who, in a twinkling of an eye, vanished into the safety of their den. Each night thereafter, when I turned up at the den and the cubs caught wind of me, they immediately went to ground. The lesson of associating my scent with danger had been well and truly learned. In the wild, you don't get many second chances.

After this last family get-together, somehow, I have no idea how, the vixen once again disperses her litter. The young vixens, it seems, stay happily within their parents' territory, but the young dog foxes are forced to leave. It will be many of these travelling dog cubs, now in their adult coats, which gamekeepers all over the land will snare in their carefully set wire loops during the coming months. Even if they avoid the traps and keep clear of the guns, their chances of being able to find enough food to survive through the cold conditions are not very good. After all, the young dogs, and vixens too, are still quite inexperienced, and winter can be heartless.

It is time to put Quippick, my Suffolk tup, in amongst the pets. I strap a harness onto his body; this holds a block of green crayon in place on his brisket. Every time he tups one of my ewes, marking her tailhead, I will make a note of the date in my diary. After 16 days, I will change the colour of the crayon so that I will be able to see any ewes that have returned to the tup. From these details, I will be able to accurately work out feeding requirements during pregnancy and the exact lambing dates. A little extra work now will greatly improve my efficiency next spring. If everything goes to plan, my pack will be all safely lambed well before my hill lambing gets under way.

The sun sets into a clear Bonfire Night, its roots stretching back far beyond the treason of that abortive Gunpowder Plot. With a bale of dry straw to set it going, the flames rapidly take a firm hold on the bonfire. Victoria's Guy catches alight as the blaze sends a vortex of sparks spiralling high into the sky. For a few moments, the glen is lit with an incandescent glow.

We let off a box of fireworks. As the fire gradually subsides into a red heat, Maggi pushes potatoes into the ashes to cook. Chick and Christine Campbell, together with their six children, walk over from the Dhu, torchlight beams shining out of the blackness, to share our fire and baked tatties. Each time I turn away from the warmth of the fire, the cold night air tweaks my nose.

Long after the Campbells have gone home and our children are tucked up in bed, Maggi and I sit quietly on a fireside log, watching the flames tell stories. Overhead meteorites burn up as they shoot across the star-filled heavens. My garden looks rather forlorn and will require a bit of tidying up. Weeds and dead heads are consigned to the compost heap, along with the cold ashes from the bonfire. When the ground is clear of everything except the winter-hardy leeks and parsnips, I make a start at turning over the sod. One spadeful at a time, I expose the fresh earth to the beneficial weathering properties of the winter frosts.

At Harthill, a disaster has overtaken my hoggs. Nine of them have been killed by marauding dogs. The local police spotted a pair of likely-looking candidates near the farm, an Alsatian and a collie – a deadly combination if the sheepdog rounds up the sheep for the Alsatian to kill; unfortunately, the dogs were able to escape. The dog which actually killed my sheep was certainly a large one. The puncture marks at the back of each victim's head looked so much like bullet entry and exit wounds that, at first, it was thought that these hoggs had been shot. Every year, throughout Britain, some 10,000 sheep are needlessly slaughtered by man's best friend.

I take a walk with my dogs, along the glen, past Ben Ducteach, to look over my hill cows. A tranquillity has descended upon the hills now that the stags have finished rutting. The hinds have resumed their everyday life in large herds while the stags have gathered together in smaller groups and gone off to the high ground to recuperate. My Blackface ewes graze peacefully over their sheep-bitten hefts, clipping down the same narrow tracks as regular as clockwork. The young eagle, showing the white wing spots and inner tail of a juvenile bird, is busy mousing amongst the heather.

Dusk is settling over Glengyle as I return homeward. A large flock of whooper swans comes bugling in overhead before landing, splashing and wallowing onto the lagoon at the head of the loch. Grazing widgeon whistle softly on the shore. Behind the darkness, the night sky echoes to the high-pitched zee-p calls of migrating redwing, interspersed with the occasional, harsher shack-shack of accompanying fieldfares. By morning, the remaining rowan berries could well be gone from the trees.

I turn my hand to some maintenance work. The saw-millers have sent me the wood I need to repair and replace gates in the fank. After the Glengyle and Portnellan sheep have been handled through the fank five times during the year, there is always a fair amount of wear and tear to be made good. Fortunately, it is the school half-term holiday and Jamie is able to help me. He sets to with his usual rural determination, measuring, sawing, hammering, fetching and carrying, for hours on end. Finally, we apply a coat of creosote to all the new wood in order to try and prolong its serviceable life. The old stone dykes about the place also need to be looked after. The little time and effort invested in servicing stock-proof dykes will be repaid manyfold. Apart from securely confining sheep and cattle, a sound wall will also provide invaluable shelter for both livestock and wildlife during the stormy winter months ahead.

It is not all work, though, particularly at this time of year. A 'challenge match' has been arranged between a scratch team from Stronachlachar and the local village's football league team, Aberfoyle Rob Roy. These periodic sorties by the men from the hills are usually hard-fought affairs and great fun, especially if we manage to win. The game is to be played at Aberfoyle and, after the fine spell of weather we have been enjoying, naturally it begins to pour with rain.

There are four shepherds in our team, Iain, John and me from the north shore, and Chick as the sole representative of the other side. The game is fast and furious, and because of the atrocious underfoot conditions, there are mistakes galore. The rain continues unabated. We change our goalkeeper every ten minutes or so, to prevent any one player becoming frozen to the spot. Puddles form all over the playing surface, hindering the progress of the ball, in fact, frequently stopping it dead in its tracks. The river Forth, alongside the ground, is rising ominously quickly. At the end of the game, 22 saturated players and a soaked referee leave the field to the flood waters. Stronachlachar have won by eight goals to six. Perhaps the conditions were more in our favour.

The hours of these lengthening winter evenings are usefully exploited in our household. Maggi steadily reduces her woolpile, spinning, weaving and knitting it up into a variety of products. Some of the ancient Celtic designs which she incorporates into a number of her patterns are extremely intricate. Celtic art, it seems was averse to using squares or parallels of any kind, revealing itself only in delicate, convoluted, interlacing curves, circles, squiggles and illusory knots.

I get down to dressing a few tups' horns into heads for shepherds' crooks. First, the hazel shank is fitted to the raw horn. From this beginning, the lines and angles of the finished article can be worked on. I use a saw to reduce the horn to roughly the dimensions required. The shank is then stood to one side. Next, the natural curl on the horn will need to be straightened out. I heat the horn thoroughly over a flame of methylated spirit burning in an old tobacco tin before squeezing it in a vice. When cool, the horn will retain its new shape. Now comes the long process of rasping, filing, carving, rubbing down and polishing until the desired effect is gained. The horn is then permanently fitted to the shank, and the finished crook is varnished several times.

It is my turn again to collect and drive the local Brownies to their weekly pack meeting in Aberfoyle. The rota system works out well; after all, it takes a gallon of fuel to get down and back. As soon as I drop the girls off at the school where their meetings are held, I retire to the Altskeith Hotel for a pint which I sip and enjoy whilst watching 'One Man and His Dog' on the television. It is nice to be able to sit in comfort and be able to see some of our top handlers putting their dogs through their paces. The programme manages to portray the intimate interaction between dog, man and their sheep. The one drawback to not having a television at home is that we do miss the occasional good programmes.

I take delivery of my two-week-old Welsh Black cross Friesian heifer calf, especially ordered through one of the Stirling calf dealers. She has come all the way from Wales but appears to be none the worse for her long journey. I decide to call her Megan and will rear her to eventually replace Tansy as my house-cow. In order for Megan to have plenty of milk, I wean Sweep and Clover, now five months old, and turn the heifer on in their place.

The two big calves will be fed on the best hay, cereal and high-protein concentrates for the next few weeks. Then, gradually, I shall introduce some urea and straw into their diet. Urea, also known as non-protein nitrogen, is a very inexpensive source of dietary nitrogen which, if properly balanced by a high starch intake, from straw for example, can be efficiently converted into lovely red meat by ruminant animals. There is no cheaper method of producing highly valuable animal protein available to farmers today.

I am always interested in finding ways to improve the lambing percentage of the Glengyle hirsel. After some consultation with the head shepherd, it has been decided that I can tup about 100 of my gimmers in-bye this time, in the West Park. The largest group of eild ewes at clipping time are always the gimmers, so it makes sense to hold them in to the tup. If I can at least get them in lamb in the first place, I am half way to solving that part of the problem.

My 200 or so gimmers are roughly equally divided between the high- and low-ends of my hill, but the high-end is much easier to gather single handed. I begin the job of taking in one cut at a time. A small winter visitor to the glen is flushed into flight from virtually underneath my boots, zig-zagging a short distance before taking cover once again. Even although I see the exact spot where the jack snipe went down, ideal camouflage makes the bird impossible to pick out from the surroundings. Above me a flock of twittering snow buntings twists and turns amongst the rocks. A fresh dressing of heather sprigs on the eyrie tells me that my pair of eagles have been reconnoitring their old nest sites, probably as part of their pre-mating ritual.

Below me, in the Braes of Balquhidder, I can see chimney smoke rising from Inverlochlarig House where, towards the end of November 1734, Rob Roy MacGregor lay in his bed, a very sick man. Rob and Montrose had long made their peace again, thanks chiefly to the intercessions of the Duke of Argyll, and the farm leases of Monachyle Tuarach had been returned to the MacGregor. When Rob and Mary eventually retired to Inverlochlarig Beg, he left Monachyle Tuarach in the capable hands of his two eldest sons, Coll and Ranald. The two younger sons, James and Robin Og, were living as freebooters amongst the hills, in true MacGregor fashion.

Now the priest explained that before Rob could die in a state of grace, he must forgive all of his enemies. Mary, a devout Christian woman, gently tried to persuade her stubborn husband to make his peace with his maker before it was too late. At last, just to please his wife, Rob agreed, looking his priest full in the eye and swore that he, Rob Roy MacGregor of Glengyle, forgave any man who had ever done him wrong. Then turning aside to his youngest son, the wild Robin Og, he quietly instructed him to look to them and settle all accounts.

Rob lingered until the evening of 28 December and even then, after a long illness, he summoned up sufficient energy to go out with a typical MacGregor flourish. One of his old adversaries, Maclaren of Invernenty, hearing that Rob was close to death, came to gloat over the demise of the great man. When Rob was informed of Invernenty's approach, he at once rose from his bed, donned his finest chieftain's garb, complete with claymore, pistols and targe, to greet his visitor. One can imagine Rob relishing Maclaren's obvious discomfort at being so well entertained by this old man who, according to all accounts, already had one foot in his grave. At length, Maclaren departed. Rob, drained by his last effort, called his piper to his side and bade him play the lament '*I will return no more*'. Even before the last sad notes had faded into the night, Rob Roy MacGregor was dead.

Gathered into small flocks on the very tops of my hill, the ptarmigan, with their complex system of three plumage moults a year, are now snow white. There is no snow, but they still are not easy to see. Both sexes have black tail feathers which can be seen when they are startled into flight, uttering a peculiar dry, croaking sound. My mountain hares, too, on the upper slopes, have changed from their summertime blue to winter white; while, lower down, the solitary hunting stoats will be wearing their ermine coats. Snow is not the trigger for these colour change mechanisms; it happens in response to temperature reduction.

It takes me several days to gather in steadily all the high-end sheep and take out all the gimmers. With the older stock ewes back on their ground, my final tally of gimmers stands at 107, just over half the number on Glengyle. It will be very interesting to see what significant difference there is going to be between the numbers of non-productive gimmers off the different ends of my ground.

The West Park has been closed off to stock since the cast ewes went away and there is plenty of good grazing in it, enough to last these 107 gimmers a few weeks. To make sure they stay in it, I go round the entire length of the fence, loaded down with fencing materials and tools, mending any potentially weak points. I have to pay particular attention to the numerous water-gates, free-swinging contraptions which guard the way out along burns and small water courses. After the recent spate of flood water, quite a few of them require some restoration. The big double set, normally hanging sedately at the point where the Glengyle Burn flows into the park, have vanished altogether. The remains of them will be floating about, in small pieces, out in the vastness of Loch Katrine. The sheer savagery of the water which sometimes comes raging down these burns is quite frightening.

Loch Katrine has been designated as one of the low-flying areas for assorted sorties by military aircraft, mostly, I believe, by our own RAF. These planes often fly past below me, screaming along the glen with only feet to spare between them and the pylons. My sheep do not seem the least bothered by these intrusions, but I nearly jumped out of my skin one day last year when a plane leapt out of the glen behind me and was gone. Only then did the noise hit me.

Today, unfortunately, one young pilot out on a training flight overdid things and buried himself and his Jaguar fighter in a deep peat bog, on the side of nearby Ben Lui. This is the fourth such accident so far this year. Apart from the tragic loss of life, it comes rather expensive at £5 million a time.

At long last I am to get my Wolfhound 'cap'; well it's really a tie, something I have dreamed of but was beginning to think would never happen. It does prove, however, that if you buy the right people enough pints, in the end you get your just rewards. The intended victims this week are Currie RFC, one of the Edinburgh clubs.

As we get stripped for the game, in Currie's brand new dressing-room complex, Big Duncan Tulloch, our captain, goes over a few points with me, making sure that I am conversant with the team codes for line-outs, scrums, and open-play variations. It all sounds very well organised. Duncan thinks that I will settle into the side all right. I simply wish that the butterflies in my stomach would settle, too.

Seven and a half minutes before kick-off, Big Duncan gathers everyone round him. In the centre of the dressing-room he lays it right on the line: we have come here to win in true and traditional Wolfhound style. There are only two minutes to go by the time Duncan has finished psyching us up. We are rearing to go. With our socks straight and our collars neatly turned up, we follow our leader – right into a large ball cupboard.

That was my very first lesson in Wolfhound rugby. Never again will I take anything seriously. We finally managed to extricate ourselves from the ball cupboard, not an easy thing to do when the people at the back keep pressing forward while those in front are struggling to get out, and hammered our unfortunate hosts out of sight. Well, we had to after that escapade.

The tups have been loaded up at Milngavie and returned to the hills. Their long summer sojourn on lush meadows is over; now they will have to prove their fitness and their worth on the rugged ground of west Perthshire.

In the fank at Edra, the new arrivals are ready to be drawn into lots for each hirsel. First of all, any tup that has only been one year on a hill is pulled out, destined to return to the same place for a second season. Then the shepherds take a turn about at selecting one tup at a time from the remainder, until each man has reached his quota. The new tups, recently bought at the tup sales, are always introduced to their job on the easier ground at the east end of the loch so I won't see them on my hill for a year or two.

Once the draw is complete, we begin branding each lot in turn. My 26 receive a single letter 'G' on the right horn. The brand is burned in, quite close to the head, so that if the end of the horn ever has to be cut off, the record will be retained. A wee spot of keel is applied to the fleece – blue on the right hip for the Glengyle tups. The warmth given out by the brazier is very welcome.

The tups are then turned out into one or other of the Edra parks, to wait for their day to dawn. The tups will go out onto the east-end hirsels a full week before I take mine to the hill.

When the nights began to lengthen, the time had arrived for ewes everywhere to come into season. From then on, the oestrous cycle is repeated every 16 days, until either the ewe is successfully mated or the year turns the mid-winter corner and the nights shorten once more.

It is the lateness of the hill spring which dictates our lambing period.

More winter visitors have appeared on Loch Katrine. They seem to be coming in by the day. The red-headed drakes identify the large raft of diving ducks as pochard. Also out on the cold water is a smaller flock: this time, the chestnut heads belong to the goldeneye females, the drakes having an almost black-sheened head with small, round white cheek spots. Golden-eye are the best of the diving ducks.

Our resident mallards, not to be outshone by these exotic upstarts, begin to take the eye with their pair-bonding behaviour. It would appear that a female mallard with a bonded mate has a better chance of surviving the rigours of winter than one without. Unfortunately for some females, getting herself a mate can be fraught with problems too. On occasion, a large number of drakes will pay court to the same female. Winter courtship culminates as usual with a simulated union on the water which is normally straightforward and uneventful. However, with sometimes as many as a dozen drakes all trying to mount the same duck at the same instant, it is not unknown for the poor female to be drowned. This is why I often refer to these particular birds as the Glengyle Chapter of Hells Angels.

A thrush clearly sings out a storm warning from the top of a gently swaying pine. The sky looks foreboding, and already small waves are running away down the loch in front of the wind. Lower down the tree, the storm cock's first cousin, the blackbird, sings a brief snatch of his song. He repeats the same few notes and then falls silent, as if disappointed at what he hears. The thrush sings on.

High above Glengyle, my pair of eagles tame the wild north winds with their mighty wings; hung up, black, against the purple sky, they look positively menacing. No wonder that Highland herds of old relied on a charm to prevent the Iolar dhub (black eagle) making off with their sheep. The charm itself was a simple enough thing. All that was needed was a piece of string, which no good shepherd should ever be without, into which a row of knots was tied while calling upon the Iolar dhub to put down his prey.

The wind takes another breath, and comes again more strongly than before, tearing at the tattered remnants of leaves still clinging forlornly to the waving branches. This night is one to rattle the roof of old Glengyle House. Snug inside is the only place to be. At 8.30 p.m. the electricity goes off. Out come the candles and matches. The summer scent of beeswax soon pervades the room. We all sit around the faithful Rayburn, making toast.

When I open the door to the morning gale, everything is crouched before the blast. Trees are down across the road and I will need to clear a way through for the school bus. My powersaw is making short work of the windfall when the Water Board foresters turn up in the Land Rover, looking for the same, and show me how it should really be done. In a matter of minutes, the road is open. The wood is mine, though, since I was here first.

The bad weather is not done. In fact, I don't think it has properly started yet. Thunder begins to growl around the glens like a bad-tempered dog and hailstones are unleashed from on high. Every time I step through the door, the wind grabs my coat and beats me round the head with it. This is definitely a day for staying close to the fireside and only venturing forth to do what has to be done.

It has been a hungry time. As soon as the winds have abated, Maggi puts extra food on the bird table for the garden birds. Outside the window, great, coal and blue tits vie with each other

The tiny garrulous pygmy shrew

to take turns on the fat-filled coconut shell. Any surviving insects still able to fly will be feeding from the honey-filled cups of the ivy flowers, indisputably the last plant of the year to bloom. My pets browse on the lower ivy leaves, sometimes standing up on their hind legs to reach the more succulent leaves higher up.

My ewes are undoubtedly in fine fettle but they are nowhere as fat as the badgers. Sometimes I can glimpse an old tubby brock out on the hillside, literally rolling in layers of submerged blubber. Although they do not truly hibernate, badgers do spend long periods snoozing in their snug nests, conserving energy and living adequately off their plentiful reserves of fat. Some of the somnolent sows would have mated last springtime, others may not have taken to the boar until the autumn. In both cases, because of delayed embryonic implantation, development of the unborn young takes place through the winter months and the cubs will make their appearance next February and March.

Grey squirrels, too, lie up in their dreys for days or weeks at a time when the weather is inclement. At other times, they can often be seen feasting on or burying a cache of acorns, or gathering scattered beech nuts.

Most animals will have adapted to the rigours of their winter regimes by this time. The tiny, garrulous, pygmy shrew faces the hardest time of all. In order to endlessly fuel a body which has a heartbeat of 500 per minute, shrews live only to eat. In winter, their supply of insects, slugs, frogs, eggs and the like is not exactly plentiful. If they cannot find a meal, or are prevented from feeding for as little as three or four hours, they will perish.

Moles have retreated to the sheltered woodland soils, and will be making greedy inroads into their stockpiles of paralysed earthworms. The hedgehog, a close relative of both the mole and the shrew, is a true hibernator. Rolled up, fast asleep in a bed of dry leaves, their torpor is so deep that even the hosts of fleas in residence among the quills leave them completely undisturbed.

The head shepherd makes the run up the lochside to deliver my tups to Glengyle. Iain herds 18 tups out of the trailer, 16 destined for the hill, plus two extra to cover the high-end gimmers in the West Park. Mona works them up into the fank. Inside the small handling pen and using a watering can, I dye their long, woolly coats a beautiful bright yellow, before slapping on a big blue keel mark onto the right hip of each animal. I should have no trouble picking them out on the hillside during the weeks to come.

I puff a little antibiotic powder into the eye of one of the tups who seems to have a mild infection. If left untreated, the eye would probably become much more inflamed and watery, eventually becoming opaque or even ulcerated. The ensuing blindness, fortunately, would be of a temporary nature, but because the disease is highly infectious there is always a danger of it spreading to other sheep. A mild case, such as this, caught early enough, should clear up completely in a few days. The animal will be immune from any further attacks.

Having assured myself that the tups are all sound on their feet and legs, I turn them into the outside weir and give them a good feed of best hay. They will wait in here, quite happily, until tomorrow morning.

A strident bellow tells me Tansy is ready to come into the byre for the night. Eager for the warmth of her stall and the fodder sitting in her trough, the old house-cow is waiting patiently at the gate, Megan standing close to her warm flank. Finn follows them up the road. She is keen to work.

The cattle are soon secured and fed, tucking noisily into their small mountains of hay and cereals. I turn my attention to the kennels. The dog meal is measured out into each dish and the newly-formed ice broken up on the drinking pails. Low temperatures never seem to bother these hardy tykes.

I push the old wheelbarrow along the graveyard footpath to load up with logs to feed the Rayburn. The high-walled MacGregor burial ground is a haven for a wide variety of life, too. A rapid succession of crisp notes and trills betrays the presence of a tiny wren concealed amongst the undergrowth of the ivy-clad inner sanctum. Above, clinging to a feathery overhanging pine branch, is an even smaller bird, a goldcrest searching for insects between the long needles. The solitary little red bird watches my approach eagerly from the top of the wall; he hops along, keeping abreast of me in case I should unearth some supper for him. White rumped bramblings and a few pink chaffinches seek food around the gravestones. Against the bottom of the wall, empty red campion seed pods contain overwintering adult ladybirds. Some insects even produce their own anti-freeze which enables them to withstand winter temperatures in the region of minus 15°C.

Close to the wall I notice that the children have put freshly-cut sprays of holly berries on Gran's grave. I stop and ponder for a moment or two. It aye brings a tear to my eye.

The daylight is going out on this, the last day of my shepherd calendar. Ice forming on the loch cracks and groans. The frost under my feet crunches as I retrace my steps to the fank to make a final check on my tups. I stand, unobserved, leaning on the gate

A tiny wren concealed amongst the undergrowth

as, one by one, they settle down under the darkness. Gentle belches send hot breath steaming out into the cold air. They munch softly on their hay. As I walk softly away I turn towards the west and cast my eye up at the red sky at night.

THE BEGINNING.

Glossary

Broke wool Small pieces of wool
Buchts Sheep pens (used in different districts instead of fank)
Clipper sheds Shearing sheds
Chaser tups Second lot of tups to be put on the hill
Crogging Bringing individual sheep to the shearer
Cut Small number of sheep from same area
Eild ewes Ewes not producing a lamb
Fank Sheep pens
Feeders Stock ewes sold for fattening
Gimmers Female sheep in their second year
Hap Waterproof cover
Heft A group of sheep which live within the confines of a particular area of hill
Hirsel An area of hill, within natural boundaries, normally herded by one man, also the hill itself
Hoggs Ewe lambs kept for breeding stock
In-bye Fields
Keb Ewe with a dead lamb
Keel/ed Coloured marking fluid, for identification
Out-bye Hills
Riggs Tup with either one or no testicles
Roughies Sheep in full wool
Shearling Young sheep, usually a tup, sheared once
Shed off Separate
Snek Latch
Speaned Weaned
Stell Sheep pen on the hillside
Tups Rams
Wether/wedder lamb Castrated tup lamb
Wearing Dog holding a cut of sheep in one place
Weir Large holding pen in the fank
Whole-luggers Lambs before they have been ear-marked

Of Dogs and Men

John Barrington
ISBN 978-1-906817-90-9 PBK £8.99

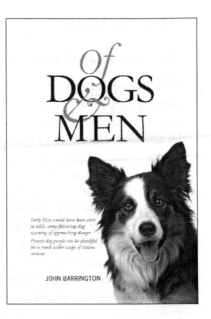

Early man would have been alert to wild, camp-following dogs warning of approaching danger. Present day people can be thankful for a much wider range of canine services.

Part autobiography and part history, *Of Dogs and Men* is a celebration of our passion for the trusty sheepdog.

Filled with lively anecdotes, poems and mythological stories, Barrington sets out to map the evolution and bond between man and dog; how dogs developed from the wild into the beloved companions as we know them today. Barrington includes heart-warming stories of collies used in life saving operations as search and rescue dogs, in epilepsy and cancer alert situations and as guide dogs.

Out of the Mists

John Barrington

ISBN 978-1-905222-33-9 PBK £7.99

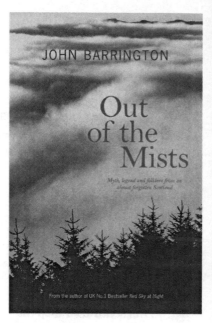

In the earliest hours of the morning shepherds gather, waiting for the mists that conceal the hillsides to clear. To pass the time they tell tales of roaming giants, marauding monks and weird witches. Enter this world of magic and wonder in *Out of the Mists*, a delightful collection of stories which will captivate and entertain you while answering your questions about Scottish history and folklore.

Why did St Andrew become the patron saint of Scotland?

How can you protect yourself from faerie magic?

What happened to Scotland's last dragon?

John Barrington uses wit and his encyclopaedic knowledge of Scottish folklore to create a compelling collection of stories that will capture the imaginations of readers of all ages.

Loch Lomond and the Trossachs: An A–Z of Loch Lomond and The Trossachs National Park and surrounding area

John Barrington
ISBN 978-1-905222-42-1 PBK £8.99

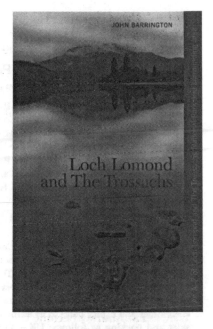

- How did the Devil form the Whangie?

- Where does the word 'blackmail' derive from?

- Which church minister was away with the fairies?

- How did Rob Roy defeat a troupe of Redcoats with an echo?

- Where can you see the Heavenly Dancers?

The answers to all these questions can be found in *Loch Lomond and The Trossachs*, John Barrington's follow up to the bestselling *Red Sky at Night*. Here, Barrington draws upon his wealth of knowledge and experience of life in Loch Lomond and surrounding Trossachs area to create a compelling historical, mythological and linguistic A to Z of the region.

This is an insider's recommendation of all you should see in this, Scotland's first national park, if you truly wish to uncover its beauty and find out all it has to offer. From the enchantments of the Aberfoyle landscape to the locality of the Zygaena moth, Barrington's love of his subject shines through as he explores the sites, characters and wildlife that make this area so attractive to tourists, historians and etymologists alike.

Details of these and other books published by Luath Press can be found at:
www.luath.co.uk

Luath Press Limited
committed to publishing well written books worth reading

LUATH PRESS takes its name from Robert Burns, whose little collie Luath (*Gael.*, swift or nimble) tripped up Jean Armour at a wedding and gave him the chance to speak to the woman who was to be his wife and the abiding love of his life. Burns called one of 'The Twa Dogs' Luath after Cuchullin's hunting dog in Ossian's *Fingal*. Luath Press was established in 1981 in the heart of Burns country, and is now based a few steps up the road from Burns' first lodgings on Edinburgh's Royal Mile.

Luath offers you distinctive writing with a hint of unexpected pleasures.

Most bookshops in the UK, the US, Canada, Australia, New Zealand and parts of Europe either carry our books in stock or can order them for you. To order direct from us, please send a £sterling cheque, postal order, international money order or your credit card details (number, address of cardholder and expiry date) to us at the address below. Please add post and packing as follows: UK – £1.00 per delivery address; overseas surface mail – £2.50 per delivery address; overseas air-mail – £3.50 for the first book to each delivery address, plus £1.00 for each additional book by airmail to the same address. If your order is a gift, we will happily enclose your card or message at no extra charge.

Luath Press Limited
543/2 Castlehill
The Royal Mile
Edinburgh EH1 2ND
Scotland
Telephone: 0131 225 4326 (24 hours)
Fax: 0131 225 4324
email: sales@luath.co.uk
Website: www.luath.co.uk